Northwestern University
STUDIES IN *Phenomenology &*
Existential Philosophy

Sartre's Ontology

Klaus Hartmann

Sartre's Ontology

A Study of Being and Nothingness

in the Light of Hegel's Logic

NORTHWESTERN UNIVERSITY PRESS

EVANSTON   1 9 6 6

Foreword

IN MY ANALYSIS of Sartre's main work I have tried to include sufficient exposition of his views to enable the reader without extensive knowledge of Sartre to follow the interpretation. The reader is, however, expected to be conversant with Hegel and, to a lesser extent, with Husserl and Heidegger.

A comment on secondary literature: I have not found, among studies of Sartre, any detailed treatment of his ontology in the light of Hegel, although I might mention W. Biemel's article ("Das Wesen der Dialektik bei Hegel und Sartre," *Tijdschrift voor Philosophie*, XX [1958]) on Hegel's and Sartre's dialectic. Biemel, however, does not attempt an analysis of Sartre's ontology but limits himself to discussing a formal statement of the dialectic as it occurs in Sartre's main work. I might also mention the writings of J. Kopper (cf. the Bibliography), who discusses Sartre in the light of Hegel's notion of spirit, his main emphasis resting on the community aspect. Of major studies of Sartre I might list the following: G. Varet, in his *L'Ontologie de Sartre,* and M. Natanson, in his *Critique of Jean-Paul Sartre's Ontology,* locate Sartre within the framework of Husserl's phenomenology and see in the philosophy of *L'Être et le néant* a newfangled or ill-advised modification of the phenomenological method. Natanson, in his above-mentioned work (pp. 73f.), has discovered a reference to Hegel, but it is the *Phenomenology of Spirit* he has in mind. W. Desan, in *The Tragic Finale* (pp. 156, 159), considers Sartre an original thinker within the existentialist tradition but has little appreciation for his dialectic and merely presumes an indebtedness to Hegel. And, although J. Möller, in *Absurdes Sein?,* is aware of the close relationship between Sartre and Hegel (pp. 105ff., 108), his main interest focuses on polemical apologetics and on an attempt at "overcoming Sartre's thought by metaphysics" (p. 161). The bulk of secondary studies on Sartre stem from adherents of scholasticism or of superficial existentialism and have proved of little value. Accordingly, secondary works, as opposed to those of philosophers in their own right, are drawn upon only occasionally.

A comment on the manner of quotation and citation: Sartre's main work is abbreviated as "EN." Where the wording is essential, quoted passages or terms are given in the original French, either in the text or as footnotes. Otherwise, I quote from Hazel E. Barnes's translation [1] (abbreviated as "BN"), except where I have preferred to give my own version. The page numbers in both the French and American editions are included. Frequently, in passages of a more expository character, Sartre's statements are paraphrased, closely following the text, with a citation of the parallel passages in the French and American editions. Where such passages approach a verbatim equivalent of Sartre's French text, they are treated as translated quotes and either put in quotation marks or set off in the text. My aim was to avoid overburdening the book with too many quotations in the original French and (to escape what would otherwise be a necessity) to quote only complete sentences or groups of sentences in translation. For a few quotes from Husserl I have felt free to offer my own translations. Quotes from Hegel's *Logic* are taken, or adapted, from the Johnston and Struthers translation (abbreviated as "J&S"). For other works by Hegel, I have consulted the available translations but have used my discretion. Reference to Hegel's *Phenomenology of Spirit* as a literary entity is made under that title; in references to the English translation, J. Baillie's title, *Phenomenology of Mind*, is used. In footnotes, quotes have often been left in the original German, especially where the claims of authenticity must prevail over those of readability. For terms like *pour-soi* in French and *Fürsich* or *Fürsichsein* in German, I have chosen "for-itself" or "being-for-itself," rather than "being-for-self," to bring out the parallelism with *en-soi, Ansich,* or *Ansichsein,* which are traditionally rendered as "in-itself" or "being-in-itself."

In conclusion, I should like to express my thanks to Professor Johannes Thyssen, Bonn, for his friendly interest in the aim of this book and for many a dispute over its substance. My thanks also go to Dr. John R. Silber and Dr. Vere C. Chappell for looking over the translation. The responsibility for torts to the English language remains, of course, entirely mine.

KLAUS HARTMANN

Bonn/Austin, Texas, September 1965

1. *Being and Nothingness,* trans. Hazel E. Barnes (New York: Philosophical Library, 1956). Material quoted with the permission of the publishers.

Contents

[xi]

Introduction

WITH THE EXCEPTION of his book on Genet and the recent *Critique de la raison dialectique,* Sartre's theoretical works were written long ago. The hectic reaction is a matter of the past. Hectic as it was, this reaction was prompted only to a small degree by the theoretical writings. The main work, *L'Être et le néant,* no less than the other books on the imagination and the emotions, had to yield pride of place to the novels, plays, and essays. Soon after World War II there appeared a number of philosophical studies of Sartre, mainly in French, but they, in turn, were largely affected by the ideological order of the day conjured up by Sartre himself. Thus, as an object for philosophical examination, Sartre seems by no means exhausted. In some respects knowledge of his philosophy, which is so rich in attempted solutions of the great problems in the field, has yet to be disseminated.

But since Part I of his new, bulky work on dialectical reason gives evidence of Sartre's continued interest in a theoretical treatment of philosophical problems, is it legitimate to analyze what now appears a mere part of his philosophical effort? Is not everything in flux, so that we ought to wait and see what line Sartre's thought will take? To this we could answer that with the appearance of the new book on the dialectic of reason the position taken in his preceding works stands forth as completed. Sartre has not abandoned the position taken in these works, but rather extends it to cover a social philosophy under the auspices of a Marxist orientation. His *existentialism* is now intended to serve as a basis for Marxism, in that it is to assemble a "truly comprehensive knowledge" of man to be integrated into Marxism once

Marxism has accepted the "human dimension" and the "existential project" as the basis for its anthropological knowledge.[1]

The phase of Sartre's thought with which we are to deal appears, taken by itself, as a philosophy not yet subservient to socio-revolutionary *praxis*. Precisely to the extent that it is not so subservient, its links with traditional philosophy come to the fore, and it can be considered the latest metamorphosis of our philosophical heritage.

The advent of a philosophy which embraces a kind of system and a comprehensive theory bearing on many traditional philosophical questions is no trivial occurrence. If only as such a piece of philosophy, EN is remarkable. It is the more so if we consider that it is intended as the upshot of the philosophies of Husserl, Heidegger, and Hegel. As its subtitle states, it is designed as a *phenomenological ontology*. This is the program, carried out in a full-scale essay. Are we then to think that EN is a syncretism of Husserl, Heidegger, and Hegel? Are not these elements, supposedly fused in Sartre's philosophy, actually incompatible? Neither Husserl's nor Heidegger's connection with Hegel is apparent. Clearly, more general consideration, transcending our immediate task, will have to be given to the problem of how phenomenology and dialectic have been wedded in Sartre's work.[2]

Before entering into the systematic context, however, let us pause and cast a glance at Sartre's intellectual development, which may to some degree make the coalescence of these philosophies plausible.

We have to picture the young Sartre as a man saturated with the philosophy syllabus of the French *lycée;* he knows the Stoics, and classical authors such as Descartes, Leibniz, Spinoza, Kant, and Bergson. In his university years he is influenced by philosophers and professors such as Alain, J. Wahl, Brunschvicg, R. Aron, and Laporte. Sartre experiences a reaction against the idealism of academic philosophy.[3] He craves "reality" in all its senses, whether socio-political, interpersonal, or sensuous. J. Wahl's book *Vers le concret* impresses him, a figure like St. Exupéry intrigues him, social depravation upsets him. He reads Marx, without a knowledge of Hegel.[4] The quest for "reality" prompts him to

1. *Critique de la raison dialectique*, I (Paris, 1960), p. 111.
2. Cf. W. Biemel, "Das Wesen der Dialektik bei Hegel und Sartre," *Tijdschrift voor Philosophie*, XX (1958), 300.
3. *Critique de la raison dialectique*, I, p. 23: "l'idéalisme officiel."
4. *Ibid.*, p. 22.

write an early literary piece centering on the contingency of the real.[5] Psychoanalysis, too, arrests him, and as early as 1932 he is in possession of a theory designed to render the notion of the unconscious unnecessary.[6] Once again, it is the theme of contingency, this time in the heart of man.

The encounter with Husserl's phenomenology marks a major intellectual experience. It begins in 1932 when Sartre reads, at the suggestion of R. Aron, the book on Husserl by Lévinas.[7] In 1933–34 he spends a brief year in Berlin as a research student at the Berlin French Institute.[8] For Sartre, Husserl promises an "overcoming of the conflict between idealism and realism," an "affirmation of the supremacy of consciousness and of the presence of the world such as it is given to us." [9] In Berlin he writes the article "La Transcendance de l'égo" (published in 1936), and it is in this period that we have to place his study of Heidegger.

After returning to France, Sartre writes a historical monograph on French theories concerning the problem of imagination, *L'Imagination* (published in 1936). The subsequent systematic work, *L'Imaginaire* (composed from 1935 on, published in 1940), clearly exhibits phenomenological training. The line he takes in these works is understandable, inasmuch as the imagination was bound to be a touchstone for phenomenology, which, for him, was tantamount to a philosophy of reality and concreteness. Now Sartre discovers the negative as something posited outside me as nonexistent, and, quite generally, consciousness is regarded as something negative and its reference to the world as negation. The elaboration of phenomenology, by itself, leads to the subsequent great theme of the negative. (Incidentally, *L'Imaginaire* constitutes the first literary evidence of Sartre's familiarity with Heidegger.) A study on the emotions—*Esquisse d'une théorie des émotions* (published in 1939), a précis of an unpublished manuscript on the psyche on which he worked for a longer period [10]— winds up the series of phenomenological monographs.

Hegel's entry on the scene requires an explanation. Sartre is not, from his university training, rooted in a French Hegelian

5. *Légende de la vérité*, 1931. Cf. S. de Beauvoir, *La Force de l'âge* (Paris, 1960), p. 50. The subject recurs in the novel *La Nausée*.
6. S. de Beauvoir, *op. cit.*, p. 134. It is the theory of "bad faith" [*mauvaise foi*]. See chap. 3, sec. 4, below.
7. *Ibid.*, pp. 141f.
8. *Ibid.*, pp. 142, 162.
9. *Ibid.*, p. 141.
10. *Ibid.*, p. 326.

tradition; he never read Hegel at the university.[11] Perhaps his reorientation was motivated by a lingering French interest in Hegel (as represented by the works of Janet, Lévy-Bruhl, and Brunschvicg) and by the renewal of this interest in the thirties. We recall the special Hegel issue of the *Revue de métaphysique et de morale* of 1931, J. Wahl's book on Hegel of 1929, articles by J. Hyppolite, and Kojève's Hegel lectures in the years 1933–39. In addition, Sartre's interest in Hegel can be made plausible from his previous study of Marx. His actual concern for Hegel does not precede the year 1939.[12] While the autobiographical remarks in the *Critique de la raison dialectique* suggest that Hegel came to attract Sartre as an intellectual instrument to comprehend Marxism,[13] we must, in view of the thematic sequence of Sartre's works, recognize that Hegel is introduced primarily as the philosopher who offers a doctrine on negation and on consciousness as negativity. In fact, we can say that Sartre found his way to Hegel via modern phenomenology—or, more correctly, via his own extrapolation: an existential phenomenology with emphasis on freedom, negation, and contingency. Thus, the Hegelian influences visible in EN constitute a recasting, however trenchant, of positions previously held by Sartre. Sartre's criticism of Hegel urges a preconceived position: for him, Hegel has flouted the contingency of being, of reality, and the individual, in an intellectual totality. His view of Hegel has been formed *ad hoc*, in connection with his phenomenological philosophy; it is not derived from the French Hegelian tradition.

There can be no doubt that Hegel was present in Sartre's mind during the composition of EN. The work gives ample evidence of his familiarity with Hegel. He quotes from the *Science of Logic*, the lesser Logic of the *Encyclopedia*, the Nuremberg writings, and the *Phenomenology of Spirit* in French translations, and argues against Hegel in two major and many minor passages. The presence of Hegelian thought in EN is thus no mere theoretical coincidence, existing without Sartre's actual cognizance.

Sartre means to be a phenomenologist, starting from consciousness or the cogito. But he does not mean to be an epistemologist, such as Husserl was, even if we grant the extension Husserl gave epistemology in his doctrine of the constitution of meaning. Sartre believes that *subjective orientation* and *ontology* are com-

11. *Critique de la raison dialectique*, I, p. 22: "Hegel lui-même nous était inconnu."

12. S. de Beauvoir did not read Hegel until 1940: *La Force de l'âge*, p. 470.

13. The use of Hegel for a refined understanding of Marx is evident only in the *Critique* itself (1960).

patible. In this he is close to the Heidegger of *Sein und Zeit*, although separated from him by his insistence on the cogito as the basis. If we grant, then, that Sartre aims at an ontological appraisal of consciousness and its object, and, further, that an appraisal of consciousness by way of the notion of substance has lost its grip ever since Brentano and Husserl rediscovered the intentionality of consciousness, we can understand that Sartre embraces notions like "in-itself," "for-itself," "for-other(s)," "in-itself-for-itself"—concepts which have their place in Hegel's *Logic*. For the time being, Hegel serves us here merely as an indication of the classical locus of these concepts. It remains to be seen to what extent Sartre's philosophy is more deeply indebted to Hegel's *Logic*.

If we are right in regarding Sartre's bent for ontology and his insistence on the cogito as joint features of his philosophy, a concurrence of Husserl's phenomenology and Hegelian concepts appears at first glance as an interesting attempt at a synthesis, rather than a syncretism—a synthesis with room to accommodate Sartre's relationship to Heidegger.

The present study takes its division of material from Sartre's main work. In its principal sections it is intended as a critical analysis of EN, with Hegel's dialectic serving as a methodological perspective, and it contains, in a final chapter, a systematic confrontation of Sartre and Hegel. It should be stressed that in this study we are dealing only with Sartre's basic ideas and leave undiscussed such otherwise important themes as the body, psychoanalysis, concrete interpersonal relationships, and concrete forms of freedom. In fact, we separate a more strictly ontological area from an anthropological ontology. Further, it should be clear that the present study is not another contribution to existentialism. Sartre's ontology is treated as such and not as an existentialist ideology in the form of an abstract code.

In accordance with our aim we will first have to inquire into the nature of Sartre's starting point. In this connection it is not essential to us that a certain form of phenomenology precede EN in Sartre's intellectual development; phenomenology is, rather, a systematic starting point on the way toward ontology. The work itself, as well as our analysis, displays this shift or movement. As for an analysis of Sartre's ontology proper, it does not appear advisable—at least not as long as his philosophy meets largely with uninformed readers—to replace his systematic order by another, possibly classical, scheme. Accordingly, we follow Sartre and subdivide into being-in-itself, being-for-itself, and being-for-others. The concluding chapter is an attempt to give room to a systematic perspective transcending these divisions. However, exposition, analysis, and systematic interpretation are not strictly separated. In the interest of the exposition, the analysis will at times adopt a provisional position which receives an *approfondissement* in subsequent passages of this study.

Sartre's Ontology

1 / The Shift to the Ontological Level

[1] The Starting Point

SARTRE BELONGS TO THE GROUP of Husserl's successors. In his early writings he made contributions of his own toward a further scientific development of phenomenology. His approval of phenomenology rests, positively speaking, on his desire to make reality immediately accessible to the subject; negatively speaking, it rests on a skeptical reserve toward views in terms of which the given is to be reduced to entities not given in the subject. Husserl's theory of intentionality, with its radicalism, offered an alternative: the world is given to the subject unmediated. But Sartre's skepticism with regard to non-given entities becomes, in turn, a touchstone for a critical examination of phenomenology. Sartre's article of 1936 ("La Transcendance de l'égo," *Recherches philosophiques,* pp. 85–123) voices criticism of the ego as a subjective entity and makes it a construct of consciousness, while Husserl, in his egology, had made the ego a center of gravity. The article points up another item of theory where Sartre does agree with phenomenology: Husserl's theory of a stream of consciousness, with its retentions and protentions, which, in keeping with the theory of intentionality, avoids immanent entities [1] and thus permits of a nonsubstantial unity of consciousness. (A theory, incidentally, which has served as a source of inspiration for Heidegger's notion of "ecstatic" temporality.) Thus, the two areas of phenomenology—intentionality theory, with its doctrine on the phenomenon, and the theory of consciousness, or object theory and subject theory—have received Sartre's attention and have been rephrased in an independent manner. Similarly, in the

1. Where Husserl connects intentionality with immanent entities—sense data —Sartre opposes him.

opening paragraphs of EN Sartre takes his stand on a phenomenology of his own radical acceptation. He is determined by a theoretical basis which was, in essential respects, readily available. The mainspring of the work is a dissatisfaction with the phenomenology of Husserl and of Heidegger, which is, nevertheless, retained in essential points. This dissatisfaction is not determined by Sartre's former skepticism; on the contrary, it concerns the question of whether phenomenology will justify the initial welcome extended to it and whether it can give any access to reality. In other words, Sartre's dissatisfaction concerns the *problem of being* as dealt with in phenomenology.

The Introduction to EN presents the reader first with an original account of the phenomenological notion of the phenomenon, tacitly presupposing familiarity with the subject, in order to pass on to a phenomenology with an ontological foundation and, finally, to a phenomenological ontology.

Sartre begins his discussion of the notion of the phenomenon by saying that "modern thought has realized considerable progress by reducing the existent to the series of appearances which manifest it." [2] In this way three dualisms could be eliminated: that of "interior" and "exterior" (or thing-in-itself and appearance), that of "potency" and "act," and, finally, that of "appearance" and "essence." The phenomenon is the "relative-absolute"; it has to appear to someone, but is what it is in its own right. The phenomenon has no reference to something behind it which would be absolute: "it is absolutely self-indicative." [3] The creativity of a person—e.g., the genius of Proust—is "the work considered as the totality of the person's manifestations." [4] A phenomenal being, lastly, is the "well-connected series of its manifestations," [5] united by the "law" or "ground" of the series; it is itself an "appearance." [6]

We notice two divergent cases: series of interconnected appearances (e.g., the sliding scale of perspectival aspects of a table), and appearances (like the various electrical phenomena) which are only grouped together as one. Referring to Poincaré's nominalism, in terms of which a physical reality is but "the sum of its various manifestations," Sartre rejects such an impoverished unity of appearances. [7] The beings Sartre has in mind, then, are

2. EN, p. 11; BN, p. xlv.
3. EN, p. 12; BN, p. xlvi.
4. *Ibid.*
5. EN, p. 13; BN, p. xlvi.
6. EN, p. 12; BN, p. xlvi.
7. *Ibid.*

perceptual things.[8] There remains a difference, however, between such an essence and an intuitive essence, which is not a synthetic unity but that which is identical in a multiplicity. Sartre's radical acceptation of the notion of the phenomenon has a nominalist ring, although he rejects such a charge and affirms an intuitive essence. The ontological consequences of assuming essences, if only as the law of an open series, are suppressed in order to bring out the thesis that the phenomenon as a unitary entity would be all that description had to take account of. But clearly, a law differs in status from a phenomenon. If a phenomenon must belong to a series, and if a series is not to be a random series, a law is necessary to the phenomenon.[9] In the Introduction, Sartre presents a position which he himself transcends in subsequent sections of EN—phenomenology serves only as an example—but in essential points he maintains the theory of the phenomenon just outlined. However, he deviates from phenomenology on the issue of objectivity in its relation to being.

In our present context, all that matters for Sartre is that the phenomenon requires nothing "behind" it. Speaking more generally, Sartre wants to say that, on the object side, no ontological

---

8. We may note that in his text Sartre equates "appearance" and "manifestation" [*apparition, manifestion*] with *Abschattung* (EN, p. 13; BN, p. xlvii). Here (and in subsequent footnotes) we register Husserl's divergent views. For Husserl, there is a significant difference between phenomenon and *Abschattung*. The phenomenon is described in the perspective of the phenomenological reduction as a noematic object sense with an object pole as its center. *Abschattungen* (shades) are ways in which the noematic content displays itself. They make it possible for us to take different points of view toward something intended as identical. Noema and *Abschattungen* are related like unity and multiplicity (*Ideen zu einer reinen Phänomenologie und phänomenologischen Philosophie,* I [The Hague, 1950], p. 203). The noema presumes object unity. *Auffassungen* (interpretations) and *Abschattungen* may vary, and, with them, noematic features. The noema itself is structured and varies when we pass to other material contents or interpretations; but an object unity intended as identical may survive (*ibid.,* § 131; cf., also, p. 272). We cannot admit, therefore, that for Husserl any variation of shade or interpretation constitutes a new phenomenon of a series. Sartre, too, relates an *Abschattung* to a unity, the perceptual thing, but it is a "profile," a thing in perspective, and an abstraction only in the sense that it has been isolated from a series in which it is located. Husserl's more flexible view—allowing for a noema standing between thing and *Abschattung*—is, in EN, replaced by a simplified and schematic theory. The phenomenon is *homogeneous*. It is in keeping with this view that Sartre rejects the "hyle," Husserl's sense data. Granted that the difference is largely one of words, Sartre's more radical position has, at any rate, implications concerning the problem of object unity. It betrays an underrating of categorial problems.

9. Later (EN, pp. 243f.; BN, pp. 193f.), Sartre speaks of an antecedent revealedness of the essence on the basis of our reference to the future.

distinction is needed. It seems that a monism in terms of phenomena has taken the place of the previous dualisms.

However, a fresh antithesis, that of *finite* and *infinite*, emerges, since a phenomenon stands in a series of other phenomena which, at least in the case of perception, is never closed.[10] Sartre emphasizes this point—which is in principle shared by phenomenology—to demonstrate that we cannot stay with this view, since this would involve the "reality of the thing" being replaced by the "objectivity of the phenomenon" which rests on a "recourse to the infinite." [11]

Sartre wonders if the possibility to go on indefinitely within a series of phenomena could serve as a foundation of their "transcendence." [12] Transcendence would not, then, be defined as a real-

10. Cf. Husserl, *Ideen*, I, p. 80: "To be in this manner incomplete in infinitum belongs to the indissoluble essence of the correlation of 'thing' and 'perception of a thing.'" In illustration, Sartre uses phenomena of our object world, i.e., spatial things with affective and practical meanings. Material for a systematic review of classes of intentional objects by their manner of givenness could be assembled from *L'Imaginaire* (Paris, 1940) and *Esquisse d'une théorie des émotions* (Paris, 1939). *L'Imaginaire*, for example, discusses the restricted explicability ("quasi-observation") of imaginary objects. In EN, Sartre emphasizes that the subject, through its varying perspective, confers infinity on a single phenomenon, or even on a single *Abschattung* (EN, p. 13; BN, p. xlvii). This is unclear. To accept this, we would have to reintroduce *Abschattungen* in Husserl's sense.

11. EN, p. 13; BN, p. xlvi.

12. EN, p. 13; BN, p. xlvii. Everything depends here on the meaning of this word. In our ontological discussion of the phenomenon we will return to this notion. For the time being, let us make sure of its authentic meaning in Husserl. For him, "transcendent" denotes: 1) the opposite of being contained *realiter* [*reell*] in consciousness (*Die Idee der Phänomenologie* [The Hague, 1950], p. 35); and 2) a kind of givenness, a mediated [*nicht selbst schauende*] cognition, in which we go beyond what is given in a true sense (*ibid.*). Thus, whatever is inadequately given, what can only display itself in terms of a multiplicity, is transcendent (cf. *Ideen*, I, p. 287). In this acceptation the universal, qua immediately intuitable, would not be transcendent. Something transcendent "appears" through a manifold given in another, unmediated, kind of givenness. Thus, "visual things" are transcendent as opposed to the *Abschattungen* "experienced" [*erlebt*]. On both counts, real things in terms of our natural attitude are transcendent. The concept is also applied within the phenomenological reduction. Husserl speaks of "this miraculous consciousness of something determined or determinable given in such and such a way . . . which is an opposite to consciousness itself, something other, unreal, transcendent in principle" [*dieses wunderbare Bewussthaben eines so und so gegebenen Bestimmten oder Bestimmbaren . . . das dem Bewusstsein selbst ein Gegenüber, ein prinzipiell Anderes, Irreelles, Transzendentes ist*] (*Ideen*, I, p. 203). 3) In this third sense the noema also is transcendent since it is not *realiter* [*reell*] contained in consciousness and since it is displayed in a manifold of shades. 4) And in yet another sense, in the phenomenological reduction, the object as a unity of noematic multiplicity (cf. *Ideen*, I, p. 207) possesses transcendence. *Objectivity* for Husserl can be considered as built up through variation in which something identical is authenticated (e.g., as that which proves identical in various intentional experiences; cf. *Ideen*, I, § 91).

ity of its own in space and time, but in terms of an infinite series of appearances. A single phenomenon, taken by itself, could not be transcendent but would, rather, remain subjective, as an affection of the subject. Only because a phenomenon of necessity has reference to other phenomena is there something non-subjective, a series tied to a ground which "does not depend on my discretion"; thus, the phenomena would cease to be moments of myself and would take on "objectivity." [13]

Sartre rejects such transcendence in the sense of mere objectivity.[14] Objectivity would be based on the series; but since the series is never closed, objectivity would always remain an un-fulfilled claim. We have a paradox in that it is not the presence of the members of a series but "their absence which gives them objective being"; their being is founded in non-being.[15] The dilemma that the ground of transcendence must be neither negative nor subjective requires, according to Sartre, the assumption of a "being of the phenomena" [16] in order that transcendence can be meaningfully asserted.

The advantage of exclusive reliance on phenomena—the disappearance of the said metaphysical dualisms—has, under Sartre's analysis, proved an illusion. The antithesis of the finite and the infinite has revived the dualisms: what appears is only "an aspect of the object"; the object "is altogether *in* that aspect and altogether outside of it." It has retained a "potency" of being exposed further and further. The essence, finally, remains "radically severed from the individual appearance," since it would take an infinite series to manifest it.[17] It is true that the antitheses to

13. EN, p. 13; BN, p. xlvii.
14. EN, p. 28; BN, p. lxi.
15. *Ibid.* The argument rests on the assumption that there could be no comparative objectivity, with a positive foundation, for an unclosed series. Sartre asks for the totality of a "bad" infinite, and since this is in principle not available, objectivity, qua requiring a totality for its foundation, is based on something negative: viz., that which, with a view to totality, remains outstanding, a nothing. Husserl discusses this question (*Ideen*, I, pp. 297f.). For him, there are objects which, in principle, appear inadequately. But complete givenness is signaled as an idea, as a system of endless processes of continuous appearance. While a closed unity is inconceivable in terms of continuous traversal, the idea of complete givenness is evidently available. This idea is not, in turn, an infinite. In transcendent intuition there is no adequate givenness; all there can be is the idea of a transcendent object and thus an a priori rule for its infinities. With this solution a *positive notion of objectivity* is possible. Husserl requires that a priori element which Sartre suggests, but fails to consider, when he speaks of "essence" and "law" in his criticism of the phenomenological position.
16. EN, p. 15: "l'être du phénomène" (or, EN, p. 14: "des phénomènes"); BN, pp. xlix, xlviii.
17. EN, pp. 13f.; BN, pp. xlvii f.

the individual phenomenon do not belong to another dimension of being, but are accounted for by an infinite progress within a single dimension, that of phenomena. What we are left with is a possible progress toward objectivity, but we fail to lay hold of *reality*. The very notion of an infinite series of phenomena leaves reality undetermined. The rationale of the phenomenological position, as highlighted by Sartre, proves an unsatisfactory position which, for him, is to be overcome by the assumption of a being of phenomena.[18]

In speaking of Sartre's starting position—the theme of this section—we also have to consider the *subject*. On this count, however, Sartre does not intend to drive phenomenology to absurdity in regard to its treatment of being; on the contrary, he accepts, subject to his subsequent reformulation of consciousness, a central point of phenomenological subject theory: the real being of the noesis or act. We defer, therefore, a discussion of Sartre's view of the subject within a phenomenological context to its place in the argument which follows.

[2] THE ARGUMENT FOR AN ONTOLOGICAL FOUNDATION OF THE PHENOMENON

THE QUESTION adumbrated by our analysis is this: in what sense is it legitimate and even necessary to speak of a being of the phenomenon? We might consider such a being a mere mystification; all that Sartre means by "being" of the phenomenon is the essence of appearance, and this simply is that it appears. But Sartre means *being*. On the one hand, he means nothing but the "is"; on the other, he insists on a "relationship" between being and the phenomenon.[19] Sartre embarks on an argument by elimination to determine the problematic referent of this relationship, the being of the phenomenon. He dismisses premature determinations of that being and rules out any idealist solution by a

18. It is clear that, in stating a disjunction of "subjective or infinite," Sartre classifies Husserl's transcendent noema, which has intentional and not real being, under the subjective heading. If all that was involved in the being of the phenomenon was "a" being, he could have found it in Husserl. It is here that we already find in Sartre a different notion of being. (We will discuss the notion of being involved in the following sections). Surely, for Husserl, a transition from mere intendedness to being as it is taken for granted in the natural attitude [*natürliche Einstellung*] can only be supported by objectivity. For Sartre, on the other hand, the assumption of a "being" of the phenomenon makes it unnecessary to require a series to establish transcendence, since even a single phenomenon is a "plenitude of being" (EN, p. 28; BN, p. lxi). Transcendence and objectivity are severed.

19. EN, p. 15: "l'objet ne possède pas l'être . . . il est." ". . . le rapport qui unit le phénomène d'être à l'être doit être établi avant tout." BN, p. xlix.

reductio ad absurdum—i.e., the argument of the non-original nature of passive being. In this connection he casts a first glance at
the subject "for" which the phenomenon is.

The being of appearance in question is not itself appearance.
We might say that being, as such, manifests itself to us, and
Sartre does indeed assert a disclosure of being "by some kind of
immediate access like boredom, nausea, etc." [20] Such an appearance would be a "phenomenon of being" [*phénomène d'être*].[21] But
in such a phenomenon of being, being is not itself appearance.[22]

Nor can being, as distinguished from the phenomenon, be
made available by moving from the phenomenon to its essence
(e.g., in an eidetic reduction). Being is not a "quality" and not a
"meaning of the object." The distinction between essence, or
meaning, and phenomenon is simply different from that between
being and phenomenon. The object "does not refer to being as to a
signification." Nor is being "presence." For, according to Sartre,
"absence, too, discloses being"; "not to be there means still to
be." [23]

Being is not what the phenomenon refers to but "simply the
condition of all revelation." [24] The idea Sartre credits Heidegger
with—that the subject [*Dasein*] could, in virtue of its comprehension of being, "pass" from beings to being—is on a level with
Husserl's passage from the phenomenon to its essence: if I transcend a table toward its being (the being-of-the-table), all I get is
a "being-qua-phenomenon" [*l'être-phénomène*] [25] which, in turn,
requires a being for a foundation, and not being itself, which is its
foundation [*fondement*]. All we achieve is a meaning of being.
Such a meaning is a phenomenon of being.[26] Clearly, ontological
comprehension cannot collapse with its referent, being. If, then,
we seek the "condition" or "foundation" of appearance, it cannot,
for Sartre, be essence or meaning, which themselves are appearance.[27]

20. EN, p. 14; BN, p. xlviii. Cf. Heidegger's interpretation of boredom in *Was
ist Metaphysik?*, 7th ed. (Frankfurt, 1955), p. 28.

21. *Ibid.* The corresponding German term, *Seinsphänomen*, is already found
in N. Hartmann, *Zur Grundlegung der Ontologie* (Berlin, 1935), 2nd ed. (1941),
p. 40.

22. Cf. EN, p. 14; BN, p. xlviii.

23. EN, p. 15; BN, p. xlix.

24. *Ibid.*

25. *Ibid.*

26. The phenomenon of being is thus not restricted to an immediate access to
being as such. Any phenomenon is in some way a phenomenon of being.

27. Cf. N. Hartmann's aporetic treatment of the transcendence of the phenomenon [*Phänomentranszendenz*], *Zur Grundlegung der Ontologie*, pp. 164–67.

Sartre follows an apagogical line of thought. He wonders if the assumption so far, that being was a condition for the disclosure of beings, does not belong to some kind of "ontological realism entirely incompatible with the very notion of appearance." Could not the being of the phenomenon consist in its being given to a subject, i.e., in its *percipi*? [28] His ensuing analysis is designed to show that this is impossible. As a preliminary, Sartre gives us an analysis of the subject in terms of which the latter proves, in turn, to be dependent on something not founded by itself. Both phenomenon and subject thus require a being of the phenomenon not residing in the subject.

The thesis that the being of phenomena reduces to their *percipi* is an idealistic one. Sartre assures us that the idealistic position, which reduces being to cognition, cannot escape the positing of being, at least in the case of cognition itself. This breach in the idealistic principle promises, as a sequel, a non-idealistic solution to the problem of the phenomenon. Were cognition itself to succumb to the principle *esse est percipi* it would lack a foundation in being and so, reduced to mere givenness, fall away "into nothingness." We cannot, therefore, say that cognition or knowledge is reducible to the status of *percipi*. [29] Even if the phenomenon has its being in its *percipi*—this, too, is rejected later—the being of consciousness, *percipere*, cannot. There is, therefore, in the subject a dimension of being which Sartre calls "transphenomenal." [30]

28. EN, p. 16; BN, p. 1. *Percipi* is Husserl's expression for the ontological status of the noema, *Ideen*, I, p. 206. Recently, O. Becker (in *Lebendiger Realismus* [Bonn, 1962], p. 4) has discussed the problem of an ontological interpretation of the phenomenon in phenomenology and in Husserl in particular. He arrives at a rejection of any such ontological interpretation and concludes "dass die 'Welt der reinen Phänomene' *ontologisch nicht charakterisiert* ist. Nach dem *Sein* eines *reinen Phänomens* zu fragen, ist sinnlos. Ein Phänomen hat sein Wesen im Erscheinen, nicht im Sein. Was die 'reine' Phänomenologie erfassen wollte, war dieses Erscheinen, gewissermassen das Erglänzen des Phänomens selbst." From this position, Sartre's approach to ontology from a phenomenological starting point can be negated, at least to the extent that this approach invokes phenomenology. It is evident, however, that Husserl (*Ideen*, I, p. 206) does not exclude ontological determinations. See also O. Becker, *op. cit.*, p. 5.

29. EN, p. 17; BN, pp. 1 f. The use of the term *percipi* and the express reference to Berkeley call for a remark. Berkeley, of course, did not hold the idealistic position referred to here, and says quite clearly that, besides the things whose *esse* is their *percipi* and which are therefore ideas, there is a perceiving being (*Principles*, § 2) and God (*ibid.*, § 147). For Berkeley, too, the subject constitutes a dimension of being of its own, not subject to the condition of being given to . . . The thesis Sartre attacks here is a purely systematic idealism which posits the subject as something unreal, the self-reference of thought.

30. EN, p. 17: "transphénoménal." The term does not imply that there is something beyond the phenomenon, as the prefix suggests—particularly in the subsequent notion of the transphenomenal being of the phenomenon, which lends

He finds an antecedent to this insight in Husserl, who considers the noema an "unreal correlative of the noesis" but the noesis something "real" [*reell*]. The reality status of the noesis indicates, for Sartre, that it is not subject to the *percipi*. The noesis presents itself as preceding any reflection bearing on it. In agreement with Husserl, then, Sartre claims for consciousness a *dimension of being* not founded on its givenness to a subject. Consciousness is not merely a self-referent knowing but a "knowing being" [*être connaissant*]; it is consciousness qua being of the type of consciousness and not qua being known.[31]

This first characterization of consciousness as a dimension of being leads to some further points taken over from phenomenology. Consciousness is *intentionality*: "All consciousness . . . is consciousness of something"; it is a "positing of a transcendent object." [32] We have already seen Sartre's account of an attempt to establish the transcendence of an object on the basis of an infinite series of phenomena. Here now, conversely, the transcendence of the object is to result from the impossibility of something infinite residing "within" consciousness. Sartre depends on a pictorial explanation. An object—more correctly, a spatial object—is something opaque, which we never quite penetrate. It is an infinite which consciousness can never finish taking stock of. Were there to be such an object within consciousness, consciousness would be absorbed in it and fail to be present to itself. For this, to use a complementary figure, it has to be translucent.[33] The object has thus to be assigned a place outside of consciousness. This holds for any cognizant consciousness. Its objects are, with reference to

itself to an oversimplified interpretation—but simply means that something does not exist in virtue of its givenness. Cf. EN, p. 29; BN, p. lxii.

31. EN, p. 17; BN, p. li.

32. *Ibid.*

33. EN, p. 26: "translucidité." Cf. also EN, p. 120; BN, p. 77. The figure of a translucent consciousness is not new. Schopenhauer uses it for the ego but, contrary to Sartre, denies that it was "durch und durch intim, gleichsam durchleuchtet"; for him it is "opak" (*Sämtliche Werke*, ed. Deussen [München, 1911], II, p. 220). W. James speaks of "diaphaneity" (*Journal of Philosophy* [1904], 477). A discussion of James appears in W. Desan, *The Tragic Finale*, p. 145. We might add that Hegel—whose theory, however different, will prove to have much relevance for Sartre—uses the figure as an illustration of his notions of *Begriff* (notion), *Idee* (idea), and *Ich* (I). Cf. *Enzyklopädie*, § 164: *Klarheit* (clearness), as distinguished from *Unterbrechung*, *Trübung* (interruption, or dimness); *ibid.*, § 237: *flüssig und durchsichtig* (fluid and transparent); *Logik*, III (*Werke*, V [Berlin, 1835]), p. 12: *sich selbst durchsichtige Klarheit* (self-transparent clarity, J&S II, p. 216); *Vorlesungen über die Ästhetik* (*Sämtliche Werke*, Jubiläumsausgabe, XII [Stuttgart, 1937]), p. 157: *das reine, vollkommen durchsichtige Scheinen des Ich in sich selbst* (the pure, completely transparent, shining of the ego in itself).

it, transcendent.[34] So far, we lack a detailed theory of consciousness as a dimension of being. But it has become clear that consciousness is a being and that its objects are transcendent with reference to it. We have now to pursue Sartre's question of whether the subject can serve as the being required for a foundation.[35]

Even if the being of a thing were to be reduced to *percipi* status, a thing has a being different from that of subjective impressions or a synthesis of impressions. Otherwise, it would be something noetic, a synthetic act. But the intentional object cannot be resolved into a component part of the reality of consciousness; it has at least a "being." It might, so it seems, be no more than intentional being, *percipi*, but from what has been said this could not be the being of the subject.[36]

Sartre now proceeds to analyze the type of being provisionally granted, the *percipi*.[37] Prompted by the liguistic form of this word, Sartre thinks that the phenomenon, if its being were tantamount to *percipi*, would be characterized by passivity. An analysis of this notion shows that something has to pre-exist if a passive being is to be determined by something else not coincident with it. Without such a foundation, it would be a creation of consciousness. Something created or posited, however, is a nothing if taken by itself; it does not achieve independence, but has to be maintained in being. Thus, it remains within the subjectivity of the creator or, in our context, the perceiver. The general paradox of creation is only adumbrated here, but for Sartre a phenomenon without independent being would precisely fit the case of this paradox. Another argument against passive being takes the line that passivity would have to be reciprocal according to the principle of action

34. Cf. EN, p. 17f; BN, pp. li f. Transcendence equally characterizes the affective consciousness. Cf. *Esquisse d'une théorie des émotions*, p. 29. The same position is taken by Husserl, *Ideen*, I, p. 244: ". . . auch die Gemüts- und Willensakte [sind] ursprünglich objektivierende. . . ." A clouding-up of consciousness would equally result from the immanence of a non-infinite object, e.g., from the "hyle." The argument for the transcendence of the object from infinity is thus dispensable on account of the subject as well: non-transparent entities are outside of consciousness; non-transparent entities are not restricted to infinite ones.

35. EN, p. 24; BN, p. lvii.

36. *Ibid.*

37. EN p. 25–27. BN, p. lvii–lx. The following argument owes its plausibility to the fact that it implies a thing-like object or a substance as a substratum for changing qualities. Theoretically, however, the argument is purely formal, so that a passive being—in our context intentional being—since it is, in a formal sense, a kind of "being," would serve as a sufficient foundation of the phenomenon. It was in this sense that such being was provisionally granted. The result of the argument is, however, that the being of the phenomenon cannot be coincident with passive being.

and reaction. Just as a hand exerting pressure suffers pressure, consciousness, in being active, would have to be passive as well—a state of affairs which, as we shall see, is incompatible with Sartre's notion of consciousness.[38]

Passivity and relativity, then, are only "modes of being," [39] but cannot affect being. The phenomenon is relative with reference to consciousness, but consciousness cannot found or constitute its being. The suggestion that a formal being, such as can be accorded to something merely relative, would suffice as a foundation of the phenomenon is thus rejected in favor of an independent and transphenomenal being proper to the phenomenon. The phenomenon has to be regarded as an object. Consciousness transcends itself toward an object existing independently. The basic insight of phenomenology, to the effect that consciousness is consciousness of something, had really been granted from the start; all that matters is the "ontological status" of such an intentional object. We would miss the intentionality or transcendence of consciousness, if the object had the status of *percipi,* since it would then be confined to subjectivity.

Now, it seems, Sartre can say "consciousness is congenitally oriented towards a being which it is not." [40] An ontological proof has been offered. The intentionality of consciousness, which itself is a being, can now be claimed as a reference to the object in terms of being [*Seinsverhältnis*]. Consciousness must have a content given to it as the object of a revealing intention not confined within subjectivity "or it is nothing." "Immanence can make itself definite only in the seizure of something transcendent." [41] Sartre's problem is not to infer the existence of objective things from a subjective phenomenon. He is not raising the epistemological question as to whether we are justified in positing subjective phenomena as objectively real. What he has in mind is a relation in terms of being, a relation between consciousness qua trans-

38. EN, pp. 25f.; BN, p. lix. The latter example is unconvincing. Taken from the area of mechanics, it fails us at the crucial point: action is not production, so why should a phenomenon produced by consciousness be subject to the mechanical analogy? On the contrary, under the analogy it becomes incomprehensible why consciousness could fail to be passive, if we assume a foundation of being in the object. Sartre also discusses Husserl's "hyle" from the point of view of passivity (EN, p. 26; BN, p. lix). It is not strictly passive since it is not intended, but a neutral givenness.
39. EN, p. 27: "manières d'être."
40. EN, p. 28: ". . . la conscience naît portée sur un être qui n'est pas elle." The translation is adapted from H. Spiegelberg, *The Phenomenological Movement,* II (The Hague, 1960), p. 488.
41. EN, p. 29; BN, pp. lxi f.

phenomenal being and transphenomenal being qua being of the phenomenon. Objectivity cannot be construed with subjectivity as its basis. Still, the being of the phenomenon is no noumenal being behind the phenomenon: "It is the being of this table, of this package of tobacco, of the lamp, more generally the being of the world. . . . The transphenomenal being of what exists for consciousness is itself in itself." [42]

For Sartre, phenomenon and consciousness are now grounded in their being. Consciousness is "revealed-revelation of existents, and the existents appear before consciousness on the foundation of their being." [43] Being, however, does not reveal itself "in person"; [44] being is foundation. It is only apprehended "through the mode of being that manifests it and veils it at the same time," i.e., the mode of being of the phenomenon. "Consciousness can always pass beyond the existent, not towards its being, but towards the meaning of this being." [45] The meaning of being revealed to consciousness is itself a phenomenon, the phenomenon of being. This phenomenon of being is an "appeal to being"; it requires being as a foundation of the phenomenon.

The phenomenon of being is, if we like, a higher-order phenomenon. As an implicit understanding it accompanies all given phenomena and is, by itself, a phenomenon. As such it requires, in turn, a being. Sartre anticipates the objection that this would introduce another being—viz., the being of the phenomenon of being—and so upset the elucidation, by way of the phenomenon of being, of the being of the phenomenon, since it would leave open another being requiring elucidation of its meaning. His answer is that this is no additional being with a meaning of its own; the meaning of the being of the phenomenon, as expressed in the phenomenon of being, holds also for the being of this meaning, i.e., for the phenomenon of being.[46] Being possesses a generality enabling it to serve as a foundation of beings (existents) as well as of the meaning of their being. The ontological proof is not restricted; it is intended to be valid for every phenomenon, including the phenomenon of being.

The bases of an ontology have become visible: they are the two "types of being," [47] the *being of the phenomenon* and *con-*

---

42. EN, p. 29; BN, p. lxii. Cf. Hegel, *Vorlesungen zur Geschichte der Philosophie*, III, *Jubiläumsausgabe*, XIX (Stuttgart, 1937), p. 575.
43. EN, p. 30; BN, p. lxii.
44. EN, p. 30; BN avoids this phrase (p. lxii).
45. EN, p. 30; BN, p. lxiii.
46. *Ibid.*
47. EN, p. 34: "types d'êtres," more correctly, "types d'être" (e.g., EN, p. 711);

sciousness as a being. So far, however, pursuant to the Introduction to EN, we have been given little more than the mere "that" of a being of the phenomenon. The further elucidation of this being, of the being of consciousness, and of their relationship is now Sartre's task. But before we join him in this, a closer study of his theses in the Introduction may be welcome.

[3] BEING AND PHENOMENON

THE SHIFT from phenomenology to the ontological level depends on an argument in which the word "being" plays an important part. So we should attempt a clarification of this notion of being, all the more so since the ontological proof depends on it, and, without that proof, the ontological level could not be considered "established," but would merely be presupposed. The legitimacy of this passage from phenomenology to ontology is not essential to the ontology to come, but the disclosure of being from a phenomenological basis does, at least in part, involve a particular formulation of being which, in turn, determines Sartre's ontology in its eventual structure.

It is obvious that a philosopher who starts from the phenomenon or the given and who, rather than plunge into ontology proper, intends to blaze a trail toward it must clear an initial hurdle: the ambivalence of the phenomenon as an entity standing between consciousness and being. To deal with this problem, Sartre adopts, apagogically, a subjectivist notion of the phenomenon, to show that it is untenable and requires us to pass on to being. With this, the starting point of the argument, the phenomenon in its neutrality is itself sublated.

The argument described above involves two stages. First, it is argued that a phenomenon, even on an idealist interpretation, has a being, since it would otherwise collapse with the subject; it has at least a being in the manner of the *percipi*. Second, it is argued that *percipi* being is, as such, nonsensical; what is required is an independent being proper to the phenomenon, such that a disclosure of phenomena is a disclosure of the world's being.

Percipi being stands for an existential moment. A phenomenon has to be there in order that it can be given to a subject to which it is related. This is what the argument from passivity is supposed to bring home. Let us consider this argument in its basic

---

cf. "manières d'être" (EN, p. 27). The vacillation between the two expressions and the merger of "type" and "région" (EN, p. 34: "région d'être") is characteristic of Sartre. Cf. pp. 41, 132, 135f., 144, below.

assumptions. The fulcrum of the argument is the idea that the relationship between phenomenon and subject, the *percipi,* involves a passion and that passion in turn involves a *subsistent* supporting it. In classical terms this means that a phenomenon has to be considered a *concretum,* a unity of essence and existence. The phenomenon would be a subjective object. It would either precede its givenness (which is paradoxical) or the *percipere* would posit both essence and existence. We would thus embrace a picture theory claiming pictorial entities in the mind, a theory which, failing the idea of *percipi* being, would suppose a production of phenomena in the subject. (Sartre's objection is that in such an event the created phenomenon could not dissociate from the creator. It is of course debatable whether consciousness is not that unique being where such production takes place, i.e., where the phenomenon is an idea and has the status of a *concretum* which can be an Other of consciousness.)

What Sartre demands as a foundation of the *percipi* is not a phenomenon as a *concretum.* That which has to precede as a foundation for passion is referred to as a "being." A "being" is required to "support" the phenomenon. With this claim, the classical view of a conjunction of essence and existence in a *concretum* is rejected. But the ontological argument which Sartre gives involves a *petitio principii* since it implies that, in the case of the phenomenon, there is no such conjunction. The argument from passivity is already committed to the ontological thesis which requires demonstration, viz., that existence has to be considered an in-itself, separate and independent of essence. We had better reverse the *demonstrandum* and say that, in order to escape the difficulties of the picture theory and to do justice to phenomenological evidence, a new ontology to interpret subject and phenomenon has to be formulated.

Since Sartre's argument clearly alludes to Anselm, let us look for a parallel between the two ontological arguments. In his *Proslogion,* Anselm begins with an idea of God in consciousness. Man understands the idea, or the word, "God," and harbors it in his mind, although this is not tantamount to evidence that God exists.[48] Anselm's thesis is that what is in consciousness, the idea of God, is, qua content, greater than anything conceivable;[49] i.e.,

48. *Proslogion, S. Anselmi Cantuariensis Archiepiscopi Opera Omnia,* ed. F. S. Schmitt (Secovii, i.e., Seckau, 1938) I, p. 101: ". . . intelligit quod audit; et quod intelligit in intellectu eius est, etiam si non intelligat illud esse. Aliud enim est rem esse in intellectu, aliud intelligere rem esse."

49. *Ibid.:* ". . . aliquid quo nihil maius cogitari potest. . . ."

that the idea is outside and inside consciousness since otherwise the greatest would not be the greatest.[50] Therefore, God cannot be conceived of as other than existing.[51] The argument says in fact that, in the first place, something is in consciousness and that it remains to be determined, next, whether this might not, in addition, have a "status of being" beyond that of conscious immanence. The idea that what is in consciousness denotes a maximum provides a bridge leading over to something beyond, or unrestricted to, consciousness, something with the status of "true being." However, it is not legitimate to identify what is in consciousness with what truly is. Initially, Anselm does distinguish the two, but goes on to identify them, since he assumes what need only be a picture of God in the mind as God's being in consciousness; the selfsame thing in consciousness has to be considered something transcending consciousness. The argument suggests that God—and not the mere idea of God—is "at least" in consciousness and that it has to be determined whether he is not something else, or is something else as well. The idea of God and God are ontologically different; God is not "at least" idea and, in addition, in virtue of the argument, transcendent God.[52]

The theoretical situation in Sartre's proof is similar. For the sake of argument, Sartre begins with a phenomenon in consciousness with the status of *percipi* (corresponding to Anselm's *esse in intellectu*). Next, he questions its status of being. The result is, as the argument from passivity is designed to show, that this cannot be *percipi* being. This general argument replaces the specific role of Anselm's maximal concept. Thus, Sartre's argument differs from Anselm's in that the *esse in intellectu* is completely negated; the status of being of a phenomenon is different—not different "in addition," as in Anselm's argument where God is *in intellectu* and *in re*. Sartre's argument therefore sublates its premiss. Apart from the apagogical assumption, there is no *esse in intellectu*, no *percipi* being.

In the argument, the immanent phenomenon (admitted by Anselm, assumed apagogically by Sartre) is mistakenly identified

50. *Ibid.*, pp. 101f.: "Si ergo id quo maius cogitari non potest, est in solo intellectu: id ipsum quo maius cogitari non potest, est quo maius cogitari potest. Sed certe hoc esse non potest. Existit ergo procul dubio aliquid quo maius cogitari non valet, et in intellectu et in re."

51. *Ibid.*, p. 103: "Sic ergo vere est aliquid quo maius cogitari non potest, ut nec cogitari possit non esse."

52. The present interpretation is indebted to B. Geyer (F. Ueberweg, *Grundriss der Geschichte der Philosophie*, II, *Die patristische und scholastische Philosophie*, ed. B. Geyer [Berlin, 1928], p. 200).

with a homonymous something with a different status of being—
God is at least *in intellectu;* the phenomenon has, for the time
being, *percipi* status—and yet again posited as different—God is
also outside consciousness, the phenomenon is only outside consciousness. An entity cannot, however, be considered irrespective
of its "status of being"; it cannot be identical with a homonymous
entity of a different status. This would contravene the classical
doctrine of essence and existence as ontological principles. On the
contrary, an idea would have to qualify for a *concretum* just as
much as the thing of which it is the idea. In the classical view,
there is no idea whose existential moment could be replaced by
another and yet remain the same.[53]

Viewing the matter from the point of view of phenomenology,
it is tempting to retain the identity of the phenomenon, since in
phenomenology we start from givenness. The given is our unquestioned point of departure; all that is left to be determined is
its status of being. A critical realism, with its picture theory,
cannot be so tempted but, in return, has the problem of an ungiven, immanent entity on its hands. With his argument, Sartre
wants to reduce the picture theory to absurdity (thus corroborat-
ing the phenomenological position) and, at the same time, believes himself in possession of a proof for the transcendent reality
of phenomena. The absurdity of a "mere" phenomenon cannot,
however, be demonstrated in this way and, just as with Anselm,
the positive thesis of the argument would prove too much: for
Anselm, any maximal concept could carry the proof of its existence with it (e.g., the perfect island); [54] for Sartre, any phenomenon could, including a fallacy.

Granted all this, Sartre's argument is not simply a mistake but,
rather, if viewed from classical ontology, a *petitio principii.* It says
that the ontological principles need not be regarded as conjoined
in the classical manner. Qua argument, it does not prove its point;
what it does is to urge a new ontology.

53. Kant's criticism of the ontological argument for the existence of God
points in the same direction. For him, the concept is no more than (fully
determined) essence. The question of its existence is left open; i.e., it is left open
whether there is a corresponding transcendent *concretum* or merely a subjective
concretum [idea, *Vorstellung*]. Nor does an essence involving the notion of a
maximum require by itself a transcendent existential moment (cf. *Critique of
Pure Reason,* trans. N. K. Smith [London, 1929], B 627f.).

54. Unless we understand the maximal concept, with Hegel, as an infinite, the
notion, which, qua in and for itself, is being and to which we, qua subjective and finite notion, rise in virtue of the dialectic. Cf. Hegel, *Vorlesungen
über die Philosophie der Religion,* II, *Jubiläumsausgabe,* XVI (Stuttgart, 1937),
Appendix, pp. 480f.

The existential moment, argued for in the above manner, has been given a special status. The division into two ontological moments, into existence and essence—or, more carefully, into "that" and "what" [55]—takes now the form of a "that," on the one hand, and a givenness for a subject on the other; this latter relativity covers the "what." The "what" is dependent; the "that," in contradistinction to it, is independent. Originally introduced as a trivial kind of being—for a phenomenon to be a phenomenon, it has to be—it now stands opposed to a dependent or relative "what"; it turns into being-in-itself. It does not exist for us, being the opposite of appearance, phenomenon, and object. Or, more correctly, it is "for" us only "qua" phenomenon; by itself, it is transphenomenal, *being*.

We see that the shift from phenomenology, with its ontological neutrality or mere intentional being, to being rests on a preconceived ontology. This ontology, with its crucial notion of being-in-itself, involves several problems. In our present context, however, they can only be mentioned briefly, if only because the present level of discussion is a provisional one. Sartre's notion of being-in-itself implies the assertion of a "correlativistic" position. Being-in-itself is neither subject to cognition nor something determinate which is the matrix of the phenomenon; instead, it turns into a givenness. Truth is a revelation since, as we shall see, the in-itself is nothing indeterminate either. The theoretical account of being-in-itself constitutes a peculiar solution to the problem of realism. It meets the claim of realism, in as much as the in-itself is not relative to the phenomenon; the latter is simply the mode of givenness of the former. There is being-in-itself without the added condition of availability as a phenomenon.[56] Sartre's view differs from realism, however, in that a representation in the subject and any *adaequatio* are rejected.

The Sartrean solution prompts many questions in connection with the problem of knowledge: Does not this theory prove too much if it accords a being-in-itself to every phenomenon? Are there no fallacies? Can fallacies be interpreted as transcendent

55. N. Hartmann distinguishes the two pairs of concepts: normally, essence already involves an identification with ideal being and a non-inclusion of accidents (*Zur Grundlegung der Ontologie*, 2nd ed. [Berlin, 1941], pp. 90f.); the couple "that" and "what" [*Dasein, Sosein*] is not fraught with these implications (*ibid.*, p. 92).

56. In Sartre, the phrase "there is" [*il y a*] is reserved to denote the presentation of the in-itself as a phenomenon: ". . . la connaissance, finalement, et le connaissant lui-même ne sont rien sinon le fait 'qu'il y a' de l'être, que l'être en-soi se *donne*. . . ." EN, p. 227; BN, p. 179.

objects? What about a dimension of immanence with which ideas, thoughts, and judgments are associated? Another question incidental to our present context concerns meaning. If phenomena are identified with objects or beings, this would lead to a revision of the pertinent phenomenological theory. The ontological distinction between being and sense [*Sinn, sens*] rests on the possibility of detaching sense as a meaning. Now Sartre does consider the givenness of sense or meaning; it is, in turn, a phenomenon with a being. Is being-in-itself, then, a unitary realm of being, or are there several—e.g., an ideal and a real realm? These questions can be only partially answered on the basis of EN; they point up difficulties in directions not pursued by Sartre's work.

From a general perspective, we find in Sartre a possible derivative of phenomenology which is also found, in different form, in N. Hartmann and M. Scheler. His theory, outlined above, acknowledges the main inspiration of Husserl's theory of intentionality— that consciousness, without the mediation of non-given entities residing in immanence, is present to the object. In the course of its development, in the theory of phenomenological reduction, phenomenology had again been led to such an entity, the noema, which could be credited with an "intentional being"; the traditional account of the problem of givenness came to loom large once more. Sartre proposes to go back on this step. In the field of consciousness and its object, Sartre urges an ontological position which, in some respects, comes close to that of Husserl in his *Logische Untersuchungen*. Understandably, intentionality theory cannot stay on the elemental level on which the Introduction to EN presents it. Accordingly, all we have done is to isolate, on the basis of this Introduction, a phenomenological position as it occurs in the context of Sartre's "ontological proof." The more detailed treatment of the field in EN is conducted in another idiom, that of negation, in-itself and for-itself, thus giving rise to a mixed form of theory to be assessed on its own terms. In our present context we can only wonder if Sartre's theory, in spite of its congenital flaw, will be able to do justice to all those problems for which phenomenology has created its refined instruments of thought.

[4] CONSCIOUSNESS

FOLLOWING SARTRE'S LINE of thought leading from the phenomenon to being, we have already considered consciousness in some of its elemental features, as intentionality and as a dimension of being. Obviously, only for an existing consciousness of something is there any point in wondering if the phenomenon might not be a mere moment of the immanent reality of the subject. Now these two features do not by themselves provide a sufficient account of consciousness. Sartre's figure of translucency points at another feature. His main thesis concerning the problem of consciousness is that consciousness must be conscious of itself, or else there would be an "unconscious consciousness—which is absurd." [57] The givenness of the intention directed to the object given by it is for Sartre a necessary condition of having a consciousness of that object. Is this consciousness of the transcending act another act referring to that act? That would make it a reflection, an act referring for its object to "consciousness" or "intention." Being conscious of the primary intention cannot, however, be reflection, since in that case consciousness would be split into subject and object, leaving a final term ungiven; we end in a regress. Intentional consciousness, so far claimed for a dimension of being, must now also be established epistemologically, i.e., it must be shown how consciousness of knowing, etc., is possible without a regress. For Sartre, the problem can only be solved if we assume that consciousness is not a "couple." [58] The requisite reference of consciousness to itself must not be objectifying or "positing," [59] but has to be considered a "non-positing" reference. Such an immediate consciousness is not cognitive consciousness; [60] it does

57. EN, p. 18; BN, p. lii.
58. EN, p. 19: "couple." "Dual" (BN, p. lii) conflicts with BN, p. 76.
59. EN, p. 19: "Elle [la conscience] ne la pose pas [ma perception]." The notions "positing" or "positional" [*positionnel, thétique*] and "non-positing" or "non-positional" [*non-positionnel, non-thétique*] call for a comparison with Husserl. For him, *Setzung* or *Thesis* (positing) signifies a character of the noesis in virtue of which a noema is accorded reality, probability, or some other existential mode. (Cf. *Ideen,* I, §§ 90, 103, 114.) Accordingly, "positing" does not mean that consciousness opposes an intentional object to itself or turns to it by way of intending it, but, rather, that it takes as real, etc., what is already an opposed content—intentional object or *intentum* qua *intentum*—the positing being coeval with the opposing of such content. For Sartre, a more primitive notion of positing applies, that of opposing an object to oneself. This use of the term is reminiscent of Fichte's use of *Setzen,* with the difference that positing in Sartre is not meant to involve a subjective status of the *oppositum.* Even in Husserl, in his *Vorlesungen zur Phänomenologie des inneren Zeitbewusstseins (Jahrbuch für Philosophie und phänomenologische Forschung,* IX, ed. Heidegger [Halle, 1928]), we find a meaning of "positing" [*Setzen*] close to Sartre's meaning. He says (p. 481) of an experience that it is "immanent 'wahrgenommen' [inneres Bewusstsein], wenn auch natürlich nicht gesetzt, gemeint."
60. Thus a child, counting without reflection, cannot "explain" what he is doing. Adding up appears to him only as an objective state of affairs characterizing the objects counted. EN, p. 19; BN, p. liii.

not pass judgment or comment like a reflective act, but is constitutive of any positional consciousness, including acts of reflection. Thus "every positional consciousness of an object is at the same time a non-positional consciousness of itself." [61] Sartre calls this non-positional consciousness of consciousness the "pre-reflective cogito" [*cogito préréflexif*].[62]

From this notion we can go in two directions: the pre-reflective cogito is, as we have seen, intended as an epistemological explanation of how a consciousness of intentional objects is possible; and it stands further for a structural unity leading on to an ontological interpretation of consciousness. In line with our present emphasis on what is predominantly a phenomenological position in Sartre, let us follow the former consideration.

The idea that consciousness has to be given unto itself, so as not to be unconscious, has a certain force to it. On the one hand, we believe we are "aware" of ourselves; on the other hand, this awareness would make consciousness a second object, in addition to the immediate object of our intention—a state of affairs not borne out by our normal experience. To explain this "functional" self-consciousness, a reflection is apparently called for and yet, at the same time, excluded. The dilemma has often been seen, and it was Brentano who first arrived at a considered answer, designed to meet the difficulty.[63]

---

61. EN, p. 19; BN, p. liii.

62. EN, p. 20; BN, p. liii. Sartre characterizes it as "conscience (de) . . ." (with "de" in parentheses, as opposed to "de" without parentheses, standing for a transcending reference to the intentional object). Accordingly, we use "consciousness (of). . . ."

63. This sounds like a gross oversimplification. In distinguishing αἴσθησις, which perceives vision [ὁρᾶν], from vision, Aristotle was the first to draw attention to the difference of awareness and perception (*De anima*, ed. W. D. Ross [Oxford, 1956], 425b, 12–25). Brentano was to resume this analysis. In the following remarks, we can only state briefly how philosophy in the modern age has hovered over the problem of self-consciousness. The notion of reflection, taken as introspection, remained for a long time a paradigm for an understanding of self-consciousness as a condition of consciousness. Leibniz opposes the view that reflection is a condition of our thinking and sensing ("Nouveaux Essais," ed. C. I. Gerhardt, *Philosophische Schriften*, V [Berlin, 1882], pp. 107f.). His alternative is unconscious perception of which, however, he is unable to show that it becomes noticeable through intensification and that noticing does not involve reflection. Locke has the notion of an accompanying reflection ("reflex act of perception accompanying [an action]," *An Essay Concerning Human Understanding*, ed. C. Fraser [Oxford, 1894], II, 27, 13), and also a notion of self-consciousness as a condition of personal identity (*ibid.*, II, 27, 16–19), but is not in a position to distinguish theoretically between such a self-consciousness and reflection properly so called. Kant, in his "I think," has brought into focus a functional self-consciousness, failing which a representation would be "impossible, or at least would be nothing to me" (*Critique of Pure Reason*, B 132). This "I think" is "pure

For Brentano,[64] the representation of an object, or the psychic act, is given in an internal consciousness. There is only one act, but a twofold object: a primary object and, intertwined with it, the act itself as a secondary object. The two representations are so closely linked with each other that the primary representation contributes to the being of the secondary one. Brentano realizes that the secondary object, though apprehended consciously in the act, cannot be an observed object—a thesis parallel to Sartre's distinction of "positional" and "non-positional" givenness. Brentano further calls for representational, cognitive and affective internal consciousness, while Sartre's pre-reflective cogito is left unspecified. In support of his view, Brentano does not urge the absurdity of the opposite assumption of an unconscious consciousness. He merely shows that such a consciousness cannot be demonstrated and rests his case on internal experience.[65] If we were to assume an additional reflective act, on the other hand, this would involve the content of the primary act being given twice over, a state of affairs not borne out by experience. Brentano thus accords each psychic act internal consciousness,[66] although the methodological basis for such an account of consciousness remains somewhat obscure. Reflection in the present is denied,[67] and it would be unsuitable since it would presuppose internal consciousness. Accordingly, the adequacy of the conceptual for-

---

apperception" or "original apperception." For Kant, however, this unity of self-consciousness serves as a condition of the unity of representations and thus as a transcendental origin of categories imprinted on objects presented to us. The "I think" as a fact subject to phenomenological consideration eludes us. We find a similar link-up of factual and transcendental self-consciousness in Fichte. Factual self-consciousness is referred back to a ground in the absolute subject. The absolute subject, it is true, does not precede the factual subject so that, in this respect, both are the same (cf. *Grundlage der gesamten Wissenschaftslehre*, ed. F. Medicus [Hamburg, 1961], p. 17). Nevertheless, as a transcendental condition, the absolute subject is something unknown and therefore unconscious, a logical activity. For Hegel, proper self-consciousness is bound up with an identification between me and the object: "I know of the object as mine (it is my representation); therefore, in it I know of myself" (*Enzyklopädie*, § 424). This view avoids the assumption that any consciousness of something features an added reference to itself. Any transcending preserves a previous return of the subject unto itself, and, by itself, constitutes a new return. We may say then that Kant's, Fichte's, and Hegel's doctrines of self-consciousness focus on the transcendental problem. They underpin empirical and factual self-consciousness by a logico-transcendental theory, leaving the "existing" unity of self-consciousness, as such, undiscussed.

64. *Psychologie vom empirischen Standpunkt*, I, bk. 2, chaps. 2 and 3 (Leipzig, 1924).

65. *Ibid.*, pp. 176, 179.

66. *Ibid.*, p. 218.

67. *Ibid.*, p. 181.

mulation, granted experience, poses a problem. There is no "structural self-evidence," in that the conceptualized description does not make it clear why the primary object is not once again contained in the secondary representation. This can only be rejected on account of experience.[68] The concepts used in the theory, such as representation [*Vorstellung*], object [*Objekt*], and consciousness [*Bewusstsein*], do not meet the case with precision but have to be qualified to fit an exception—namely, that the secondary representation is a representation, but without the usual characteristics of a representation—a difficulty echoed in Sartre when he calls the pre-reflective cogito, in contrast with the cogito, a "nonpositional" cogito.

Brentano's view appears as a compromise: the conscious givenness of a psychic act must be regarded as something like a reflection but not as a "proper" reflection. Similarly, in Sartre consciousness is given unto itself in something like a second cogito, or a quasi-reflection, a reflection without the decisive characteristic of reflection, objectification. Accordingly, Sartre argues for a "homology" [69] of self-consciousness as a formal condition of consciousness and explicit reflection, a form of self-consciousness not constitutive of consciousness.

Husserl, in turn, rejects Brentano's theory of an "internal conciousness." [70] For him, there is no evidence of a "continuous action of internal perception." He does admit internal perception, however, as a specific kind of consciousness. The distinction essential to Brentano, that the secondary representation of the act is not observational, receives less attention in view of the fact that Brentano does not hesitate to call this internal consciousness an "internal perception"—a term which, for Husserl, stands for a

68. *Ibid.*, pp. 178f.

69. Cf. EN, p. 117: "Ce cogito [the pre-reflective one], certes, ne pose pas d'object, il reste intraconscientiel. Mais il n'en est pas moins homologue au cogito réflexif en ce qu'il apparaît comme la nécessité première pour la conscience irréfléchie, d'être vue par elle même." BN, p. 74. It is remarkable that Sartre's prereflective cogito has been confused with his cogito. W. Desan (in *The Tragic Finale*, p. 9) writes: "Sartre makes a distinction between the prereflexive Cogito, which is ordinary and immediate knowledge (e.g., I know a table, I know Peter) and authentic reflection . . . (e.g., I know that I know the table)." This passage is, to say the least, confusing, since the term "pre-reflective cogito" is designed to single out, within the cogito, an element qualifying it—and not the cogito so qualified—and, in turn, to contrast it with a reflective cogito. The occasion for the confusion might have been a passage like EN, p. 118: "C'est que la conscience préréflexive est conscience (de) soi." Here, the pre-reflective cogito appears as a unity of intention and self-givenness, not as the element of self-givenness as such.

70. *Logische Untersuchungen*, 2nd ed. (Halle, 1913), II, 1, V, p. 356.

"primary" intention. Thus, Husserl's criticism of Brentano involves a terminological misunderstanding.

Husserl's basic notion in the field of consciousness is that of an experience [*Erlebnis*]. In one sense of "consciousness," discounting that of internal perception, an experience is a "having"; it involves the fact that "certain contents are elements of a unity of consciousness, [*i.e.,*] of a phenomenologically homogeneous stream of consciousness of an empirical ego." [71] This unity of consciousness is, by itself, a "real [*reell*] whole composed of a manifold of parts as its real [*reell*] constituents, and each such part is called 'experienced.' " [72] In terms of this notion of consciousness, an experience is not divided into content and experience of content: "Something sensed [*das Empfundene*], e.g., is none other than the sensing [*Empfindung*]." [73]

An experience can refer to "an object other than itself." [74] We then speak of an "intentional experience," standing for a third notion of consciousness. In an intentional experience "the sensa and, equally, the acts apperceiving them . . . are experienced [*erlebt*] but they do not appear as objects [*gegenständlich*]; . . . The objects, in turn, appear; they are perceived, but not experienced." [75] Something other than the experience is intentionally present in the experience. We are "absorbed" [*gehen auf*] in such an act,[76] and no reference to an ego is involved.[77] For Husserl, the givenness of an intentional object is bound up with the real [*reell*] act; the givenness of the act is accounted for simply by its belonging to a stream of experiences as a unity of consciousness.

The problem of the unity of consciousness and self-consciousness corresponds to that of the two "aspects" of an experience: an intentional experience refers to its object, and qua experience constitutes an element in a complex of experiences constituting itself as a unity. The problem is apparently solved by urging these two aspects, that of intention and that of real constitution. The question of how an intention can be conscious is analyzed into two aspects: an absorption of consciousness in the object, on the one hand, and a belongingness of an experience to a self-constitutive

71. *Ibid.*, p. 352.
72. *Ibid.*
73. *Ibid.*
74. *Ibid.*
75. *Ibid.*, p. 385.
76. *Ibid.*, p. 376.
77. Cf., however, Husserl's change of view in the problem of the ego: *ibid.*, pp. 354, 361, 363.

unity of consciousness as a complex of experiences, on the other.

In his *Vorlesungen zur Phänomenologie des inneren Zeitbe-wusstseins,* Husserl states that every act is "conscious" [*bewusst*]. "Every experience [*Erlebnis*] is 'sensed,' immanently 'perceived' (internal consciousness [*inneres Bewusstsein*]) although, of course, not posited or intended. . . ." [78] Husserl is aware of the regress argument:

Every "experience" in the strict sense is internally perceived. But the internal perception is not in the same sense an "experience." It is not in turn internally perceived. . . . "Perceiving" means nothing but a temporally constitutive consciousness with its phases of fluent retentions and protentions. . . . What we call an experience, what we call an act of judgment, of joy, of external perception . . . , all these are unities of temporal consciousness and thus perceivednesses [*Wahrgenommenheiten*]. [79]

In his monograph, "La Transcendance de l'égo," [80] Sartre draws on Husserl's analyses in the *Logische Untersuchungen* and the *Vorlesungen zur Phänomenologie des inneren Zeitbewusstseins* when he interprets consciousness as something which unites itself in a game of retentions and thus continuously refers to itself. [81] However, when he says "elle [la conscience] est purement et simplement conscience d'être conscience de cet objet [sc. transcendant]," [82] we notice a reinterpretation of Husserl. The unification of the stream of consciousness, especially if we consider that it is to account also for self-consciousness in the phase of the actual present, is not identical with what is, in effect, a notion stemming from Brentano—the pre-reflective cogito, through which a cogito is conscious of itself. Husserl does not deal with an internal consciousness purely in the present, such as Sartre assumes. [83]

78. Heidegger (ed.), *Jahrbuch für Philosophie und phänomenologische Forschung,* IX (Halle, 1928), p. 481.

79. *Ibid.,* pp. 481f.

80. *Recherches philosophiques,* 1936–37, pp. 85–123.

81. *Ibid.,* p. 89.

82. *Ibid.,* p. 90.

83. According to Husserl's later view, which cannot be fully discussed here, a pure ego is assumed. The act is seen as a ray originating from the ego as point of departure, and the complex of experiences now receives a foundation in something identical (cf. *Ideen,* I, p. 109); the stream of consciousness is not now restricted to a series uniting itself synthetically. The question of awareness, which would now be one of the ego and which Natorp considers an irreducible surd, is not, as far as we can see, discussed in any of Husserl's subsequent writings available to Sartre when he wrote EN. It is true, in his posthumous *Erste Philosophie,* I (The Hague, 1956), p. 111, Husserl once more raises the issue of internal consciousness: "Auch jenes universale Bewussthaben, durch das alles einzelne Erleben seinerseits bewusst ist, das sogenannte 'innere' Bewusstsein, ist

It seems, then, that we can distinguish two different phenomenological views: one, according to which consciousness is absorbed in its object and unifies itself in *time-consciousness,* such that no presence of consciousness unto itself as actually experiencing is expressly stipulated; and another, according to which an *accompanying consciousness, homologous to a reflection,* is assumed for every act. In his early monograph, Sartre is closer to the former view; in EN, however, he reapproaches Brentano, so that in fact we find a combination of both views. In Husserl, Sartre finds a theory of intentional consciousness clearly separating the intentional object from the confused notion of a representation; real and intentional spheres are distinguished and consciousness transcends toward its object. Regarding the latter point, though, Sartre raises a criticism concerning the ontological status of the intentional object in Husserl. Further, Sartre finds in Husserl a theory of consciousness as time-consciousness. In Brentano, on the other hand, he finds an interpretation of self-consciousness, however much restricted to a "characteristic" of an object representation which, without such secondary representation, would "not be unthinkable." [84]

Sartre's new emphasis is twofold. From Husserl's division of real [*reell*] and intentional spheres he moves on to a division of consciousness and being-in-itself. Consciousness now stands opposed to the existing object; as the "other" being it stands to the object in a relationship of being. In Husserl, the idea of seeing the reference of consciousness to its object as a relationship of being does not occur. Consciousness for him is a being, but he discounts the reality of its correlative. As for consciousness itself, Brentano's view of awareness comes to the fore in Sartre: consciousness has a quasi-reflective structure, is *self-referent being,* being turned back upon itself. Sartre draws also on Husserl's analysis of time-consciousness, which constitutes its unity through fluent syntheses. But this unity remains different from the one Sartre demands. For him, the protentions and retentions of Husserl are references in terms of intuition and not in terms of being; Husserl's

---

ein wahrer Wunderbau feinster intentionaler Strukturen, obschon freilich tief verborgener." Again, Husserl adumbrates the notion of a descriptively complex structure contrary to Sartre who assumes a pre-reflective structure simply in terms of principle. In the above-mentioned monograph, "La Transcendance de l'égo," Sartre tries to show that the assumption of a pure ego constitutes an obstacle to the synthetic self-unification of consciousness. Such an ego would be something opaque, blocking the pure self-reference of consciousness.

84. F. Brentano, *Psychologie vom empirischen Standpunkt,* I (Leipzig, 1924), p. 180.

consciousness "is," for him, instantaneous or restricted to the present.[85] In his own view, on the other hand, Sartre moves closer to Heidegger's idea of an "ecstatic" subject [Dasein]. Sartre also departs from Husserl in his denial of Husserl's immanent entities like the "hyle," whose incorporation into the unity of consciousness is incomprehensible to Sartre.

Consciousness is translucent, has reference to itself, appears to itself. In this way it excludes all other being from itself. It is a type of being of its own. Its transphenomenality consists in its "being" a self-givenness instead of being "for" a knower. It has no transphenomenal "ground" of which it is the appearance.[86] Consciousness is still formulated phenomenologically in terms of cogito and pre-reflective cogito, but its notion is already guided by a formal structure, that of the for-itself. We have not yet reached this level of analysis. But on the preliminary level of a phenomenology with ontological foundation, such as we have been discussing, Sartre gives us provisional interpretations of consciousness as a type of being.

The structural emphasis Sartre places on the notion of consciousness is visible in his accentuation of *unity*. Consciousness exists as a circle: I must be transcending in order to be conscious of my transcending act; and yet I can only execute such an act if I am conscious of it. These are reciprocal conditions and thus indivisibly one. Consciousness involves the unity and co-originality of its two moments. The pre-reflective cogito is the mode of existence of a consciousness of something, or its law or constitution. Consciousness is not substance, for this notion involves, according to Sartre, a "minor being," the being of quality.[87] The co-originality of

85. EN, p. 152; BN, p. 109. This instantaneous consciousness is not, of course, emphasized in Husserl as a presence unto itself in the present, and thus as basically non-temporal self-consciousness. Sartre's criticism of Husserl can, in turn, be criticized. Sartre believes that, in Husserl, the temporal unity of consciousness is merely intentional, and thus of lesser ontological status than an experience in its reality. In his skepticism concerning merely intentional being, Sartre considers this kind of conscious unity insufficient. It is debatable, however, whether "ecstatic" references constitute a radically different solution. See chap. 4, sec. 3, below, on "Temporality."

86. J. Möller, in his critique, wants to assume such a transphenomenal ground, of which consciousness would be the phenomenon. For him, therefore, there is a transphenomenal subjective being which is not reducible to consciousness (*Absurdes Sein?* [Stuttgart, 1959], p. 163). He intends thereby to introduce a being which encompasses consciousness and the world as a ground.

87. EN, p. 21, using pleasure as an example: "il n'y a pas plus d'abord une conscience qui recevrait ensuite l'affection 'plaisir.' . . . Le plaisir est l'être de la conscience (de) soi et la conscience (de) soi est la loi d'être du plaisir." BN, pp. liv f.

the two conditions excludes this. Consciousness, rather, is "existence through and through." [88] Another consequence is that consciousness cannot be considered determined by something external to it. Otherwise, we would have to assume that such a cause (an organic disturbance, an unconscious impulse, an experience) would trigger a psychic event which would, in turn, produce an awareness of it. In this view, the pre-reflective awareness would be a superimposed quality, a view contrary to the unity and co-originality of the two moments of consciousness and conducive to the substance model. If determinable from outside consciousness would be a thing, something unconscious.[89] By way of contrast, we are dealing with a unitary, indivisible being for which neither cogito nor pre-reflective cogito have priority although, in a phenomenological formulation, these two appear as an asymmetrical dyad. Consciousness is a being characterized by self-appearance.

Consciousness is *existence*, this term being taken both in the sense of existential philosophy, which uses it as a notion for the subject, and in a strict sense, as we saw in connection with Sartre's rejection of the concept of substance. Similarly, becoming, or any transition from potency to actuality, is unthinkable; consciousness cannot precede itself. Potency would simply mean that a condition is missing which is a condition for consciousness. What precedes consciousness in such a case would be, ontologically speaking, entirely different from consciousness and thus constitute no potency of it. Consciousness either exists as this dual condition, or else it is not. If it exists, it is a "plenum of existence." [90] In contributing both of its conditions it is determined by itself. Since no other can participate in it, it exists "by itself." [91] It is not the "result of a logical construction . . . but the subject of the most concrete experiences. And it is not at all relative to this experience because it *is* this experience." [92] In all this it is "pure

88. EN, p. 21: "existence de part en part." BN, p. lv.
89. Cf. *L'Imaginaire*, p. 41, and the discussion of "motif" and "mobile" in EN, pp. 522ff.; BN, pp. 445ff. We see that the thesis of invariable awareness follows from the unity of the subject. With this thesis, Sartre stands opposed to all views which assume a transition from unconscious to conscious: e.g., to psychology, psychoanalysis, and many philosophical doctrines (such as those of Spinoza and Leibniz, and all doctrines of emergence and epiphenomenalist theories). Sartre's thesis is that such a transition from unconscious to conscious is incomprehensible. The only relationship into which consciousness can enter is that something is "for" it.
90. EN, p. 22: "un plein d'existence." BN, p. lv.
91. *Ibid.*
92. EN, p. 23; BN, p. lvi. Sartre also uses the concept "conscience" for a single

appearance because it is a total emptiness (since the entire world is outside it)." [93]

In its existentialist slant, Sartre's notion of existence is based on Heidegger. Like Heidegger, Sartre wants to say that the human subject [*Dasein*] is "concerned about its being." Its "existentiality," this precedence of existence, contrasts with a "what" which it projects with a view to making its being possible. Man is not a "particular instance of an abstract possibility" [94] preceding him. This account of consciousness reverses the case of the phenomenon: while the phenomenon was a "being whose essence implied existence," consciousness is a "being whose existence posits its essence." [95]

Certainly, consciousness, considered as a unity of cogito and pre-reflective cogito, does not yet fully match the existentialist notion of existence; existence in its existentialist meaning is brought in by way of anticipation. The possibility of embracing that meaning is, however, rooted in the above ontological determinations. The definitive interpretation of human existence in terms of the for-itself will encompass the idea of a self-conscious cogito, as well as that of existence. [96]

[5] THE IDEA OF A PHENOMENOLOGY WITH ONTOLOGICAL FOUNDATION

LET US REVIEW the progress of our investigation. We said that Sartre is influenced by a theoretical basis readily available, namely, phenomenology. We now see more clearly the extent of phenomenological orthodoxy. What Sartre finds convincing in phenomenology is its start from the cogito and from phenomena. But he is dubious about the ontological status of the phenomenon, especially since Husserl reduces it to unreality and eventually to a

---

concrete experience [*Erlebnis*]. Cf. *L'Imaginaire*, p. 11. We touch here the problem of how the a priori structure of consciousness is related to its factuality.

93. EN, p. 23; BN, p. lvi.

94. EN, p. 21; BN, p. lv.

95. EN, p. 29; BN, p. lxii.

96. In spite of the differences urged by M. Müller, we find Sartre's notion of existence largely in agreement with that of Heidegger in *Sein und Zeit* (cf. M. Müller, *Existenzphilosophie im geistigen Leben der Gegenwart* [Heidelberg, 1949]). Clearly, Sartre is not influenced by a notion of existence in the sense of *Ek-sistenz*, the meaning Heidegger (and M. Müller) have imputed to the notion as it occurs in Heidegger's early work. Sartre has nothing in common with Heidegger's turn toward being in what he calls the *Kehre*. And it is thus understandable that the overall orientation of the two thinkers, as well as their ideological pathos, are bound to differ, Sartre's being that of finite and yet absolute freedom, Heidegger's that of an "obedience over against being."

construct of consciousness. Sartre argues that the phenomenon cannot keep its status of unreality, but has to be accorded a supporting being, and he thinks he can offer an "ontological proof." His criticism of phenomenology is a criticism of a mere objectivity of phenomena. It is true, granted an objective context of experience, that Husserl does establish the transcendence of the objects given to man in his natural attitude, if not for each single case outside its context. For Sartre, however, any single phenomenon is considered supported by a "being." With this move phenomenology is modified in terms of an ontological perspective different from that of a subject ontology, such as we might impute to Husserl.

Sartre's modification of the phenomenological notion of consciousness consists in introducing the unity of cogito and pre-reflective cogito and its ontological interpretation as a structured type of being. In view of Sartre's "realization" of the phenomenon, consciousness stands opposed to being-in-itself, the other type of being. We find, in fact, a division of beings in accordance with two types of being, of which one, consciousness, is related to the other, being-in-itself. The intention of consciousness is a relationship in terms of being.

We have interrupted our investigation at this point because we regard Sartre's theory so far as a "possible" position, that of a phenomenology with an ontological foundation.[97] By this we mean a philosophical position which takes over certain insights of a descriptive phenomenology—e.g., the doctrine of phenomena, transcendent acts, time-consciousness—but rejects the ontological non-commitment of Husserl's phenomenology and, instead, regards subject and object as types of being. Certainly, Sartre gives no "positive" ontology on this level which would show how the relation between subject and object is founded in an encompassing being. Sartre will introduce the great theme of the negative to solve the problem of this relation, but it has not yet been struck, except for the hint that consciousness excludes all being from itself.

The position of Sartre sketched above denies some of the essential aims of Husserl's phenomenology. Husserl's very first methodological step, to describe experiences whose intentional objects are available as ingredient in them when the naive thesis

97. We find attempts in this direction, albeit with divergences, in M. Scheler (*Philosophische Weltanschauung* [Munich, 1954];) and in N. Hartmann (*Grundzüge einer Metaphysik der Erkenntnis*, 4th ed. [Berlin, 1949]; and in *Zur Grundlegung der Ontologie*, 2nd ed. [Berlin, 1941]).

is suspended—a method already used in the *Logische Untersu-chungen* and perfected in the *Ideen*—is not taken by Sartre. His interpretation of consciousness leads to a more radical description of the natural attitude: the sphere of immanence is, for Sartre, one of awareness and not of contents, except where these are given to reflection. Nor does Sartre share Husserl's theoretical aim of describing the "performances" of subjectivity,[98] and thus of giving a foundation to science. For Husserl, what is to us unquestioned experience has to be made evident as a performance [*Leistung*] of subjectivity, which constitutes it just as it given to us. Experience is first reduced to the level of subjectivity, in order to be built up again in the light of comprehension. This method presupposes that the bases of evidence on the level of a transcendental and pure ego are superior to those of concrete experience and that, on returning to the level of experience, experience is established in its rationality. That such knowledge of a transcendental dimension is no mere fiction for Husserl follows from his belief that this dimension is available to description in reflection.

In contrast to Husserl's desire for the justification and foundation of experience and of science, Sartre's philosophy, to the extent that it can be considered phenomenology, stresses description and hermeneutics—much like Heidegger's philosophy in *Sein und Zeit*. Sartre's phenomenology takes over the full range of Heidegger's descriptions, and sometimes even extends them. But his descriptions combine with a structural motif—we have already noted a "structure," the circle of cogito and pre-reflective cogito—which comes to the fore in his ontology proper.

98. So we look in vain in Sartre for a detailed theory of categorial intuition, if we discount a hint in his example of a counting child (EN, pp. 19 f.; BN, p. liii), and there is no penetrating discussion of the a priori problem.

2 / Being-in-Itself

SARTRE'S PRELIMINARY INVESTIGATION, designed to establish the shift to the ontological level, took its clue from intentionality, i.e., the givenness of phenomena for a subject. It is for these two, phenomenon and subject, that the Introduction to EN establishes a "being." The resulting division of beings (existents) is into subjective being and the being of phenomena. Sartre's ontology is based on this disjunction; it constitutes an ontology of intentionality. As such, it must contain an elucidation of the relation between the members of this disjunction, for any being of the subjective type is itself in relation to the other, the being of phenomena. But, similarly, it must provide an explication of this being opposite the subject. In fact, Sartre's ontology is essentially limited to these two topics. The classical categorial titles of substance, quality, relation, space, and time are located in being, but as phenomenal categories, while relation, regarded as negation, is primarily a subject principle. In the light of the basic division mentioned above, the theory of the categories is relegated to insignificance in Sartre's work.

We begin our discussion of Sartre's ontology with being-in-itself as the simpler type of being, although an account of the in-itself will clearly not be possible without some anticipation of the for-itself. In our interpretation we will, therefore, have to find a compromise, doing justice both to the close interconnectedness of the two types of being and to the separate consideration of each of them.

The being of the phenomenon had been called, prematurely, "being-in-itself." This designation had no terminological relevance then, but was intended to bring out its non-relativity with reference to the subject. The being of the phenomenon is the "founda-

[33]

tion" of the phenomenon; we characterized it as an independent existential moment. It "is" even where there is no phenomenon.

To elucidate the being of the phenomenon, Sartre rests his case on the idea of an interpretation of the phenomenon of being. This interpretation leads, however, to something completely different from Heidegger's hermeneutics. Sartre discloses a "transcendental" meaning but no material content. It is not claimed that being is a mystical agent—with analogical predicates like dispensation [*Geschick*], sympathetic power [*Mögendes*], clearing [*Lichtung*], etc.—however much being in this acceptation may be a theme of metaphysics, a discipline whose legitimacy Sartre in no way denies. What we find is, rather, a formal explication combined with some further ontological and pictorial determinations. The latter are no more than similes for formal determinations.

The characteristics of being are, for Sartre, concentrated in three formulas: "being is itself," or, "being is in itself"; "being is what it is"; and, "being-in-itself is." [1]

The first formula—"being is itself," or "being is in itself"—emphasizes the contrast of Sartre's conception of being with created being, which he rejects. [2] He further comments that activity and passivity, affirmation and negation, are excluded from it. These latter concepts do not stand for absolute characteristics: activity and passivity presuppose human conduct (man is active when he has reference to a purpose through a means which, as determined by that purpose, is passive); affirmation and negation require an act distinguishing something from itself. Both the act and what it affirms or negates have to remain distinguished if they are not to collapse. The case of the in-itself is the opposite: it "is not reference to itself. It is itself [*soi*]." But even this formulation is only an approximation, for the in-itself is at bottom "beyond the 'self.'" The words "in-itself" and the French *soi* (itself) involve a reflexivity which has a linguistic basis. Being is the limiting concept of a self-reference, or, more correctly, not of one such reference but of an "infinity of self-affirmations." It is "filled with itself" and thus "opaque to itself." [3] Another expression for this is that it is "solid" [*massif*]. [4]

This idea is taken up in the second formula, "being is what it

1. EN, pp. 32–34: "l'être est soi," "l'être est en soi"; "l'être est ce qu'il est"; "l'être-en-soi est." BN, pp. lxv–lxvi.
2. EN, pp. 31f.; BN, p. lxiv.
3. EN, pp. 32f.; BN, p. lxv.
4. EN, p. 33; BN, p. lxvi.

is," which interprets this collapsing into itself as *identity*. If the synthesis of the in-itself is so close that we have to consider it undifferentiated and unstructured, it has no inner or outer and maintains "no reference to what it is not." And this, for one thing, in the narrower sense of a reference to something it will be or has been—i.e., that of a negative reference to itself—and, for another, in the general sense of a reference to what is other: ". . . it cannot even not be what it is not," "it never posits itself as other than another being." It "exhausts itself in being." In view of this absence of relation, being is not temporal. "It is, and when it collapses one cannot even say that it no longer is" without presupposing a consciousness as witness. It "does not exist as a lack there where it was; . . . It was and now other beings [*autres êtres*] are. . . ." [5] The in-itself is identical precisely because it merely is what it is and maintains no relation to another.

The principle of identity, thus associated with the in-itself, does not, according to Sartre, hold for the for-itself and therefore constitutes a synthetic and contingent principle of the in-itself.

The third formula, "being-in-itself is," points out that being-in-itself is in its own right and "can neither be derived from the possible nor reduced to the necessary." It is *contingent,* or, in anthropomorphic terms, "in excess" [*de trop*].[6]

This characterization of being reminds us, even down to details, of Parmenides' account of being. Parmenidean being is identical and solid, without origin, not subject to necessity, without deficiency, and thus non-referential.[7] Its continuity corresponds to Sartre's thesis that being is "everywhere." [8] But the opposite of Parmenidean being is different from that of Sartre's being-in-itself. While Parmenides opposes to it natural coming-to-be and passing-away, Sartre, in his determinations of being, is guided by a logical interpretation, such as Hegel inaugurated in his *Logic,* and opposes being-for-itself to being. Sartre's being-in-itself, qua the identical, is the opposite of being-for-itself, i.e., being as mediated by an Other. It is to being-for-itself that Hegel assigns "true" identity, though Sartre does not do this.[9] His in-itself therefore lacks that identity which consists in not-being-an-Other.

5. EN, pp. 33f.; BN, p. lxvi. (The translator of BN misses the double negation "cannot even not be.")

6. EN, p. 34; BN, p. lxvi.

7. Diels, *Fragmente der Vorsokratiker,* 10th ed. (Berlin, 1961), Parmenides fragments 7, 8: Ταὐτὸν τ'ἐν ταὐτῷ; ὄγκῳ; ἄναρχον; τί . . . χρέος ὦρσεν; οὐκ ἐπιδέες; συνεχές.

8. EN, p. 270: "l'être est partout." BN, p. 217.

9. Cf. EN, p. 116; BN, p. 74.

Sartre's identity is not even "abstract identity," "the product of a relative negation taking place outside it"; [10] it carries no determinateness.

Failing otherness, being-in-itself is not conditioned or grounded,[11] for this would involve otherness within a basic identity.

Being-in-itself is groundless not by way of identification with a ground—this would make it an absolute, or for-itself—but through the absence of otherness. It is immediate groundlessness. It is what Hegel's immediate being is prior to any reflective determinations. Its groundlessness, therefore, does not imply a possibility of being other or being not at all. Possibility must be discounted altogether. The in-itself is not, qua the contingent, conditioned by anything; it is the non-conditioned, though not the unconditioned in the sense of the self-conditioned or absolute. It is groundlessness. It does not enter into any reflection—unless we consider the for-itself the reflection of the in-itself—but is fixed as the contingent in-itself.

Can we say, then, that the in-itself, in view of these abstract determinations, has turned into an abstraction? Or is it Hegel's immediate being? Sartre expressly rejects an abstract acceptation of the in-itself. For him, its relation to the phenomenon is not like that of the abstract to the concrete.[12] His criticism of Hegel turns on this point of abstract being. For Hegel, according to Sartre, being is reduced to a "meaning of beings,"[13] whereas it is not, in truth, "one moment of the object" or one of its structures but "the ground on which the characteristics of the phenomenon will manifest themselves."[14]

What Sartre rejects is, in Hegelian terminology, the "ingre-

10. Hegel, *Wissenschaft der Logik*, II, in *Werke*, IV (Berlin, 1834), p. 30: "Sie [die wesentliche Identität] ist insofern nicht abstrakte Identität, oder nicht durch ein relatives Negieren entstanden, das ausserhalb vorgegangen wäre, und das Unterschiedene nur von ihr abgetrennt, übrigens aber dasselbe ausser ihr als seiend gelassen hätte, vor wie nach." (J&S, II, p. 38.) When Sartre says, as we have seen above, that the principle of identity is synthetic, he means to say that there is a region of being where it does not hold and, therefore, that it is "informative" to assert it of a region. For Hegel, the principle of identity is of a synthetic nature since it involves "a movement of reflection, Identity as the disappearance of otherness" (J&S, II, p. 43). *Logik*, II, p. 37: "Der Satz der Identität aber enthält . . . die Reflexions-Bewegung, die Identität als Verschwinden des Andersseins."
11. EN, p. 34: "sans raison d'être." BN, p. lxvi.
12. EN, p. 49; BN, p. 13.
13. EN, p. 49: "signification de l'existant"; cf. "l'être des choses," *ibid.* Wherever possible we try to render *Seiendes* (or, *l'existant*) in English by the plural of the gerund "being."
14. *Ibid.*

dience of negation in being." [15] He feels that negation has to leave a "nucleus" of being untouched; "being is and nothingness is not." [16] Sartre takes Hegel to mean that being and non-being are coeval contraries whereas, in truth, non-being is the contradictory opposite of being and thus posterior to being (as the positive).[17] Non-being presupposes an "irreducible act of the mind." Now in Hegel, too, being has precedence, but, according to Sartre, Hegel can make the transition from being to nothingness only by making nothingness implicit in the being which serves as his starting point.[18] This is tantamount to the charge of triviality and, in Sartre's eyes, of illegitimacy, for "one cannot cause [being] not to be." [19]

In his criticism Sartre is unaware of Hegel's point. It is for the mind thinking the *Logic* that pure, immediate, and positive being results in nothingness, a thesis which corresponds to what Sartre claims in his criticism. There is, however, this difference: the *Logic*, attaching itself to the process of thought, posits determinations which result from the mutual passage into each other of being and nothingness—viz., becoming and determinate being [*Dasein*]—determinations in which being is preserved. For Hegel, too, being has priority and conforms to a "prevalence of the positive." [20]

Sartre thinks about being in terms of another "logic": an "ingredience of negation in being" does not take place, since this would merely be a mediation in thought. Being is the basis for a negation "on" or "at" it.[21] Sartre views the problem in the light of the subject-object opposition. Only the for-itself is a unity of being and nothingness; it is, subject to a more detailed analysis, the case of an ingredience of negation in being, the only one admitted by Sartre.

Let us return to being-in-itself. As we have seen, Sartre rejects Hegel's movement from being to determinate being. But in that way, all he retains is being as characterized by identity and contingency. In what respect does it differ from Hegel's abstract

15. Hegel, *Logik*, I, p. 174 (in the plural: "Einbildungen der Negation in das Sein"). J&S, I, p. 170, has the misleading expression "adaptations."

16. EN, pp. 50f.; BN, p. 15.

17. EN, p. 50; BN, p. 14.

18. *Ibid.*

19. EN, p. 50; BN, p. 15.

20. The expression is used by J. Cohn in his *Theorie der Dialektik*, (Leipzig, 1923), p. 159. Cf. EN, p. 52: "préséance logique"; *ibid.*, "postériorité du néant." BN, p. 16.

21. Cf. EN, p. 52: "il n'y a de non-être qu'à la surface de l'être." BN, p. 16.

being? Hegel's being, being in terms of thought,[22] is the first concept of the *Logic*. In the thought movement of the *Logic*, it is seen to determine itself as essence and notion, and, transcending the *Logic,* as nature and spirit. Being in Hegel is thus abstract only qua "not yet" determined in itself. The entry into determinateness belongs to it; being is not itself abstract. The scales are tipped the other way: Sartre's being can be thought of only in the abstract, as opposed to Hegel's being, which, in the eyes of thought, determines itself.

Sartre, then, has to consider being in the abstract because, according to him, it does not determine itself. What he has in mind is *existent being.* Such being cannot undergo determinateness at the hands of nothingness, for nothingness is not. The fact that being is does not involve an opposition over against nothingness. Before there can be determination of being by negation— this will be determinateness "on" or "at" it—nothingness has to "emerge" first. This possibility for the in-itself to acquire determinateness lies, for Sartre, in the opposition of subject and object; the for-itself is the *nothingness of being.*[23]

The for-itself is the only opposite of the in-itself; it stands in immediate opposition to it. Through this opposition the subject is confronted with the entire determinateness of the object.[24] There is no room for a determination of being by stages as in Hegel. The in-itself has to be, by itself, plenitude [25] in order to prove fully determinate when negated by the for-itself. Insofar as determinateness is joined to negation, the in-itself is not, by itself, determinate, and yet it "is" all that which it is under the impact of negation.

This plenitude, the simultaneity of undifferentiated content, is not comprehensible in formal terms. Being-in-itself involves no principles like essence and existence, causing it to be finite, determinate beings. Accordingly, it appeared to us above as a mere

22. In admitting this, we understand that Hegel joins the opening concept of the *Logic,* being, onto the *Phenomenology of Spirit,* at the end of which pure knowing has collapsed into the unity of object and (subjective) certitude, constituting indifference, immediacy, or, "to call it by its true expression . . . pure being." J&S, I, p. 81; *Logik,* I, p. 62.

23. For the relationship between the for-itself and nothingness, see chap. 4, sec. 1, below.

24. Cf., however, the distinction of "basic reference" and "concrete negation," chap. 4, sec. 4, below.

25. "Plenitude" [*plénitude*] is to be taken here in the dual meaning of "fullness" (as contrasted with *décompression:* EN, p. 32; BN, p. lxv) and of "transdeterminateness" (as "condition of all revelation": EN, p. 15; BN, p. xlix). The for-itself, as negation, "adds nothing to the in-itself": EN, p. 269; BN, p. 217.

existential moment. Formally, it reduces itself to Hegel's immediate being. The subject, in turn, appears in formal terms as nothingness, such that the opposition of subject and object in Sartre's
ontology coincides with the opposition at the beginning of Hegel's
Logic, but remains arrested there. In view of its "beingness," as
opposed to its emptiness in terms of mere thought, it meets the
negation by the subject fully determinate. In the case of the
subject, Sartre will be able to push further ahead with a formal
analysis, but not, however, in the case of the in-itself. The in-itself
is the being of the phenomenon.

Perhaps we would do well to once more consider the in-itself
character of being in the light of Hegel. By its very notion, the in-
itself implies a negation. To follow the indeterminateness of pure
being to its logical conclusion is to admit that it is affected by its
contrary, determinate being. Its "indeterminateness constitutes its
quality"; [26] it is determinate being [*Dasein*], being-in-itself. For
Sartre, the logical "realization" of indeterminateness is not, as for
Hegel, tantamount to its having passed into determinate being.
Being remains neutral over against determinateness but, as ingredient in the determinate, it is not indeterminate either; it proves,
rather, to be non-indeterminateness, or plenitude. It is determinate being "for" a subject. [27] Outside of this relativity, which makes
it a phenomenon, it is, qua non-relative, fixed as in-itself.

The "latency" of content in the in-itself and the immediate
availability of the in-itself to the negation of the for-itself throws
light on the relationship between being and phenomenon. The in-
itself is, as it were, subsistent being, the ground for all finite
beings, but its relation to the phenomenon is immediate and not
mediated by ontological principles. But whereas subsistent being
is that in which finite beings participate or originate, while it itself
is regarded as removed to simplicity, Sartre's being-in-itself involves the coexistence of contents in undifferentiation. [28] Thus,
quality is closely allied to it. Being is not "in itself" (or "per se")
quality, "although it is neither more nor less. The quality is being

26. J&S, I, p. 93; *Logik,* I, p. 77.
27. This "being-for" would be a "realization" taken as a concrete intentional
reference. So Sartre says: "connaître, c'est réaliser aux deux sens du terme" (EN,
p. 228; BN, p. 180). "Le réel [i.e., the phenomena] est réalisation" (*ibid.*).
28. We find analogies, for example, in Bergson (in the relationship between
élan vital and fixed matter and form); in Whitehead's early philosophy of nature
(in the relationship between "event" and "object" [cf. *The Concept of Nature,*
Cambridge, 1920]); and even in Wittgenstein. (For Wittgenstein, atomic propositions do not contradict each other; negation and all other truth functions are
introduced only by our operations on atomic propositions [*Tractatus Logico-
Philosophicus,* London, 1922, 4.211, 5.2, 5.21, 5.2341].)

as a whole revealing itself within the limits of the 'there is' [*il y a*]."
"But in order for there to be quality there must be being for a
nothingness [i.e., consciousness] which by nature *is not* being." [29]
Consciousness, then, does not produce quality but rather, in being
directed to a "this," discloses a certain whole of interpenetrating
qualities. It assembles them, as it were. The qualitative, then, is
an undifferentiated constituent of being, although any determinate quality, as a quality of something, presupposes that we posit
it as single and discrete. The phenomenon is, thus, for its material
content, dependent on the in-itself.

But the difficulties of regarding being as identical and as
undifferentiated plenitude of content come to the fore once we
remember that the same qualities do not appear everywhere. The
availability of certain qualities and discrete units cannot be referred simply to our negation of being. Discreteness must some-
how be grounded in being-in-itself.

The phenomenon is closely allied to the in-itself in virtue of its
dependence on it for material content. It is a discrete "thing"
[*chose*] which is in-itself; in-itself also, from another angle, by
virtue of its opposition to the for-itself. Its being-in-itself constitutes its reality and its "mode of being," which is its "solidity." It is
a non-for-itself; it has identity.

Things which have the status of being-in-itself are, for Sartre,
connected to others by "external" negation—we might also say, by
an inessential otherness. Thus, a crescent moon is a full in-itself
unless a human subject takes it as incomplete with reference to
the full moon. In itself, the crescent moon is complete and is what
it is. It is not what it is only with reference to the full moon, a
reference which consciousness would have to establish.[30] But
there is something else which it is "not." It is with this idea of
external negation that Sartre accounts for the whole sphere of the
discrete, of things whose discreteness cannot be grounded simply
on our negation. But can we say that being-in-itself—which we, in
our analysis, regarded as non-discrete—can be the ground for the
discreteness as such?

This notion is involved in Sartre's contention that being-in-

29. EN, p. 236; BN, p. 187. J. Thyssen (in *Realismus und moderne Philosophie* [Bonn, 1959], p. 126) has this to say: "Dass nicht echte Getrennte da sind,
bedeutet, wie bei Leibniz, dass der gesamte Weltbestand, soweit er mir jemals soll
begegnen können, von vornherein in meiner Reichweite liegt (z.B. wenn ich zum
erstenmal die Wolkenkratzer von New York erblicke, ist das nicht ein mir von
diesen als selbständigen Realitäten her Kundgegebenes, sondern er gehört zu dem
mir verfügbaren Ansich, das ich dann als diese Objekte bewusst mache)."
30. EN, pp. 129f.; BN, pp. 86f. Cf. EN, p. 239; BN, pp. 189f.

itself can cease to exist, that it is destructible, or, generally, that something "comes from being." [31] A natural event—an earthquake, for example—introduces something into our world of phenomena; it founds the discrete appearance qua discrete.

Thus, these four must be distinguished: (1) paradoxical being-in-itself containing, qua plenitude, undifferentiated determinateness; (2) being-in-itself as the ground for changes in our world and, thus, as the ground not only for qualitative contents but also for their discreteness; (3) being-in-itself featuring discreteness, place and temporal location "objectively," and "in truth" or for science; and (4) being-in-itself as a phenomenon available to me qua concrete consciousness.

The various cases coincide in the notion that the in-itself cannot have an Other which is "for" it. Sartre considers the in-itself structurally: it possesses no self-constitutive reference, no relation, in terms of being, to something else; it is neutral over against the distinction of *beings,* each of which is in-itself [*Ansichseiendes*], and *being*-in-itself [*Ansichsein*]. Plurality can be predicated of it only in a quasi manner.[32] Seen from our angle, being-in-itself is determinate and discrete, but the discrete has a constitutive relation to something else only with reference to us. It is external to beings qua being-in-itself. Similarly, identity, as a feature of being-in-itself, is neutral over against the distinction between being-in-itself and beings of in-itself status: identity may mean the self-equality of being-in-itself (although, properly speaking, there is no "what" it could be equal to), and it also holds good for beings improperly regarded as beings per se and for beings for us (phenomena).

The quest for what is in-itself (or per se) is abandoned in favor of the question of how the in-itself is. This latter question is given a formal answer in terms of a *mode of being.* If being-in-itself founds changes in our world and, more generally, every

31. EN, p. 257: "Mais précisément quelque chose vient de l'être: ce que nous appellerons, faute de mieux, abolitions et apparitions." (BN, p. 206.) Such appearances and disappearances are, for Sartre, a topic of metaphysics. The same difficulty holds in fact for any movement. Cf. EN, pp. 260–65; BN, pp. 209–14. Similarly, metaphysics would have to account for the emergence for me of the other person and the plurality of other persons (EN, p. 358; BN, p. 297). See p. 111, and chap. 6, sec. 5, below.

32. Thus, Sartre himself speaks of being as non-related to us in the plural: "Mais lui-même [l'être] n'existe pas comme un manque là où il était: la pleine positivité d'être s'est reformée sur son effondrement. Il était et à présent d'autres êtres sont:voilà tout." (EN, p. 34; BN, p. lxvi.) Cf. the paradox (EN, p. 712; BN, p. 618), where an individual in-itself is played off against a being in general as the referent of the for-itself.

discreteness in it, we feel impelled to posit the discreteness, place, and determinateness of beings in being-in-itself. The formula which defines being-in-itself as that which is what it is apparently permits us to assume in it a "what." But the identity of being is regarded as non-otherness, the what is not differentiated from another what, and so discreteness, the basis for a place and condition of a what, is lost again. On the other hand, once we posit discreteness in being-in-itself, negation cannot be due to the subject exclusively; the reinterpretation of Hegel's opposition of being and nothingness in terms of being and subject breaks down.

Like Hegel, Sartre wants to say that the immediate is the undifferentiated which receives explication only through negation. For Hegel, too, differentiation in the immediate is not simply "not," but is "in itself" [an sich], ready for explication. It "manifests" itself by way of negation. But since Sartre starts from an "existent" being which, as such, is not affected by negation, the problem of its latent contents is not one concerning categorial determinations occurring in a dialectic of logical thinking, but one as to what being is in-itself or by itself. In this conflict of two rivaling modes of thought, a logico-dialectical and an ontologico-realistic one, Sartre's being-in-itself approaches Kant's thing-in-itself, which stands in a similar conflict between subjective determination and real being. The difference between Sartre's being-in-itself and Kant's thing-in-itself lies in the fact that Kant does not consider the opposition of the thing-in-itself to us in logical terms only; its relation to appearance is also accounted for by affection.

Kant's doctrine of affection calls in doubt the identity of the thing-in-itself and appearance. Sartre's being-in-itself is separated from the phenomenon only by negation, considered as explication; existentially, the phenomenon retains its identity with the in-itself. The subject "adds nothing." [33] Kant's embarrassment with regard to the question of whether the thing-in-itself occurs plurally or not highlights the same basic problem; it echoes the fact that, for him, negation is a subjective category. Thus, discreteness is to be referred to the subject, and yet the thing-in-itself is the real being of anything discrete.

Like Kant, Sartre abstains from answering the question of what the in-itself is. But now the question is located in a Hegelian context. The reason for abstaining is not that we must not transcend appearance; we are on the level of an ontology which can speak about being-in-itself. But the in-itself is, like Hegel's being,

33. EN, p. 269; BN, p. 217.

the logical zero instance of determination. As with Hegel, being retains its identity with the determinate, but is not itself the determinate. Determination is not the process of thinking out the implications of being, but befalls being factually, "from outside," from its Other. The paradox that being, as logically conceived, is real and that, in view of its identity with the determinate, it cannot be indeterminate, brings us to the basic problem of thought and being in Sartre's philosophy.[34]

34. We might here recall similar difficulties in Jaspers' notion of "transcendence." Cf., e.g., his *Philosophie,* 3rd ed., III (Berlin, 1956), chap. 2, "Das formale Transzendieren."

3 / The Approach to the For-Itself

SARTRE HAS OPPOSED being-in-itself and conscious-
ness. Now that the in-itself has received an interpretation in terms
of plenitude and identity, we have to inquire into subjective being.
The in-itself being what it is, it must fall to the subject to establish
contact with it. What kind of being will it have to be to do this?

Two important points have already been made: consciousness
is intentionality, i.e., reference to being-in-itself, and it is reference to itself or self-appearance. An explication of these two
moments as moments of a unity is called for, and we have already
noted that this explication in EN is formal in character: consciousness is regarded as *being-for-itself* and, as such, a counterpart
of being-in-itself. Consciousness is not only opposed to being-
in-itself in view of its different "structure," that of the for-itself,
but it constitutes a counterpart of being-in-itself qua being. In this
perspective consciousness is the opposite of being and, therefore,
nothingness. We noticed this opposition when we compared
Sartre's being-in-itself with Hegel's immediate being. Thus, consciousness permits of four interpretations: as a unity of cogito
and pre-reflective cogito, as existence, as being-for-itself, and as
nothingness. They will coalesce in the interpretation of the for-
itself as a being which is its own nothingness.

For an interpretation of consciousness as nothingness, Sartre
does not, as we did by way of anticipation, draw on the idea that
being-in-itself can only be determined by nothingness, thus presupposing a certain ontology. He intends to show phenomenologically that consciousness requires this interpretation. In several
steps he assembles evidence to show that we encounter a negative
which can find its explanation only through the above interpretation. This project can be called a "regressive analysis" or an "ana-

[44]

lytical regress," [1] starting from the concrete and intended to lead to the "origin" of the negative. The interpretation of consciousness as nothingness is to be authenticated, so as not to remain a mere assertion. In a way, the analysis runs parallel to the preceding interpretation of being-in-itself, which was not to remain a mere thesis either but allegedly proceeded from an elucidation of the phenomenon of being.

[1] THE REGRESSIVE ANALYSIS

SARTRE TAKES HIS STAND with a "concrete" description in terms of Heidegger's analysis of the human subject [*Daseinsanalytik*], which discloses a concrete whole, man's being-in-the-world. Under its terms, we need not start from an abstract consciousness, taken up in isolation, in order to pass from there to a reconstruction of its relationship to the world. Such a procedure would fail to account for the totality of man's reference to the world. In addition, Sartre has sought to establish, by his ontological proof, a theoretical foundation for this reference. It is within this concrete unity of reference that concrete forms of reference can be singled out and analyzed as to the conditions of their possibility.

Sartre discusses several types of human conduct which should permit us to delve down to the "basic reference" [2] spanning in-itself and for-itself. The kinds of conduct discussed for their structures form a sequence moving toward ever greater disclosure of the true meaning of man's reference to the world. A phenomenological analysis, as such, would be aimless and unlikely to yield the desired result, however, were it not for a guiding thread which Sartre discovers in the asking of questions as a pattern of human conduct. The selection of this pattern, however, betrays the presence of an ulterior guiding thread pre-empting the desired result, the negativity of consciousness. What Sartre is seeking is typified convincingly in the pattern of asking questions. [3]

1. EN, p. 83: "régression analytique." BN, p. 44.
2. EN, p. 39: "rapport primitif." BN, p. 4. EN, p. 149, has "relation originelle." BN, p. 105.
3. Cf. Heidegger, *Sein und Zeit*, 7th ed. (Tübingen, 1953), p. 5: "Als Suchen bedarf das Fragen einer vorgängigen Leitung vom Gesuchten her." The analysis is thus circular. Sartre differs from Heidegger in his quest for the meaning of being in that he intends to find something less generally admitted—in a sense, being is the best-known concept—viz., the negativity of the phenomenon and, eventually, the negativity of consciousness as responsible for the former negativity. Sartre's regress back to consciousness reminds us of Fichte's regress from the reflection of the philosopher back to the grounding ego. Reflection constitutes the explicit and concrete form of an act which, inexplicitly and unconsciously, founds the ego.

When I ask a question,[4] I stand before a being already familiar to me, no matter what I am going to ask about it. The question is situated within the limits of the basic reference of man to being-in-itself. I stand before a being which I question in expectation of an answer. A question presupposes one of two possible answers, yes or no. Both alternatives are transcendent and objective facts; a negative answer is just as much a fact revealed by being. On the other hand, the questioner is in a state of indetermination: he does not know whether the answer will be affirmative or negative. Sartre therefore posits "two non-beings," the "non-being of knowing in man" and the "possibility of non-being in transcendent being."[5] And, finally, a question claims the truth; the answer requires that it be "thus and not otherwise." This is a "third non-being,"[6] the non-being of limitation. In the field of worldly beings, any something "is not" some other.[7] Sartre's analysis thus transcends the positive and shows that non-being has to be included in the investigation. Non-being has been disclosed in being as well as in man.[8]

Non-being appears as a component of the real. But on the other hand, if we can be sure that the in-itself cannot give negative answers, must not the negative be located in the judgment? Sartre rejects such a thesis.[9] Ontologically speaking, the being which is the theme of the judgment is positive, and so is the judgment as a psychical fact. The requisite negation would be supported only by positive facts; it would be unreal like a noe-

Similarly, in Sartre, the question is the concrete pattern of conduct serving as a starting point for a regress to the grounding dimension. For Fichte, the common feature of the two dimensions is reflective reference; for Sartre it is negativity.

4. Cf. EN, pp. 38–40; BN, pp. 4–6.

5. EN, p. 39; BN, p. 5.

6. EN, p. 40; BN, p. 5.

7. J. Wahl has drawn attention to the fact that a question involves indeterminateness rather than non-being: no wonder we are surrounded by non-being if indeterminateness is a non-being just as much as determinateness ("Essai sur le néant d'un problème," Deucalion, I [1946], 43). This is precisely the case as long as we operate with an indeterminate notion of non-being and are looking for a mere negative "factor" in the world. A specific analysis of the question, however, could not be maintained at this level of generality. J. Wahl pinpoints the difficulty involved in a reduction of concreteness to such formal concepts as being and nothingness; they do not permit of an unambiguous phenomenological description.

8. EN, p. 40; BN, p. 6. The non-being of limitation is not in conflict with the notion of an "external negation," mentioned above. External negations are relations between things given or imagined and, as such, belong to their determinateness. A "this" is not "another this" (cf. EN, p. 239; BN, pp. 189f.). External negations are thus constitutive of things. The law of contradiction holds good in the world. Such negations are "external" in that a thing does not, qua in-itself, relate itself to others.

9. EN, pp. 41–46; BN, pp. 6–11.

matic correlative, "an unreal encompassed by two full realities, neither of which claims it." [10] It is incapable of existing by itself and calls for a nothingness as its origin which is a structural feature of the real. Sartre considers, next, whether negation could be a category.[11] If so, it would be a "positive process" in the mind which is "suddenly released by the presence in us of certain affirmative judgments" and "comes suddenly to mark with its seal certain thoughts which result from these judgments." [12] Negation which is "refusal of existence" would have disappeared. It might be a free invention, in contrast to prior judgments establishing a fact. The connection between negation and what is negated would be ruptured, leaving negation as an "irreducible event." On the level of consciousness, however, negation is consciousness of negation; there can be no category which would "inhabit consciousness and reside there in the manner of a thing." [13] Nothingness is an "intuitive discovery." "The necessary condition for our saying *not* is that non-being be a perpetual presence in us and outside of us, that nothingness haunt being." [14]

After the rejection of the two challenges, Sartre can claim the negative as a phenomenon. There is an "infinite number of realities . . . experienced . . . by the human being . . . which in their inner structure are inhabited by negation. . . ." [15] Among them are "distance . . . absence, change, otherness, repulsion, regret, removal, etc.," realities which Sartre calls *négatités* (negative beings).[16]

[2] NEGATIVE BEINGS

SARTRE'S REGRESSIVE ANALYSIS has led to negative beings. It has shown that we encounter the negative. The next step will be to discover the negative in consciousness as that on which negative beings depend. Without losing sight of this ulterior aim of Sartre's analysis, let us discuss a few examples of negative beings.[17]

We have seen that the question, as a pattern of human conduct, involves an understanding of non-being. The same is true of destruction. For destruction to be possible, its object has to stand

10. EN, p. 41; BN, p. 6.
11. EN, p. 46; BN, p. 11.
12. *Ibid.*
13. *Ibid.*
14. EN, pp. 46f.; BN, p. 11.
15. EN, p. 57; BN, p. 21.
16. *Ibid.*
17. EN, pp. 42–46, 55–57; BN, pp. 7–11, 20f.

out from among other beings as "fragile"—a feature involving the possibility or probability of non-being. It is man who is responsible for such non-being. On the basis of his fundamental reference to being, man maintains "a reference of individualizing limitation" to a being, and this reference "causes fragility to enter into this being as the appearance of a permanent possibility of non-being." Such a being either invites destruction or protective measures which keep non-being on the level of "mere possibility." A being considered worth protecting can be destroyed by natural events which, otherwise, could not be called destructive.[18]

Missing someone [19] is another example which, for Sartre, permits of an even clearer intuition of non-being. The place where I am missing someone indicates, by itself, that the person missed is absent. I am looking for Peter in the café: the café presents itself as background for a center, the person looked for; the café is intuited as "nihilated." [20] The center with reference to the nihilated background is itself unoccupied, so that it affords a second intuition of nothingness.

Finally, we might mention distance.[21] We can take it as two points separated by a length, or as a length limited by two points. Or it can be a given extension I have to clear to reach a goal. In all of these cases the positive has a negative admixture.

Sartre advocates a broad notion of *négatités*. In some cases the negative will mean no more than a "condition of the sharpness of [the] outlines" of realities otherwise positive, while in others it constitutes nothingness proper, whose "positivity is only an appearance." [22] Negativity and positivity appear as "mixed."

Transcending this oversimplified view, we can distinguish two cases: *négatités,* or negative beings that have a negative index; and others, which contain a negative constituent and so could be called "objectively" negative beings. Something rejected, suspected, removed to a distance, or missed can, with essential continuity of its objective features, become something affirmed, welcomed, or brought to proximity or inspection. In Husserl's language, what we have here are noetic characters [*Aktcharaktere*] conditioning the meaning of the noematic correlatives.[23] The negative would be objective qua correlative of a negative act. A length as a limited line, on the other hand, possesses a "noematic" negative; it

18. EN, pp. 43f.; BN, pp. 8f.
19. EN, pp. 44f.; BN, pp. 9f.
20. EN, p. 45: "cette néantisation est donnée. . . ." BN, p. 10.
21. EN, pp. 55–57; BN, pp. 20f.
22. EN, p. 57; BN, p. 21.
23. Cf. *Ideen,* I, §§ 105, 106.

is, as Sartre says, a *Gestalt*. This could in turn be accentuated affectively or pragmatically. Sartre is not concerned with the specific point of the latter example. All he wants to bring out is the common feature of a negative which is a "component" within the positive.[24] The negative is encountered in reality.

[3] NEGATIVE CONDITIONS IN THE SPHERE OF IMMANENCE

IN THE NEXT STEP of his regressive analysis, Sartre intends to give evidence of a negative which is a nothingness in the sphere of immanence and not simply an objective negative. What is offered, though, is not so much phenomenological evidence as a discursive argument. It corresponds to that part of the Introduction to EN which makes the shift from the phenomenon to the being of the phenomenon. While Sartre there presented phenomena as a monistic realm of being, he now presents the same phenomena viewed as negative. The Introduction proceeded by way of argument to a grounding being, and so Sartre argues in similar fashion for a nothingness which grounds negative beings [*négatités*]. By analogy to the "ontological" proof, he means to give us a "meontological" proof.

Let us briefly consider this project. The objective negative is claimed as a starting point for an elucidation of consciousness as the original negative. We might make the objection that negative beings [*négatités*] are special cases, selected by an arbitrary guiding thread, and that, apart from such cases, consciousness is confronted with positive phenomena, such that the inference of a negative consciousness is unconvincing. We might admit that things experienced share pragmatic and affective determinations and that, therefore, a negative is always present in experience, although this fact would not militate against the basic positivity of the given. Nor would the fact that any given is a limited given

24. Cf. EN, p. 52: "deux composantes . . . du réel," viz., "l'être" and "le néant." BN, p. 16. In a later passage (EN, pp. 231f.; BN, pp. 182f.), Sartre construes the spatial given from a "this" in relation to other "thises." A "this" as a generality conceals the problem of spatial limitation. A "this" is, in this context, taken as a *Gestalt* on the background of unarticulated "thises." (Similarly, for Hegel a "this" might be a tree, a house, etc. Cf. *Phänomenologie des Geistes*, ed. J. Hoffmeister [Hamburg, 1952], p. 82; *Phenomenology of Mind*, trans. J. Baillie, 2nd ed. [London, 1949], pp. 152f.). If pressed concerning why a *Gestalt* appears to be spatial, we could reduce the "this" to a point and then the *Gestalt*—e.g., a length —would have to be construed by transcending from a "this," the one terminal point, to the other. What is simultaneously spatial is dissolved into succession. Viewed in this way, distances as things to be cleared in an effort, and distances as intuited lengths, are not in principle different. Viewed phenomenologically—or, in Hegelian terms, in immediacy—a *Gestalt* is irreducible, in contrast to a successive construction in terms of negativity.

make any difference. The analytic regress inferring an original negative, the subject, from a derivative negative, the phenomena, infers a ground for a given in one-sided interpretation from such given. Later, when the evidence for a negative consciousness is taken for granted, the given qua negative receives a fresh interpretation to the effect that it is negative because consciousness excludes the given or has to be negativity to be consciousness. The argument hinges, as we can see, on the generality or equivocal meaning of negativity, or, to be more precise, on the equivocation of a phenomenologico-objective nothingness and an ontological negative regarded as that which stands opposed to a for-itself.

But let us pursue Sartre's argument a little further. His argument takes this form: [25] Nothingness is encountered in the world of objects. It cannot, however, be referred to being-in-itself since this is pure positivity. Nor can it proceed from a nothingness since this is not. It can, therefore, proceed only from a being, but a being subject to the qualification that it maintains a nothingness. Such a being has to constitute a unity with a nothingness, and such nothingness must not "befall" being because, otherwise, the problem would only be pushed back to that being which performs this feat on the former. We end in a regress because nothingness can never be shown to issue from a positive being. But even if being maintained nothingness within itself, this might be a "transcendent in the very heart of immanence." [26] Being and nothingness have to be so unified that being is concerned for its nothingness; [27] such being "must be its own nothingness." [28] That is, we are not dealing once more with a negation, a nihilating act, issuing from a positive being—which is impossible—but with a type of being of its own: a being which forms a unity with nothingness in such a way that it is "its own nothingness." It is thus distinguished from the phenomenon, which is also a unity of being and nothingness. Being of the type now discovered is the disjunct of being-in-itself. The opposite of being-in-itself is not simply nothingness but a unity of being and nothingness.

Once more we see the equivocation. The phenomenologically negative—the negative being or *négatité*—is not indigenous to

25. Cf. EN, pp. 58f.; BN, pp. 22f.
26. It might be transcendent in that it is not "the" immanence but only something encompassing immanence as a negative, such as present or past.
27. EN, p. 59: ". . . un être en qui, dans son Être, il est question du Néant de son Être." The French phrase is designed as an equivalent of Heidegger's phrase, coined for the *Dasein*: "Das Seiende, dem es in seinem Sein um dieses selbst [sein Sein] geht. . . ." (*Sein und Zeit*, p. 42.)
28. EN, p. 59; BN, p. 23.

positive being. It has to be introduced from outside being as if it were a special product. The producer is consciousness as something "ontologically" negative, as a being which is its own nothingness. Viewed in this way, the connection between producer and product is the identity which consciousness as a negative shares with its product as the objective negative, or *négatité*.

This relationship between origin and product is undialectical. But by way of anticipation we might say that consciousness, as the "ontologically" negative, is dialectical: it is because it is its own nothingness that it negates being. Only in this way can it remain negativity. Its relationship to the objective negative is precisely not identity but negation. The specific negativity of negative objects will be construed by further dialectical steps presupposing this "basic" or "fundamental reference."

The replacement of an intention with negative noetic character (producing, as it were, its negative correlative) by a negation as the ontological relationship between the for-itself and being can thus be seen to constitute the basis for Sartre's synthesis of phenomenological and ontological analysis.

Skirting the ontologico-dialectical analysis, Sartre, once more in an undialectical spirit, draws attention to a negative presupposition of intentionality: the subject of the intention must not collapse with the intended, but must disengage itself from being. This is an adumbration of the eventual dialectical solution, in terms of which negation is itself the intentional reference to being. Otherwise, the cogency of this point is insufficient. (The common solution would be to remove the subject, as a being of special reality status—the status Husserl calls *reell*—from the real in the natural acceptation, regarding, however, its reference as a positive act.)

For Sartre, this disengagement is twofold: disengagement [*recul*] [29] from being which, by this disengagement, becomes an object, and disengagement [*décrochage*] [30] of the subject from itself, such that it will not be determined causally by its own past. Without the latter disengagement the subject would be fused with its being and, therefore, also with being generally.[31] This "immanent" disengagement is co-original with the "intentional" disengagement and opens the view toward the core of negativity exhibited in the "presence-to-itself" of consciousness. For the time being, its phenomenological counterpart is the relationship of "re-

29. *Ibid.*
30. EN, p. 64; BN, p. 27.
31. Husserl's problem of psychologism is here phrased in these terms.

tention," which Husserl regarded as a connection with the past rather than a separation from it.

It will not be necessary in this context to enlarge on the distinctions Sartre makes in this interim stage of the analysis. He deals with a psychical sphere of impressions and experiences which have to "nihilated" in order that perception and imagination may become possible. The analysis is a hybrid since it joins phenomenological entities with pure negation and even with a plurality of negations (one of them being the imagination). In a subsequent analysis the psyche is regarded, more formally, as an in-itself.

The negations referred to are no more than presuppositions. If consciousness is not to owe its being to a positive spontaneity, the ground which makes its reference to itself and to the world possible remains to be presented. We can expect a final clarification only from an ontological study of the unity of cogito and pre-reflective cogito.

Nevertheless, Sartre gives us, on the provisional level of the analysis, an account of *freedom* [32] which, in a subsequent analysis, is regarded as the being proper of man. Its essential feature on this level is the disengagement of man from his own past. Insofar as it is not yet, in this acceptation, grounded in its ground, Sartre calls it "empirical freedom." [33] It is no more than a condition of consciousness—and therefore precisely nonempirical—a caesura which, as it were, is "undergone." Freedom thus refers us to an analysis of consciousness as its own ground.

Sartre goes on to discuss freedom in a wider sense, including its reflective mode of awareness, anguish.[34] For our purpose we can ignore this side issue. His account of anguish in EN, apart from its importance as an anthropological description, serves the purpose of leading over to another theme which, in turn, can contribute to an elucidation of consciousness as a grounding dimension. Anguish appears as something to be avoided; man flees freedom, which causes him anguish, toward himself, interpreted as "being." This is the origin of a dialectic which Sartre calls "bad faith" [*mauvaise foi*]. It is the most revealing aspect of consciousness available to phenomenology and psychology,[35] pointing to, or even exemplifying, its negativity.

32. EN, pp. 61–83; BN, pp. 25–45.
33. EN, pp. 62, 83; BN, pp. 25f., 44.
34. EN, pp. 66–83, esp. 66, 71, 75, 77; BN, pp. 29–44, esp. 29, 33f., 37f., 39f.
35. Cf., however, p. 53f., below.

[4] BAD FAITH

SARTRE'S AIM in his analytical regress, to give evidence of features of consciousness which can have their foundation in its negative structure only, reaches its climax in his analysis of "bad faith." In his account of it anthropological description, largely inspired by Heidegger's analytic of *Dasein*, occupies much space. However, in the framework of the analytical regress proposed by Sartre it serves as a supreme piece of evidence: bad faith is not to yield another structural element—such as the disengagement from being qua negation of the intentional object or qua negation of the past—but the central structure of consciousness, which alone can suffice as condition of the concrete patterns of conduct in bad faith.

A remark about the choice of this phenomenon: Bearing in mind that we are to regress from phenomena to the conditions without whose supposition these phenomena are unthinkable, we can once more, as in the case of negative beings, ask to what extent the condition inferred from the chosen phenomenon can be generalized—or, in other words, to what extent the inferred condition (if it is, as Sartre is anxious to show, a negative) can be connected with a dialectical negative. For bad faith, such a connection will be claimed. Viewed superficially, the chosen phenomenon might appear peculiar or farfetched. Sartre selects his pieces of evidence in such a way that essential anthropological descriptions result, however much personal or ideological idiosyncrasies enter into this account of man. Just as asking questions was a basic pattern of human conduct—a pattern which, incidentally, is constantly at work in philosophy—and just as negative beings appeared as objects of our everyday world, so, in Sartre's hands, bad faith will prove a basic feature of man, his everpresent menace.

The notion of bad faith, more so than the thesis of objective non-being to be encountered in patterns of conduct like questioning or other patterns related to negative beings, poses the problem of whether we are in fact dealing with a phenomenon. Perhaps this phenomenon is a *hidden* phenomenon,[36] and convincing as such only in connection with its interpretation. In pursuing the analysis of negative beings we noted that it followed a path stemming from an ontological rather than a phenomenological considera-

36. Sartre speaks of an "evanescent" phenomenon [*phénomène évanescent*]. EN, p. 88; BN, p. 50.

tion. The same was true of man's disengagement from being, which stands for intentionality. For our present issue, bad faith, the ulterior ontological project is even more decisive—so much so that, without it, the phenomenon is perhaps questionable. In terms of its function in the overall plan of the work, this would mean that the last step of the analytical regress could not figure as an inference from a phenomenon to its condition, but that the alleged structure of consciousness would have to be posited synthetically, as in Heidegger's analytic of *Dasein*.

Sartre's basic idea is that man can "take negative attitudes with respect to himself." [37] Bad faith is one of those patterns of conduct exhibiting this possibility. The question, then, is, what must man be, in terms of his ground, to be capable of bad faith?

Sartre claims that bad faith occurs in connection with the anguish before freedom. I feel anguish and repress it. I can stand at a distance from what I am; I am able "not to be" the anguish which I am.[38] Another intuitive basis of bad faith is, for Sartre, the resistance of the patient in psychoanalytic treatment.[39] This resistance cannot reside in the id or the ego, but only in the superego or censor. But this, in turn, would require all the features of knowing and reacting: it must know that the complex is to be withheld from the psychoanalyst, know what the analyst is up to, and be able to synthesize this twofold awareness. In short, the censor has to be self-consciousness. The censor is "consciousness (of) being conscious of the drive to be repressed, but precisely in order not to be conscious of it." [40] Consciousness thus has the character of bad faith: I am . . . in order not to be it. This phrase expresses the evanescence of the phenomenon. While we tend to explain such "phenomena" by the assumption of an unconscious, Sartre emphatically rejects such an explanation. For him there exists "an infinity of types of behaviour in bad faith" appearing "in the translucency of consciousness" [41] which can serve as examples.

In his analysis Sartre rests his case on a basic duality of human reality, which takes several forms. Man is facticity and transcendence, for-himself and for-others, past and future. Each dual aspect of man must be "capable of a valid coordination"; bad faith, however, is the art of affirming "their identity while preserving their differences." [42] It slides from one aspect to the other,

37. EN, p. 85; BN, p. 47.
38. EN, p. 82; BN, p. 44.
39. EN, pp. 9of.; BN, pp. 51ff.
40. EN, pp. 91f.; BN, p. 53.
41. EN, p. 93; BN, p. 54.
42. EN, p. 95; BN, p. 56.

monopolizing one of them. It thus offers a possibility of warding off reproaches, for in terms of bad faith I am not *facticity* but *transcendence;* I am beyond what I have done.[43] Conversely, my transcendence can be silenced by my facticity: I couldn't help doing what I did; I claim my facticity for an excuse.[44] I "am" transcendence or facticity, as if these did not stand in opposition to their other, which I equally am. In bad faith my being is an in-itself.

A similar scheme applies to the unstable unity of another pair of opposites, that of *being-for-itself* and *being-for-others*.[45] I can view myself with my own perspective or from the vantage point of others. Both aspects are of equal validity, and so a game between them is possible. A case in point is the role I play for others and my attitude to it.[46]

Yet another application of the scheme is the *game with the temporal dimensions* or *ecstases:* I either want to be the one I was or, rather, to disengage myself from my past.[47]

The examples, and the abstract scheme to which they can be reduced, show that bad faith constitutes a negative attitude with respect to oneself which is grounded in a duality of the human subject. It is an immediate structure of consciousness, i.e., it belongs to it in its instantaneity. A negative attitude with respect to myself is possible because at any time I am, and yet am not, such and such. Otherwise, I would be an in-itself, a thing, and such a negative attitude would be impossible. On the other hand, I monopolize what I want to be to an unambiguous "I am such," although I am just as much something else.[48]

This game between two aspects of a unity is not, for Sartre, a special case but the immediate and constant menace of man's existential project. For the counterpart of bad faith, *sincerity*, is equally in bad faith.[49] Sincerity involves the demand "man ought to be *for himself* only what he is." [50] It posits for man the ideal of the in-itself. The ideal calls for an opposite, and the being posited by the ideal therefore does not apply to man. Man is no in-itself. If he tries to make himself an in-itself—e.g., by playing a role—he will always remain at a distance from it. Nor can he maintain an

43. EN, p. 96; BN, p. 57.
44. EN, p. 97; BN, p. 57.
45. EN, *ibid.*; BN, pp. 57f.
46. EN, pp. 98–100; BN, pp. 58–60.
47. EN, pp. 103f. (analysis of an incriminated homosexual); BN, pp. 63f.
48. EN, pp. 107f.; BN, pp. 66f.
49. EN, pp. 103, 108; BN, pp. 63, 67.
50. EN, p. 98; BN, p. 58.

emotion without distance from it, so the ideal of sincerity is thus an impossible ideal. Sincerity, i.e., subordination to the ideal, is itself insincere, in bad faith.[51]

Sincerity need not ignore transcendence: it may demand the admission of a negative, which I am, and expect me to change henceforth. It requires that consciousness be what it is, i.e., be for itself what it is, in order to change or not be what it is. Faced by an interlocutor, I would be called upon to make myself a "thing" in order to regain freedom after forgiveness. The sincere person admits his baseness and by that very fact acquires merit and ceases to be base. The sincere person "constitutes himself as what he is in order not to be it." [52]

Sincerity requires that I coincide with my being. Potentially, I am already, in the mode of the in-itself, what I have to be.[53] Sincerity is simply the project of making my whole self an in-itself. In contrast, bad faith requires that I be what I merely share in (transcendence and freedom, on the one hand; facticity, past, and objectivity for others, on the other).[54] Sincerity is in bad faith if it proposes in-itselfhood for me, for in doing this it presupposes that I am no in-itself, or else there would be no demand, and suspects, moreover, that I cannot fulfill it. It is precisely this margin, this incapacity of being an in-itself, this being as well as not-being, which is a condition of bad faith. I am not what I do not want to be, but not absolutely not, or else I would be in "good faith." [55] Similarly, I am not absolutely not what I am not but want to be; it is a possibility for me, or else I would be in "good faith." Bad faith thus presupposes this dual structure of the human subject.

Bad faith now seems conceivable, but what remains to be made clear is that it occurs, that man believes in his own lie.[56] Consciousness "believes" in its self-assessment. In French as in English, terms like *mauvaise foi* (bad faith) and *foi* (faith, generally) carry a linguistic persuasion with them: one's reference to oneself is believing, not knowing. This explains why, in the project of imposing upon myself, there is a margin for bad faith and

51. EN, pp. 98–103; BN, pp. 58–63.
52. EN, p. 105; BN, p. 65.
53. EN, p. 106; BN, p. 66.
54. *Ibid.*
55. EN, p. 107: "de bonne foi." BN, p. 66.
56. This part of Sartre's analysis serves to elucidate bad faith for its own sake —or rather, another condition of its possibility—and not to elucidate the structure of consciousness as the ground of negativity. However, it is included in the interest of giving a fuller picture.

truth to play in. Believing lacks the full self-evidence of certainty, which would prevent any insincere project.[57] The possibility of deciding in favor of bad faith has to be understood from the nature of faith or belief itself. Believing in this manner, I do not believe that I can find true certitude; my faith is not ignorant of the fact "that faith is decision." One assumes this kind of resigned belief "as one goes to sleep." [58] The resignation of this belief means that it is a belief which is "resigned . . . to not being persuaded." [59] That such belief occurs, however, has yet to be more fully demonstrated, and without religious analogies.

Sartre discusses the possibility of a belief which does not intend to be fully persuaded. Believing is something immediate which is sublated by the structure of the pre-reflective cogito, once this pre-reflective cogito is interpreted as knowing: "to believe is to know that one believes," [60] and such believing is now interpreted as the knowledge that one "merely" believes. Belief is thus discredited and upset. Sartre admits that the pre-reflective cogito is not the same as knowing but serves simply as a basis for knowing. Still, in his opinion, it destroys belief. And yet, belief is impossible without pre-reflective cogito. Belief is therefore a self-destructive structure. Good faith can never be faith pure and simple; good faith is an "ideal of being-in-itself." [61] Sartre is not thinking of a sublation of belief into knowledge but rather of a dual structure, disturbed belief [*croyance troublée*].[62] Belief or faith is itself in bad faith. Bad faith is by its very project the "utilization of this self-destruction [of faith] in virtue of consciousness [(of) itself]." [63] If I know that I can never believe fully, then "there is a place for every impossible belief." [64] It is here that the decision in favor of bad faith wins its plausibility. My belief is debased belief, and that is why I confuse the reasons for its failure: for one, that immediate certainty is insufficient for believing; and for another, that belief by its very structure fails me. I want to believe that I am what I am not, and by realizing the impossibility of true belief (or good faith) I come to believe in an inauthentic manner what I could not believe authentically. I possess no counteragency of knowledge which could destroy my contradictory belief. If, for example,

57. EN, p. 108; BN, p. 68.
58. EN, p. 109; BN, p. 68.
59. *Ibid.*
60. EN, p. 110; BN, p. 69.
61. *Ibid.*
62. EN, p. 117; BN, p. 75.
63. EN, p. 110; BN, p. 69. My version adapted.
64. *Ibid.*

I want to believe myself courageous, there is no apodictic agency telling me that I am a coward, for I am not a coward in the mode of the in-itself. To doubt my belief that I am courageous is not to know that I am the opposite. Nor could I ever *know* that I am courageous. Such a possibility would surpass pure reflective certitude.[65] It seems that the destruction of good faith produces a balance between what I want to disengage myself from and what I want to embrace. In this field of potentials the will has its say and it has no reason not to choose the alternative of bad faith. The will to flee "what one is," which for some reason carries a negative accent, is mediated by the self-destruction of belief.

While good faith is the will to overcome the internal disintegration of the for-itself in favor of the mode of the in-itself, bad faith is the will to flee the in-itself in favor of disintegration. But it denies that it flees anything (which it would otherwise take into account); it negates itself as negative and aims at an in-itself which "one" wants to be.[66]

The analysis of bad faith can be seen as a contribution to anthropology: it points out a constant possibility of man. The analysis asserts a phenomenon and gives an explanation based on the insight that man is none of his determinations absolutely, i.e., in the mode of the in-itself. Bad faith is, in the light of this explanation, a self-interpretation of man as an in-itself. To that extent Sartre's analysis is a theoretical account of Heidegger's inauthenticity [*Uneigentlichkeit*], with the difference that bad faith is not an absorption of the subject in the world or the crowd but, rather, an *undialectical* attitude of man to himself, an absorption in the in-itself. Sartre construes, if we like, a *Gestalt* of consciousness in the manner of Hegelian *Gestalten* in the *Phenomenology of Spirit*.

Consciousness, in the predicament of bad faith, exhibits a close resemblance to one of Hegel's figures, that of "dissemblance" [*Verstellung*].[67] The conflict Hegel has in mind here is admittedly a different one: it is the conflict between consciousness, as satisfied by its moral act, on the one hand, and as positing its object outside itself in a beyond, on the other. Consciousness is in fact moral (sincere), but in view of the transcendence of the moral

65. EN, p. 111; BN, p. 70.
66. *Ibid.*
67. Hegel, *Phänomenologie des Geistes*, pp. 434ff. The fact that Sartre's doctrine has a close relationship to Kierkegaard as well is here ignored. It might be called a systematic simplification of the various forms of anguish Kierkegaard distinguishes in *The Concept of Dread*.

demand it alternates between itself and an in-itself which it is not and never can be.

At the same time, it is conscious of its contradiction and *dissemblance*, for it passes from one moment, *immediately in its relation to this very moment*, right over to the opposite. *Because* a moment has for it no reality at all, it affirms that very moment as *real*: or, what comes to the same thing, in order to assert *one moment* as per se existent, it asserts the *opposite* as the per se existent. It thereby confesses that, as a matter of fact, it is in earnest about neither of them.[68]

The conflict resembles that between bad faith and sincerity in Sartre. Hegel, it is true, places his emphasis differently: the reference of consciousness to an in-itself results from the fact that the in-itself is regarded as a demand which asks the impossible. Consciousness realizes the contradiction and reunites the opposites in itself. It becomes conscience. Sartre, in turn, stresses the tendency of consciousness to be absorbed in the in-itself, and what is demanded of it, and what is so difficult for it to live up to,[69] is precisely its being a self. It is clear that Sartre's account of consciousness deviates materially from Hegel's, especially in its understanding of the in-itself of which consciousness is the constant transcendence. For Sartre, the projection toward the ideal is in bad faith in view of the structure of man, which defies fixation; for Hegel, this is so in view of the dialectic of the ideal itself, at the stage where it occurs, while consciousness can move on to a synthesis with its in-itself.

In points of method, moreover, we find similarities between Sartre's treatment and the treatment in Hegel's *Phenomenology of Spirit*. In Sartre, bad faith, sincerity, and belief are being personified, and the whole analysis is a case of applying a richer content to elementary features of consciousness in terms of a systematic analysis. Sharing these features with the Hegelian analysis, it cannot possess strictness. Consciousness is credited with a capacity for reflection it cannot have in the case of a phenomenon on the fringes of the unconscious. As a *Gestalt* of consciousness, bad faith has the features of an abstract myth.

But let us return to our context. What is essential for the purposes of Sartre's regressive analysis is not bad faith for its own sake, but the disclosure of the *condition* which alone makes bad

68. *Phenomenology of Mind*, trans. J. Baillie, 2nd ed. (London, 1949), pp. 629–30. (The italics follow the original German).

69. Cf. Sartre's footnote (EN, p. 111; BN, p. 70), where an escape from bad faith is regarded as not altogether impossible.

faith possible. Bad faith as the will-not-to-be-such-and-such or the will-to-be-such-and-such presupposes, or permits the inference of, a certain structure of consciousness. Consciousness must be capable of not being what it is and of being what it is not in order for the undialectical negation of what I am to be possible. The undialectical is to be founded on the dialectical. What is essential is not bad faith—although it is intended as a description with anthropological validity—but the structure of consciousness to be inferred from it. Bad faith appears within the project of the regressive analysis because it implies a negative structure of consciousness and because, in terms of the guiding thread of the analysis, it constitutes the greatest advance, reaching consciousness itself. Its analysis yields the formula which is later used to characterize the for-itself. Bad faith is only possible if what I am is in question, if in some way I am not what I am and in some way am what I am not. The formula, that the human subject, or consciousness, "is what it is not and is not what it is," [70] will come up for discussion later. In our present context it stands for the unity of any opposition within consciousness (e.g., cowardice and courage); consciousness is and is not its determinateness. The existential polarity of facticity (determinateness) and transcendence (openness) is also covered by the formula.

If we are to see in this approach to consciousness as a for-itself a first systematic assertion, its import is that consciousness is its determination but *also* its opposite. Taken in this way, the result of the analysis of bad faith is still a provisional notion, compared to the proper ontological interpretation of consciousness, although the pertinent formula has already made its appearance.

70. EN, p. 103; BN, p. 63.

4 / Being-For-Itself

THE REGRESSIVE ANALYSIS was designed to prepare for the ontological consideration of consciousness as being-for-itself and to motivate its interpretation as negativity. It is not obvious that consciousness has to be taken as a self-negation and that an analysis of its structures on this basis has any cogency. The whole build-up of Sartre's ontology hinges on this departure. Without a reflection on method to motivate a certain idiom of the analysis, the further analysis of consciousness beyond mere phenomenological determinations would be directionless and at random. The regressive analysis now is designed to ward off the impression that an interpretation of consciousness in the Hegelian terms of negativity and being-for-itself is an arbitrary project. Backed up by this analysis, the new interpretation of consciousness supervenes on the former phenomenological account and wins the upper hand. Of course, the resulting philosophy is not intended as an "interpretation"—this is a reflective term. What is intended is an original grasp of the subject and its reference to being.[1]

As we have seen, Sartre derives his motive for the interpretation of consciousness as being-for-itself from phenomenology. He

1. We might here recall Hegel's objection to Fichte (*Logik*, I, pp. 71f; J&S, I, p. 88). In Fichte's start from a pure ego, rather than from immediate self-consciousness, "the advantage is lost which is to arise from this beginning of philosophy, namely that it is something thoroughly well known which everyone finds immediately within himself as the starting point of further reflection." He incurs, instead, "the disadvantage of the illusion that we are speaking of something known, namely the ego of empirical self-consciousness, whereas in fact we are speaking of something remote from this consciousness." A similar comment might be made on the starting points from phenomenology and negativity, respectively. Sartre's regressive analysis is an attempt to take the basis of phenomenology as a clue and to justify the new basis phenomenologically.

stresses the character of consciousness as a unity of cogito and pre-reflective cogito and provides in his regressive analysis evidence for an understanding of this unity in terms of negativity.[2] These two conceptions—the *structural unity of presence-to-itself* and *negativity*—are to join in the interpretation of consciousness as being-for-itself. The function of negativity in this connection is so far obscure. The justification of a subject notion couched in these terms depends on its fruitfulness in providing an understanding of the structures of consciousness, the ease with which it fits into a comprehensive ontology, and its ability to survive criticism.

[1] THE INTERNAL STRUCTURE OF THE FOR-ITSELF

IN THE PREPARATORY ANALYSES, evidence was given of derivative negations belonging to consciousness. But, in terms of the guiding idea that consciousness is a unity, their ground or origin was still missing. This is also true of the conditions of bad faith, the study of which had led to a formula for consciousness as a whole.

Sartre's next step comes somewhat as a surprise. It is to locate this origin in *instantaneous consciousness*, regarded as the unity of cogito and pre-reflective cogito. This unity is, for Sartre, the ontological sphere of origin of all derivative structures of consciousness.

Consciousness is appearance-to-itself, presence-to-itself, and as such, as we have seen,[3] homologous to reflection. A concrete consciousness—an act of believing, for example—is "consciousness (of) belief," [4] and in this manner a being in absolute immanence. If we try to lay hold of it, it becomes dissociated into a duality, like reflection. We are confronted with the difficulty of a phenomenological description of this unity.

To formulate this dual unity, Sartre sees several choices open to him: a pictorial account, linguistic evidence, and the formulation in a judgment. Pictorially speaking, consciousness is a "game of reflections" [*jeu de reflets*].[5] This account corresponds to the figure, discussed above, of the translucency of consciousness. Consciousness is "shine and countershine," "shine recouping it-

2. We have urged objections to this procedure. Cf. p. 50f., above.
3. Cf. p. 24, above.
4. EN, p. 117; BN, p. 75.
5. EN, p. 118; BN, p. 75. The figure is not obvious. In the phrase *"reflet-reflétant"* the word *"reflétant"* involves the meaning of *"réfléchissant."* However, Sartre intends to stress the reciprocity, as opposed to the asymmetrical unity, of cogito and pre-reflective cogito.

self" [*reflet-reflétant*] [6] in one.[7] Consciousness is thus something decompressed,[8] a "phantom dyad" [*dyade fantôme*].[9] It dirempts itself into cogito and a witness.[10]

Language gives us a clue in the word "itself" [*soi, se*].[11] It expresses a special relationship of a subject to itself, an "ideal distance" to itself. Language, in using reflexive pronouns, avoids the identical expression—the noun to refer to the noun—and thus offers an analogy to the identity within non-identity, which Sartre calls "presence-to-itself" [*présence à soi*].[12]

Sartre's meaning is also borne out by the judgment. The cogito "is" pre-reflectively given cogito, or, in concrete terms, "belief is consciousness (of) belief." This is no judgment of identity, for the two referents differ and yet they are, by the copula, posited as the unity of one being. We may call such a judgment a "speculative judgment." [13] It expresses a tension within a unity. Sartre objects to the idea of expressing the for-itself in a logically identical, i.e., tautological, sentence.[14] For him, logical form and ontological structure bear an analogy. The "being" of the sentence corresponds to being-in-itself; for the sentence to be an expression of the for-itself the identity in terms of being-in-itself has to be dissolved by a diversity of subject and predicate.

Sartre's meaning is expressed once more in a pictorial account, in which presence-to-itself is interpreted as a being with a "fissure." The figure suggests a duplicity of beings separated from each other, such as a real cogito and a real pre-reflective cogito, and thus seems to urge a "bad" kind of unity. What is meant, however, is a fissure within consciousness [*fissure intraconscientielle*],[15] a fissure within a unity. What separates is an "ideal distance," a "nothing" [*rien*]. The separative nothing is nothing determinate (like a spatial distance, for example), for that would militate against the posited unity and translucency of consciousness; consciousness is "nothing other" than consciousness (of) itself. The

6. EN, *ibid.;* BN, p. 76. I offer here an interpretative translation.
7. Hegel, in connection with his doctrine of the "notion," speaks of "Scheinen in sich selbst" (*Enzyklopädie,* § 159), a "shining within itself." Cf. pp. 11, n. 33, above.
8. EN, p. 116: "décompression d'être." BN, p. 74.
9. EN, p. 221; BN, p. 173.
10. EN, p. 117; BN, p. 74.
11. EN, pp. 118f.; BN, pp. 76f.
12. EN, p. 119; BN, p. 77.
13. Following Hegel, *Phänomenologie des Geistes,* p. 51 (J. Baillie, trans., p. 120).
14. EN, p. 117; BN, p. 75.
15. EN, p. 120; BN, p. 78.

fissure is the "pure negative," "nothingness" [*néant*]. This nothing-ness, as such, "is not"; it is sustained or "made to be" [*est été*].[16] Only in this way can being be its own presence-to-itself. Nothing-ness is the pure negative as inherent in a being.

In his interpretation of presence-to-itself as being with a noth-ingness, Sartre applies the idea of a determination of the in-itself through nothingness.[17] The nothingness discovered in the for-it-self possesses this basic relevance. The in-itself appears here as a subject which, in an "ontological act," brings forth a nothing-ness.[18] The in-itself, by receiving a nothingness, reduces its positiv-ity. The for-itself is the result of the nihilation of the in-itself.[19]

Sartre's presence-to-itself involves a reference of conscious-ness to itself such as is expressed, with more or less articulation, in any notion of the ego. What is normally an accompanying spectator within the ego, or a self-awareness, is now interpreted as a cogito which is separated from its pre-reflective cogito by a rift or nothingness. More generally, a self is a being which is its own nothingness and, thus, a negation of identity. "Being" here stands, for example, for the cogito of belief which is only con-scious (of) itself with this nothingness. For Sartre, this structure occurs only in consciousness, and so the formulation in terms of a being which is its own nothingness is sufficient to denote it unam-biguously. Presence-to-itself is a unity of being and nothingness. Now such a notion retains a certain vagueness: without an expli-cation, we do not see why it is a conceptual equivalent of pres-ence-to-itself, why it involves a unity, or, finally, why it stands for the origin of the negative in the world.

Nothingness regarded as a fissure is, first, separation—a rela-tionship of otherness between beings. The separated entities, how-ever, must make up a unity if consciousness can be presupposed as a unity of immanence. The separated entities are not each the "other" of the other, their relationship is not one of otherness, because the other maintains an identity with the one. Thus, this unity is, by its very form, a whole negating something which is no

16. EN, p. 120; BN, p. 78. This expression has been misunderstood by several authors, e.g., by J. Möller, who considers the phrase a present perfect (". . . es [das Nichts] ist nicht, es ist gewesen," *Absurdes Sein?*, p. 45), and by M. Natanson, who renders the phrase by "is-was" (*A Critique of J.-P. Sartre's Ontology*, p. 59). "Il est été" is a present passive and not a present perfect active. A proof is offered by EN, p. 361: ". . . le soi-object pour *être* devrait s'éprouver comme *été* par et pour une conscience. . . ." BN, p. 300.

17. Cf., above, p. 37f.

18. EN, p. 121: "acte ontologique." BN, p. 79.

19. *Ibid.*

Other for it. By its logical form it is Hegel's being-for-itself.[20]

Hegel's being-for-itself is a categorial stage of determinate being; it is "infinite being," [21] "absolute determinateness." The concept involves that determinateness in virtue of an Other has been received into being proper and the difference between the two resolved. It is the culmination of a notion already foreshadowed by an earlier type of determinate being—*Dasein*—or, more specifically, "something" [*Etwas*] which Hegel calls *Insichsein* (being-within-itself) and which is finite. In being-for-itself Hegel reaches a concept in terms of which the independence of the Other disappears by entering into the unity of the One. The Other is a "moment," "being-for-one." [22] Being-for-itself, as conceived by Hegel, is a stage of determinate being and as such an abstraction, a determination of thought.

It is through this comparison with Hegel's formal determination of being-for-itself that we now understand the phenomenological unity of consciousness as a unity of determinate being.

But is it really true that Sartre's presence-to-itself is a for-itself in the sense of the Hegelian concept just outlined? Might it not be mere *Dasein* or "determinate being," a being "including Not-being," [23] the "simple oneness of Being and Nothing"? [24] Presence-to-itself now is no "simple" unity of being and nothingness, no immediate unity. Nothingness here is a separation within a unity,

20. In contrasting Hegel's and Sartre's concept of being-for-itself, we are clearly isolating a notion from Hegel's philosophy. In doing this we in fact discount Hegel's comprehensive notion of "spirit" and compare a mere "form" or "scheme." This is not unobjectionable. On the other hand, it will be interesting to see if all that Sartre has taken over from Hegel is a "scheme." The reader is referred to the final chapter.

21. *Logik*, I, p. 173; J&S, I, p. 170.

22. "Sein-für-Eines" (*Logik*, I, p. 176). J&S, I, p. 172: "This moment expresses the manner in which the finite exists in its unity with the infinite, or as ideal in nature. In Being-for-Self negation is not applied as a determinateness or limit, not, therefore, as relation to another and distinct Determinate Being. . . . Thus Being-for-One and Being-for-Self are not true determinatenesses relatively to one another. But let the distinction be granted for a moment; then, if we can assume a Being-for-Self, it is Being-for-Self, as cancellation of otherness, itself, which relates to itself as to the cancelled Other; it is thus for One, and in its Other relates itself to itself. That which is of ideal nature must needs be for One, but not for an Other: that One for which it is, is merely itself.–Ego, or Spirit in general, or God, are of ideal nature because they are infinite; but, as being for themselves, they are not distinct, ideally, from that which is for One. For then they would be merely immediate, or rather, they would be determinate beings, or being-for-other; for that which for them is would then be an Other and not themselves, if they had not the moment of being for One."

23. *Logik*, I, p. 125; J&S, I, p. 131.

24. *Logik*, I, p. 112; J&S, I, p. 121.

an opposition of moments of consciousness in a totality, and, therefore, what we have is being-for-itself. And yet, in terms of the formal abstraction, all there is, is a nothingness sustained by being. Presence-to-itself is thus being-for-itself *and also "Dasein,"* determinate being, or, again in Hegelian terms, infinite and finite being in one.[25] (We will return to this relationship between being-for-itself and determinate being in Sartre.)

The coincidence of the two determinations reminds us of Hegel's more concrete notion of "subjective spirit." This has a twofold characterization: spirit is "absolute negativity" [26] and "universality being for itself," [27] but it is also *Dasein,* "determinate being." [28] In stages of its own development it distinguishes itself qua for-itself from itself qua merely being.[29] No more than an external parallel in our context, Hegel's notion of "spirit" serves here as evidence of a unity of negativity, which is an expression of being-for-itself, and determinate being. As we said, spirit in Hegel is a more concrete notion and, correspondingly, its negativity is more fully determined as a "return from nature." [30]

For Sartre, negativity is pure nothingness, and so he is led to regard being-for-itself in a speculative fashion as an "ontological act," as a stepping down of the positive by the reception of a nothingness, or as the emergence of a nothingness within being, a speculative process resulting in presence-to-itself.

This speculative interpretation calls our attention to the problem of unity. The step from being to presence-to-itself is conceivable only if being is taken as being in Hegel's sense: being stands in an antithesis to nothingness and, as in Hegel's dialectic at the beginning of the *Logic,* they enter in a unity. The very opposition is already the unity of presence-to-itself. Such a mediation is a mediation of thought determinations. If we took being as "existent being," it would remain unaffected by nothingness. By itself, it is no unity, nor does nothingness involve a reference to unity, as is the case in Hegel's notion of spirit regarded as (more fully determined) negativity: the relationship would remain undialectical,

25. With a view to Hegel, Sartre objects to calling presence-to-itself "infinite" (EN, p. 118; BN, p. 76). In saying this he is, however, misconceiving Hegel's notion of the infinite as a qualification that would reduce consciousness to an in-itself. See the discussion on the following pages.
26. Hegel, *Enzyklopädie,* § 381.
27. *Ibid.,* § 382.
28. *Ibid.,* § 383.
29. Cf. *ibid.,* § 398.
30. *Ibid.,* § 381.

the constitution of a unity incomprehensible. And, to be sure, the being Sartre has in mind here is being-in-itself as a mode of being; by receiving a nothingness into itself, something of the mode of the in-itself is turned into a presence-to-itself, and yet, it is still opposed to being-in-itself. In no way has all being-in-itself (or being-in-itself as such) been turned into presence-to-itself. Presence-to-itself exists only as a subject already constituted which negates being. And this is precisely the situation Sartre means to do justice to. Being is to remain the opposite of the subject and its "moment." [31]

We are faced with a conflict: Sartre regards presence-to-itself as a speculative unity of being and nothingness with reality status. But the mediation of the two moments can be successful only in dialectical thought. The abstract synthesis of being and nothingness, in turn, cannot cover the opposition of subject and being. The fact that presence-to-itself is a determinate and individual finite being is expressed only in a game between presence-to-itself in the sense of a nothingness of being and in the sense of a human reality opposed to being. The notion of being is equivocal, standing for a thought determination and a real and specific existent.

Hegel accounts for the relationship of being-for-itself (as a form) and being in his discussion of the subject in terms of the "notion" [*Begriff*], which is regarded as a synthesis of essence [*Wesen*] and being.[32] For the subject to be an existent and to have beings opposed to it means that it comes under the notion of the "notion," i.e., that it becomes a unity with its opposite. The subject in Hegel passes through a development of assimilating being, which is opposed to it and yet already united with it. Thus, for Hegel, the subject can be considered as mere form—being-for-itself—and, once more in formal terms, as the notion which involves a relationship between being-for-itself and being. Similarly,

31. Cf. the revealing passage, EN, p. 121: "Le néant est la possibilité propre de l'être et son unique possibilité. . . . Le néant étant néant d'être ne peut venir à l'être que par l'être lui-même. Et sans doute vient il à l'être par un être singulier, qui est la réalité humaine." BN, p. 79.

32. *Enzyklopädie*, § 159: "Der Begriff ist hiermit die *Wahrheit des Seins und des Wesens*, indem das Scheinen der Reflexion in sich selbst zugleich selbständige Unmittelbarkeit und dieses *Sein* verschiedener Wirklichkeit unmittelbar nur ein Scheinen *in sich selbst* ist." "Thus the notion is the truth of Being and Essence, inasmuch as the shining or show of self-reflection is itself at the same time independent immediacy, and this being of a different actuality is immediately only a shining or show in itself." (*The Logic of Hegel* [i.e., *Encyclopedia*, Part I], trans. W. Wallace [Oxford, 1892], p. 283.)]

negativity is exempted from the precarious status of being one with being, on the one hand, and not being so, on the other; it integrates itself successively into being.

Sartre's presence-to-itself remains paradoxical: it is negativity and yet being, a unity of being and nothingness, an existent being-for-itself *sui generis*.

Leaving aside the problem of its speculative derivation, it appears as a structure to be "applied" to a concrete subject. Sartre does not acknowledge a progressive dialectic of material content which leads to the constitution of the subject and to its further specification. The unity of being and nothingness stands for a nihilated psychical being, a being which appears to itself.

This unity, taken by itself, is comparable to Hegel's notion of psychic immanence, the "feeling soul," [33] which is "simple ideality." [34] Proceeding from this point Hegel gives an evolution of the subject to spirit as a consciousness which transcends toward objects.[35] Spirit moves from reflection within itself to consciousness and self-consciousness; its stages form a line of succession. Each stage can be regarded as simple, as presence to an object or as return from the object to itself. In the stage of transcendence the previous stage of presence-to-itself is sublated and preserved. Thus, there can be no problem as to how a consciousness, in being conscious of objects, can "simultaneously" be conscious of itself. A descriptive approach to the psychic subject, designed to show that it transcends to its object and is equally present to itself, is in Hegel replaced by a succession of steps evolving within the a priori unity of being-for-itself.

For Sartre, transcendence toward an object is tantamount to an opposition of presence-to-itself to being, and thus a simultaneity of presence-to-itself and transcending consciousness is apparently covered. Being-for-itself is both presence-to-itself and consciousness. Both relations, that of consciousness to itself and that of consciousness to being, are phenomenologically a unity and co-original. The dialectical account has to do justice to this state of affairs. Being-for-itself is nihilated being and thus "is not" being-in-itself which, by that very fact, stands opposed as something specified, as phenomenon and situation for the for-itself. Sartre's non-successive account of the two relations as a simultaneous unity possesses the character of a formal description which matches the phenomenological given. On the other hand, pres-

33. *Ibid.*, § 403: "die fühlende Seele."
34. Cf. Sartre's expression, "dyade fantôme." EN, p. 221; BN, p. 173.
35. Cf. *Enzyklopädie*, § 412.

ence-to-itself is considered the origin of a fuller, though merely immanent, structure, the self proper, which is developed in stages of dialectical construction.

Sartre proceeds on two paths to unfold from the internal structure of the for-itself its fully developed structure. First, he unfolds the so-called "immediate" structures of being-for-itself from this very being, a process which we might call a "subjective logic" of being-for-itself, regarded as a unity of being and nothingness. To this we find added an account of the temporality of the for-itself. The second project is to unfold the structures of the for-itself as transcending consciousness, i.e., as opposition to being. This latter analysis can presuppose the self and, thus, benefits from greater concreteness.

The analyses in EN implementing this program serve a twofold aim: Sartre intends to establish intentionality on an ontological basis and to receive Heidegger's analytic of *Dasein*, or human reality, into his philosophy. The analysis of the "immediate" structures, in particular, is designed to accommodate this latter intention. It provides constructive analogies with Heidegger's existentialia (such as facticity, possibility, purpose)—constructive in as much as they are developed from presence-to-itself as their origin.

[2]   THE IMMEDIATE STRUCTURES OF THE FOR-ITSELF

PRESENCE-TO-ITSELF is the *ground* of being-for-itself in its various structures; they have to be developed from it. We can, therefore, speak of the deductive character of Sartre's analyses. In them he deduces a total structure from a ground which thus proves abstract if taken in isolation.

The Being of the For-Itself

PRESENCE-TO-ITSELF is appearance-to-itself; a phantom if we like, but not nothing. Since it is the systematic origin of all further structures, we have already given a fuller ontological account of it. It stands before us as an existent being-for-itself *sui generis*. Sartre, in his account of it, has so far left aside the aspect of its existence or being in order to discuss it now as a separate structural moment. The for-itself "is," if only "in the manner of a being which is not what it is and is what it is not." [36] To make his point clear, Sartre brings in determinations of the world: an individual was and is a particular individual in a situation. What

36. EN, p. 121; BN, p. 79.

remains "independent" then in being-for-itself—its component be-ing-in-itself—is not restricted to the unity of presence-to-itself but is extended to intentional consciousness. The for-itself is presence to the world [*présence au monde*], or situatedness.[37] Human reality [*Dasein*] is, to use a Heideggerian equation, its "being-there" [*Da-sein, le simple* fait "*d'être là*"].[38]

We have already discussed Sartre's meaning: The notion of being-in-itself is, as it were, neutral over against the alternative of being-in-itself as such and the being of being-for-itself. The for-itself is negativity for which being is in the form of a world and a situation. So far, this being is the in-itself of consciousness. The "event" of the for-itself means that being-in-itself as such is lost and turns into being-for-itself. We can call the latter a "wide" for-itself, in contrast to the presence-to-itself in immanence; it involves the idealization of being through a negativity which happens to it. What is idealized here remains being-in-itself. Qua "ideal," being-in-itself is phenomenon; qua being, being-in-itself is the "being of the phenomenon."

But then again the for-itself, in a narrower sense, although a nihilated being, "is." It has an existential moment, which is not exhausted in ideality, in the phantom dyad of presence-to-itself, for otherwise it would not "be." A nothing, a negativity, cannot subsist by itself; it has to be sustained by a being, has to be negativity of a being. The for-itself is related to a being, but "its" being is not that of phenomena—these are transcendent with reference to it—but one of immanence. It is a being of its own over against the world.

In the notion of being-in-itself the two cases are collapsed. With reference to man's existence [*existenziell*], being-in-itself stands for *facticity*.[39] This existential determination of man, which Heidegger adumbrates in a hermeneutic of human reality, is, for Sartre, a result of the logic of being-for-itself. In view of its in-itself status, being-for-itself carries the feature of contingency which, for Sartre, belongs to being-in-itself.

Being-for-itself finds itself particularized in a particular world. It "is" all that, it "is" so-and-so and such-and-such "ideally" [*ideell*], i.e., as the negation of all that. But it is not its ground. Being-for-itself "is" the factual, which is a moment of it, but the factual is not grounded in it the way a moment is grounded in the whole; it is in-itself. Qua "for" a for-itself—i.e., entering in it as a moment

---

37. EN, p. 122: ". . . délaissé dans une 'situation'. . . ." BN, p. 79.
38. EN, p. 126; BN, p. 83.
39. EN, p. 125; BN, p. 83.

—the factual is already received into its interpretation.[40] Qua by itself, not grounded by the for-itself, it is groundless and contingent. By being a unity with an in-itself and a reference to an in-itself, being-for-itself shares this contingency. It is *Dasein,* being-there.[41]

On the other hand, being-for-itself is its own ground, not qua being, but qua non-being, or consciousness.[42] Taken in this way, the for-itself is a closed sphere. It lives in its world of meaning; it is its own aspect from within. Where there is being there is meaning for consciousness. In this way the phenomenon belongs to the sphere of the for-itself. This sphere corresponds to Heidegger's notion of "being-in-the-world" [*In-der-Welt-Sein*].

Qua being-for-itself, consciousness is conditioned by itself and therefore necessary. Again, in view of its being-in-itself or being-there, it is contingent. It is a "factual necessity." [43] Being-for-itself is responsible for its being since it chooses the meaning of its situation and itself as ground for itself in that situation. But then again, it is not justifiable, in so far as it cannot choose its position in the world and its existence.[44] This account of the relation between in-itself and for-itself is the basis for the major ideological statements of Sartre's existentialism.

The being-in-itself of the for-itself, at this stage of exposition, concerns its instantaneity, its presence-to-itself. It is its "being." Interpreted as facticity, however, it suggests a transcendence of instantaneity. Due to the in-itself, the for-itself possesses a basis from which to distinguish itself, a basis in its back, as it were, which it negates. Thus far, the temporal character of the in-itself is left undetermined: facticity is present as well as past being. As that which the for-itself "is already," [45] facticity betrays its temporal character, which Sartre is to bring out later in a special analysis of temporality. Prior to a specifically temporal interpretation, however, facticity, as a dimension of the for-itself, stands opposed to another such dimension, the for-itself's possibility.

The For-Itself as Lack

BEING-FOR-ITSELF is the negation of its being-in-itself. Viewed from being-in-itself, it is thus incomplete, lack of

40. Cf. EN, p. 126: "librement construit." BN, p. 83.
41. Cf. pp. 75, below.
42. EN, p. 124; BN, pp. 81f.
43. EN, p. 126: "nécessité de fait." BN, p. 84.
44. *Ibid.*
45. Cf. "Schon-Sein" in Heidegger, *Sein und Zeit,* p. 327.

being [*défaut d'être, manque*].[46] This is to render plausible the fact that consciousness is dynamic and reaches out beyond itself to complete itself. The for-itself strives for a complement to be "whole." It transcends itself to eliminate its lack of being.

To exemplify this point, Sartre states as a fact that it is consciousness alone which notices incompleteness in the world and transcends it toward completion. Only man can view the crescent moon as lacking something compared to the full moon. Man supplements what is there [*l'existant*] by a complement [*manquant*] to make it a whole [*manqué*]. The projecting of a whole precedes. Man transcends toward an ungiven totality in terms of which the given is determined. To make this possible Sartre argues that consciousness "must be itself a lack." [47]

In the argument Sartre considers desire [*désir*], or hunger and thirst. Desire must itself be a lack since, otherwise, as Sartre shows in reviewing historical positions, no connection between desire and the desired can be established. Desire taken as a psychical state is purely positive; such a state is what it is. A "conatus" gives rise to something else but does not desire it; even if it is lacking something, an organism displays merely positive features. It is only for the spectator to speak of "desire." In its own perspective, however, desire is the case only if it transcends, if it is outside itself and present to the desired object. Desire is a "lack of being"; it is "haunted" by the being it lacks.[48] Desire as a lack appears "on the ground of a totality," which is itself in the form of satisfied desire. Desire and the desired stand out as moments to be fused in the "missing totality." [49]

Desire is a concrete for-itself, and the for-itself is, as such, a lack. This notion has a fallacious simplicity: on the one hand, the for-itself must "be" a lack, i.e., there must exist a unity whose being is deficient compared to its "full" being. On the other hand, however, the for-itself has to "posit" itself as a lack; it must be "for" it that it is a lack. Sartre expresses this in saying that the for-itself must be "its own" lack.[50]

Sartre tries [51] to rationalize the for-itself's qualification as a lack and its "self-positing" as such lack. The for-itself negates in relation to itself a certain being or mode of being. "What it denies or nihilates . . . is being-in-itself." But this is not just "any" be-

46. EN, pp. 128, 130, and *passim;* BN, pp. 85, 87, and *passim.*
47. EN, p. 130; BN, p. 87. Cf. Heidegger, *Sein und Zeit*, p. 243.
48. EN, p. 131; BN, p. 88.
49. *Ibid.*
50. EN, pp. 130, 131; BN, pp. 87, 88. Cf. Hegel, *Enzyklopädie,* § 359.
51. EN, pp. 131f.; BN, pp. 87ff.

ing-in-itself, for human reality is above all "its own nothingness." "What it denies or nihilates in relation to itself as for-itself can be only itself. The meaning of human reality as nihilated is constituted by this nihilation and this presence in it of what it nihilates," i.e., of the "self as the missing being-in-itself." Now, "since human reality in its primitive relation to itself is not what it is, its relation to itself is not primitive and can derive its meaning only from an original relation which is the null relation or identity. It is the self which would be what it is which allows the for-itself to be apprehended as not being what it is." This positive relation to itself, the relation of identity, is given as "perpetually absent" but has to be posited as the basis. The meaning of the for-itself as a "troubled" and non-identical for-itself results only from the identity which haunts it. The for-itself itself lacks being-in-itself. The missing in-itself is not the in-itself of facticity but the absent in-itself of the for-itself as a totality, as the "foundation of its being and not merely the foundation of its nothingness." The being of the for-itself is "failure," but failure has meaning only as "failure *in the presence of* the being which it has failed to be," i.e., totality. Totality is "coincidence with itself." The for-itself apprehends itself as "incomplete being" with reference to its totality. Sartre sees here an analogy with Descartes' inference from an imperfect being to a perfect one,[52] though with this difference: that the perfect being is no other than the for-itself, but itself as totality.

This argument calls for closer examination, all the more since it provides the basic rationale for developing a fully concrete subject from an abstract form of it in terms of presence-to-itself. In spite of the abstract level of discourse, it is meant to provide the constitution of an existential self. The reader is faced with the difficulty that the argument is a logical one (to that extent Hegel can be brought in as a precedent), while, at the same time, it concerns an "existent," or factual, subject. It involves a conflict of two modes of thought. In addition, the argument in its formal presentation is too condensed to be intelligible.

The for-itself is negative reference to the in-itself. Now for Sartre, what the for-itself negates in not just its "moment" of facticity but itself qua non-negated, qua whole. It thus refers to itself qua in-itself. This could be taken as a "logical" short cut: the for-itself negates being-in-itself; still, it "is" for-itself; therefore, it refers to itself qua in-itself-for-itself; (where the "in-itself" stands for the "being" of the for-itself). The for-itself's reference to what

52. EN, p. 133; BN, pp. 89f. Cf. Descartes, *Meditations,* Third Meditation in *Œuvres,* ed. C. Adam and P. Tannery (Paris, no date), VII.

it is—in-itself-for-itself—logically precedes the reference to what it is not. Here again the "prevalence of the positive" holds.

To help us understand Sartre's point, let us investigate the parallel Hegelian argument for a passage from finite, determinate being [*Dasein*], which is not yet being-for-itself, to the ought and to infinity. Hegel's passage from *something* to *finite being* and from there to the *infinite* is based on the dialectic of the *limit* and is reflected in an ambivalence of the notions of "determinate being" [*Dasein*] [53] and "being-in-itself" [*Ansichsein*].[54] "Something" ("a" determinate being, *Daseiendes*) is in its determination (its being-in-itself) limited over against an Other; on the other hand, its limitation stands opposed to it, so that it is being-in-itself in as much as we are discounting limitation. "Something" therefore has its "determinate being" [*Dasein*] within the limit, but at the same time it has its "being" [*Sein*] beyond the limit. Being-in-itself is both a restricted and unrestricted "something"; that which is "inherently null" [55] and "that which is in-itself," [56] i.e., completed being.

The argument is a logical one: something and Other are shown to be the same qua immediate determinate being and qua determined by the limit they share. They are thus negatives of one another and identical with one another. The negation of the negation is the positing of something as being (being-within-itself of something, and thus, as yet, just becoming, finitude).[57] The argument for the passage of the finite to the infinite invokes a parallel dialectic of the barrier. At first, the passage beyond the barrier is only a "finite egress," [58] but it involves the final passage to the infinite as a collapse into itself.[59]

What now about Sartre, if viewed in the light of Hegel? We find two major divergencies: for one, Sartre is not concerned with *something* and *Other* (as forms of determinate being) but with *being-for-itself* and *being-in-itself*. For another, the logical argument serves the case of a factual subject. Qua factual, the for-itself is thus represented by the abstract notion of *Dasein* (or, "determinate being" in a Hegelian context). Sartre is dealing with ontology; he intends to understand the factual subject and, to be

53. *Logik*, I, pp. 134f.; J&S, I, pp. 139f.
54. *Ibid.*, pp. 140f.; J&S, I, pp. 144f.
55. *Ibid.*, p. 152; J&S, I, pp. 153f.
56. *Ibid.*; J&S, I, p. 154.
57. *Ibid.*, p. 137: "Insichsein des Etwas," "Werden an ihm selbst," "Endlichkeit." J&S, I, pp. 141f.
58. *Ibid.*, p. 145; J&S, I, p. 148.
59. Cf. *ibid.*, p. 161; J&S, I, p. 160.

exact, to construe its existential constitution dialectically. He intertwines the formal derivation—which remains a play with words unless the proper dialectical analysis is brought out—with an account in terms of phenomenology or "fundamental ontology," respectively, the idea of man's projecting himself toward a totality being a thesis of Heidegger's analytic of *Dasein*. To the extent that Sartre has recourse to the latter, the dialectical derivation can take second place.

It is remarkable that Sartre discusses the ontological constitution of the factual subject with the conceptual means of what Hegel, in his *Logic,* calls "qualitative being." The reference of the for-itself to being (in the ambiguous sense of its own being—facticity and coincidence with itself—and the object) is a more determinate relation than relations on the level of qualitative being. Hegel discusses such a relation, discounting facticity as a temporal factor, in a later section of the *Logic* on the level of the "notion" [*Begriff*], and again, in the *Encyclopedia,* on the level of "spirit" [*Geist*]—the latter representing the notion of a subject which has integrated the determinations of "externality." The beginning of Hegel's *Logic*—if we are right in considering it a paradigm for Sartre—is too indeterminate for his purpose. Sartre in fact reduces the relationship between subject and being to the interplay of the abstract determinations of "determinate being" [*Dasein*] and "being-for-itself."

Like Hegel's determinate being, Sartre's being-for-itself is ambivalent as to its determinateness or in-itself status, respectively: on the one hand, being-in-itself is a "moment" of the for-itself (corresponding to the one acceptation of "being-in-itself" in Hegel: the for-itself as something positive with ingredient negativity); on the other hand, being-in-itself is coincidence, synthesis, totality, "being" (corresponding to the other acceptation of "being-in-itself": the for-itself as something negative which, by egressing beyond itself, turns positive). Sartre's being-for-itself is subject to the dialectic of the limit.

Now Sartre presupposes the being of the for-itself, in the sense of totality, on the ground of a "prevalence of the positive." The for-itself has not, at the beginning, a negative of itself opposed to it (analogous to another determinate being beyond the limit, as in Hegel); it is, by itself, a negative, a lack, over against its own totality. Thus, the "being" of the for-itself is not "developed" out of a dialectic of double negation. It is, rather, the presupposed point of orientation which the determinate and finite for-itself would reach if it could traverse a logical and categorial sequence (which it cannot do since it is defined as a finite, ontic magnitude). Sartre will re-establish the parallelism with Hegel's dialectic of determinate being and the limit, and follow the path of mediation; he will do so by subsequently devising a "complement" of the for-itself,[60] which is to enable it to coincide with itself. This complement will then be the outstanding "beyond" of the for-itself. But as we have seen, Sartre's original emphasis is on a totality opposed to the for-itself, which corresponds to Hegel's infinite as opposed to the finite. The infinite is the positive, the in-itself of the for-itself, in the face of which it determines itself as a lack. We see in Sartre a complex dialectic which can be resolved into two Hegelian dialectics: one of determinate being [Dasein] and one of being-for-itself; or a real dialectic, which deals with finite being, and a logical one, which is concerned with totality. The logical import of Sartre's being-for-itself is indicated in the formulation that a finite subject is "haunted" by its totality.

In our context, the attempt to urge a parallelism between Sartre and Hegel has to face the tie-up, on the level of qualitative being, of being-for-itself and determinate being [Dasein], such that being-for-itself stands for a finite and factual entity. Sartre's being-for-itself is an existent; its reference to its own infinity is one in terms of a "bad" infinite rather than its transformation into a higher stage of determination. The determination of its Dasein is equated with Hegel's notion of externality,[61] so that the above "existential" dialectic corresponds to Hegel's dialectic of time. To be outside of itself is the way for the for-itself to be finite and determinate [daseiend]; for this it need not, like a "something," be opposed to another being of its own type. Its dialectic is "unipolar," [62] a dialectic of the finite for-itself with itself. Ontologically, as opposed to logically, we have a twofold opposition: that of for-itself and being (taken as facticity and the object), and that of for-itself and for-itself as an immanent coincidence. Logically, however, both are leveled to a *single* opposition because of the indeterminateness of the notions of qualitative being which Sartre uses to account for the subject.

With his more determinate dialectic, Hegel, on a higher level, can do justice to the multiple oppositions which in Sartre's account are collapsed into one—although we must bear in mind that Hegel thinks in terms of a categorial and not a temporal dialec-

60. See chap. 4, sec. 2, below, "Complement."
61. Cf. Hegel, *Enzyklopädie*, § 247.
62. A term taken from J. Cohn, *Theorie der Dialektik* (Leipzig, 1923), p. 273.

tic.[63] As we have seen, Hegel accounts for the relation between the for-itself and being on the dialectical stage of the notion [*Begriff*] and of spirit [*Geist*]. His aim is to establish a totality, intended as the identity of subjectivity and objectivity. The being-in-itself the for-itself is to attain is not, as in Sartre, subjective but, rather, objective being. With this opposition of subjectivity and objectivity, Hegel can demonstrate the movement of the subject toward its totality. He develops it out of a conflict of the subject over against an Other; the subject traverses various stages of identification with being-in-itself. In couching the subject in terms of notion and spirit—which are more developed forms of unification of subject and object—Hegel is able to regard the self-transcendence of the subject as an egress toward an Other, which is already implied in it and therefore is "its" Other, and thus precisely as a transcendence toward itself.[64] Hegel's basic idea would seem to be that the subject can win its totality only through a *mediation with the object* and, to the extent that it has not so won it, by egressing toward objectivity.

Sartre tries to show how a subject *taken in its immanence* amounts to a lack and transcends toward itself as totality. In Sartre's abstract dialectic this is the obvious result of the poverty of the dialectical determinations. Totality is a "logical" extrapolation of an existent for-itself which wants to attain its "being." One might object that, in characterizing Sartre's dialectic as one of immanence, we are overlooking the fact that for him, too, the subject stands in opposition to an object and so, through the object, is mediated with itself. We will discuss this negation in a later section,[65] but at this point it might be said, by way of antici-pation, that such negation of being does not, as in Hegel, aim at an identification of subject and object. Rather, it excludes the object. Surely, Sartre intends to do justice to what is called "being-in-the-world," and the notion of the for-itself involves an immedi-ate opposition to the world. But the "construction" of a totality

63. Cf. chap. 4, sec. 3, below, "Excursus on Hegel."
64. If we characterize the subject on the level of the notion, it can be interpreted as "subjective purpose": individuality "stamps the subjectivity of the notion, pre-supposed as against objectivity, with the mark of a defect, in compari-son with the complete and rounded totality, and thereby at the same time turns outwards" (W. Wallace, *The Logic of Hegel* [i.e., *Enzyklopädie*, Part I], § 207). On the level of spirit it can be interpreted as an "abstract self-consciousness": this is already "affected by an external object, formally speaking, with a negation of itself; . . . certain of itself over against the object it is the *impulse* to posit what it is in itself—i.e., to give the abstract knowledge of itself content and objectivity . . ." (*Enzyklopädie*, § 425).
65. See chap. 4, sec. 4, below.

reference of the for-itself to itself and, more generally, of all its existential structures, remains within the immanence of subjectivity and exhibits a formalism indifferent to concrete content.

The For-Itself as Totality

LET US GRANT the transcendence by the for-itself toward its own totality. The for-itself stands in a relation to, reaches out toward, an absent self, which is its totality. But in reversal of Hegel's view, the totality is unattainable. The for-itself cannot become an in-itself-for-itself. This would be a coincidence with itself involving no otherness, a positivity which is *identité à soi*.[66] Sartre urges here the same incompatibility that exists between the two types of being. The attainment of totality, the in-itself-for-itself, would mean the destruction of the for-itself. The unattainability of totality is based on an ontico-ontological impossibility. For man, totality is a limiting concept, or an ideal.[67] Consciousness is thus "by nature an unhappy consciousness" but, as in the case of the Kantian "idea," "committed" to, or "engaged" in, this ideal.[68]

Consciousness does not refer to this totality in the manner of a positional consciousness, for that would make it an object.[69] Totality "haunts non-positional consciousness" as its "meaning." Without this haunting totality consciousness would not be consciousness, inasmuch as this means to be a "lack." Both notions of consciousness, that of lack and that of totality, form a "dyad." [70]

It becomes apparent that the structures construed successively on the basis of presence-to-itself are co-original as moments of a whole. The for-itself forms a structural unity which Sartre calls "selfness" [*ipséité*].[71] The development of the immediate structures of the for-itself constitutes a transcendental theory in synthetic progression which is designed as a "deduction" of the existential features of the subject. Its paradox consists in the fact that its starting point is itself a concrete consciousness, man's presence-to-himself.

Taken in its existential import, totality for Sartre is value [*valeur*].[72] The characteristics attributed by Sartre to the self as

66. EN, p. 133; BN, p. 90.
67. EN, p. 140; BN, p. 96.
68. EN, p. 134; BN, p. 90.
69. All negations within immanence—except reflection proper—are non-positing. This is an indication of the structural unity of immanence.
70. EN, p. 134; BN, p. 91.
71. EN, pp. 147f.; BN, pp. 102f.
72. EN, p. 136; BN, p. 92.

totality correspond to those normally accorded to value—viz., "to be unconditionally" and "not to be," i.e., to be valid unconditionally. Value is the "unconditioned beyond of all surpassings" of being and thus the "beyond of the very being which surpasses," i.e., of the for-itself. It is unattainable but, inversely, "my surpassings presuppose it." Value is the missing totality [*totalité manquée*], the self qua absolute, identical, pure, permanent, and the foundation of its being; it is the "meaning" of all surpassings, which haunts freedom. It does not exercise an "attraction" for the for-itself, but it is that which the for-itself "has to be." "In a word the *self*, the for-itself, and their inter-relation stand within the limits of an unconditioned freedom . . . and also within the limits of concrete facticity—since . . . the for-itself cannot be the foundation of its being." [73]

The difficulty of regarding totality as value is revealed when determinations of consciousness, which we consider negative, are raised in a similar manner to the status of value, i.e., to a totality of such determinations. Thus, the for-itself as a consciousness of thirst is haunted by a self featuring thirst as a value. Although a lack tends toward its satisfaction, a lack interpreted as a total self is not suppressed but exalted: "It loses its character as lack while making itself be thirst in and through the satisfaction." [74]

Earlier, we were dealing with a lack of "being," which was to be overcome; the for-itself projects itself toward a coincidence with itself where consciousness and being are one. Whereas this was a formulation of the *structural* paradox of an in-itself-for-itself, granted that consciousness is a lack by its very structure, any consciousness with *concrete* content may now stand for such a lack. And, quite generally, Sartre says that man does not aim at suppression of desire but at making it eternal. This seems to be an obvious confusion of structure and content. Only the fact that certain feelings stand for a lack leads him to identify such feelings with the lack which stands for a structure. The confusion suggests that, no matter what the concrete determination may be, the for-itself wants to raise itself to the level of "being." Sartre's example of desire (or thirst, respectively) suggests in fact that the for-itself, as thus determined, is imperfect and, as thus determined, wants to be perfect. On the other hand, the for-itself wants to transcend and negate its determination (i.e., in this context, cease to be thirst). The assertion that the for-itself wants to be thirst totally is matched by the other one, that it wants to negate

73. EN, p. 138; BN, p. 94.
74. EN, p. 146; BN, p. 101.

its determination. Sartre's thesis of the "eternal" thirst, which the for-itself wants to be, is misleading inasmuch as the ideal is posited as homonymous with the restrictive determination which is to be transcended. My demand to exalt my determination is not determined as to concrete content. On the one hand, the determination in mind is a "mode" or "being" of the for-itself; on the other, it is its restriction, an Other of the for-itself which is to be overcome. What the for-itself wants can only be expressed in terms of structure: viz., to coincide with itself. If desire were meant as a structure rather than a determination in an obvious concrete sense (e.g., thirst), man would have the desire to be desire "eternally." This would be the call for a finitude raised to a higher power; man's factual finitude would have entered reflection and become a human project. The dialectic outlined corresponds to that of externality, or temporality. To back up his iridescent account of desire, deriving from an equivocal interpretation of the dialectic, Sartre can point to basic human experiences which, if they are to be believed, suggest that man strives for increase of, as well as liberation from, desire.

The For-Itself as Complement

THE FOR-ITSELF stands in a purposive relationship to itself as totality. The latter, as its *raison d'être*, is, however, unattainable. The for-itself remains the lack of a coincidence with itself. The project toward its own totality refers it to a "mean" through which it can integrate itself with itself.

In Sartre's account, this relationship is likened to an objective lack. Just as in the example of the crescent and the full moon, Sartre regards the for-itself as made up of three moments: presence-to-itself, as that which is a lack; totality, or the in-itself-for-itself; and the "complement," as that which presence-to-itself is lacking to be totality.[75] What in the purposive relationship appears as a mean or means is here the complement of the for-itself.

The complement has to fit in with the interpretation of the for-itself as a lack. It must itself be a for-itself, because, together with it, the for-itself is to coincide with itself. "The lacking for-itself is a for-itself which I *am*." On the other hand, I am not the complement "in the mode of identity," for this would be the case of an impossible coincidence. Sartre determines the complement in the light of the totality presupposed: "I am the lacking for-itself in the mode of having to be the for-itself which I am not, in order to

75. EN, p. 145; BN, p. 100.

identify myself with it in the unity of the self." [76] Within the framework of an ideal of the in-itself-for-itself which haunts me, I refer to an absent for-itself which I am but which is yet lacking. This complement of the for-itself which I am, taken in its existential meaning, is my *possibility*.[77] The for-itself, which now appears as a "trinity," [78] has three co-original deployments: factual presence, possibility, and self-purpose. It is a construct designed to reproduce Heidegger's existentialia.

On closer scrutiny, Sartre's doctrine has its difficulties. The object analogy is problematic: according to it, a whole is composed of an existent and a complement. In man's comprehensive grasp of things in the world, a complement cannot be demonstrated; we have to infer it. Applied to the for-itself, the analogy would suggest that the for-itself, once it has projected itself toward its totality, need only find the additional term of a sum in order to make itself a whole. Once the term is found, the for-itself would already be the desired totality. If the term is not attainable, however, what is the difference between it and the "haunting" totality? Can the analogy make it clear that possibility is distinct from that which it is to make possible?

We have already given the analysis necessary for a dialectical understanding of the complement.[79] With the help of this notion the passage from presence-to-itself to totality is now *developed* or *construed*, whereas before it had been merely presupposed. The complement follows the dialectic of determinate being and the limit. Since the for-itself is also determinate being [*Dasein*], its "being" is to be sought for in the mediation with a negative of itself, the complement, which it is not yet. Under the object analogy, this opposition appears as undialectical—as an opposition of two positives—but it is in fact a subject-oriented dialectical opposition which logically mediates totality through double negation. The for-itself transcends itself toward a beyond in order to be.

In terms of the logical dialectic of being, this would be too much since it would involve the attainment of totality as a higher categorial stage, an attainment not within the reach of a finite for-itself. Possibility would be tantamount to the haunting ideal. The mediation of the for-itself with its possible must, therefore, be interpreted in terms of the complex dialectic suggested above. The for-itself in its reference to itself is external to itself. If it has, in

76. EN, p. 140; BN, p. 96.
77. EN, p. 145: "mon possible." BN, p. 101.
78. EN, p. 131; BN, p. 88.
79. See p. 74–76, above.

time, realized a possibility, it is still external to itself and so has new possibilities. For the finite for-itself, totality remains an ideal (of a higher categorial stage); all the for-itself has is its possibility which promises totality.

Again we are referred to the dialectic of temporality, which is based on the finite determinateness, in the sense of self-externality, of the for-itself so that anything attained by the for-itself in time changes into negativity. The existential dialectic which concerns us here is in a certain way opposed, as well as complementary, to that of temporality. The latter is rooted in the existence of the for-itself, taken as a negative (viz., its externality), and thus exhibits the unrest of the for-itself in terms of the "bad" infinite. In it, the ideal, or totality, is not a constitutive element, for it belongs to a higher categorial sphere. The distinction between complement and totality of the for-itself betrays a conflict between finite (real, factual, external) dialectic and infinite (logical) dialectic. In Sartre, both are collapsed without mediation.[80]

The dialectic of the for-itself, deployed into presence-to-itself, complement, and totality, leaves a difficulty: granted that possibility constitutes the for-itself as a lack and remains outstanding even if its "content" can be realized in the present, will this leveling of possibility and ideal not entail the leveling of *means* and *end* as well? The difficulty can be regarded as a consequence of the fact that we are dealing here with what was earlier called a "unipolar" dialectic. Such a dialectic provides only *one* Other for the for-itself: itself. Sartre's dialectic is a dialectic of immanence and does not, by itself, give expression to the necessity that another Other than myself is required to establish possibility, an Other enabling me to strive for my totality which, as a finite being, I cannot attain. It is a dialectic of the nullity of the for-itself, a nullity which does not derive from an existent Other restricting it, although the poverty of Sartre's dialectical determinations seems to cover this case too. Logically, the in-itself is not sufficiently determinate to figure as a means in a purposive relation. But is it not precisely the object which constitutes the means for my purpose and which is subjective and objective in one? Once more we raise our earlier objection to accounting for the purposive relation of the for-itself in terms of immanence. Can the interdependent moments of presence-to-itself, totality, and possibility be meaningful as restricted to subjectivity? How does the for-itself's reference to the world fit into this context?

80. Cf. p. 92f., below.

If only in view of the analysis of facticity as the for-itself's being in a world, it is plain that the for-itself is not limited to its subjectivity and cannot constitute a worldless subject. On the other hand, the reference of the for-itself to itself is a reference within immanence, leaving possibility and ideal as merely formal determinations. To escape emptiness, however, they will have to be connected with the world. The purposive relation connotes an "enablement," which involves a reference to the world and the use of a utensil as a means. But how are we to understand such a possible if it is, on the one hand, a for-itself while, on the other, it is tied to a worldly means?

Let us once again discuss Sartre's example.[81] Thirst "is never sufficiently thirst"; it wants to be thirst-itself in the mode of being-in-itself. For this it is "lacking a certain for-itself which would realize it as satisfied thirst and which would confer on it being-in-itself." What is required is an act of drinking, as a reflection from the aim onto the for-itself. "The possible of the consciousness of thirst is the consciousness of drinking"—i.e., in abstract terms, the projection of a for-itself beyond the for-itself which is presence-to-itself. Both presence-to-itself and possible for-itself have, in virtue of their character as for-itself, a *correlative* in the world. The for-itself of thirst which wants to be satisfied thirst has a glass before it; the possible for-itself has for its object-meaning the reference from the full glass to the emptied glass. The object side constitutes the correlative of the subjective structures and therefore features corresponding references.[82] My aim is the objective correlative of my possibility.[83]

According to Sartre the possible for-itself is separated from the for-itself as presence-to-itself "by nothing" and yet by the totality of what there is in the world,[84] inasmuch as the possible for-itself is a presence to the world. The project toward coincidence with itself traverses the world. It is "beyond the world or distance of infinite being" that "man must be reunited with his possible." This relation is the *circuit of selfness* [*circuit d'ipséité*]. The world is the "totality of being insofar as it is traversed by the circuit of selfness." In this way Sartre outlines a relationship between for-itself and world which is to transcend mere presence to the world and is to make purposive action in the world possible.

81. EN, pp. 145f.; BN, p. 101.

82. EN, pp. 149, 251; BN, pp. 104, 200f.

83. Note that the means is discussed only as something readily available to me. It is something at hand in the world, which is understood in terms of a possibility and so used.

84. EN, p. 146; BN, p. 102.

Sartre wants to meet two demands. On the one hand the for-itself refers to the world in purposive action, realizes aims in the world for its own sake, and makes known to itself what it is in terms of the world. On the other hand, the realization of an end in the world, as that which makes it possible for me to be, must be consciousness of that end. The possible is an anticipation by the for-itself (of) a for-itself which is a consciousness of objects in the world.[85] Phenomenologically, the two references are distinct as positing and non-positing consciousness. I refer to my possible for-itself pre-reflectively, while my reference to an aim in the world is that of a cogito. But since this is the cogito of a possible for-itself, my reference is mediated by a pre-reflective cogito of that cogito.[86]

Contrasted with Hegel's view, Sartre's account of the interrelatedness of for-itself and world is merely formal. The transcendent opposite pole of the subject, the world, is not a dialectical opposite. The subject's relation to the world simply runs parallel to its own structural moments. These are, as we have seen, fused with material content such as the for-itself would have in its world (e.g., thirst). And whatever my determination happens to be, I project myself toward being it totally. This aspect of subjective totality is counterpointed by the other aspect, equally restricted to my sphere of immanence, that I am negation of myself and so disown my factual determination. Thus, there is room here for a projection of "new" possibilities and a new, non-homonymous ideal, for a choice of myself, again with wordly correlatives to match the subjective structures of the for-itself. Both aspects of the for-itself, projection toward totality and self-negation, form a dialectical conflict in terms of extreme abstraction: I am not my in-itself-for-itself, i.e., it merely haunts me; and I am not what I am (since, otherwise, I would be an in-itself) and, therefore, I am always beyond myself. The dialectical construct which, as we saw, results from an equivocal notion of the in-itself, is unsatisfactory. In terms of it, the possibility of the for-itself is characterized as identical and yet as non-identical with the for-itself.

To overcome this subjective formalism—which is clearly apparent from its unipolar dialectic—the relationship between subject and world would have to be more than a correlation: the

85. EN, pp. 148f.: "Le possible, en effet, qui est mon possible, est pour-soi possible et comme tel présence à l'en-soi comme conscience *de* l'en-soi." BN, p. 104.

86. This corresponds to Husserl's thesis that I can, by way of anticipation, intend objects in protentions. Cf. *Vorlesungen zur Phänomenologie des inneren Zeitbewusstseins*, § 43. Sartre extends this idea to pragmatic references.

world would have to "supply" possibilities and constitute a dialecti-cal "mean" for myself, so that I could make known to myself, in terms of the world, what I want to be. (We will return to this question below.)

Only as deployed into its "immediate" structures is Sartre's for-itself what the word implies, i.e., a *self* which refers to itself. Presence-to-itself, facticity, totality, and possibility together form a structural network of co-original moments, of which presence-to-itself as actual consciousness constitutes the ground for the non-actual or "negative" dimensions. Presence-to-itself, qua nega-tivity, is the starting point for a construction of the self. What this is in terms of content is prefigured in Heidegger's existentialia. Sartre's own contribution is the construction.[87] We now have a better insight into its problematic character, which is due to Sartre's choice of negativity as a ground. Such a ground does not permit a dialectic of unequivocal content; it requires us to either supplement determinateness by drawing on phenomenology or to associate content from the resources of Hegel's higher dialectical stages. But we have not yet come to the end of our analysis.

[3] TEMPORALITY

BEFORE EMBARKING on a discussion of how the for-itself transcends to the world, we have to consider another of its immanent structures, or another aspect of the one structure al-ready discussed: temporality. This analysis follows on that of the immediate structures of the for-itself in such a way that together the two analyses form an account of the for-itself in immanence. In a sense, the account in terms of temporality is a repetition of the preceding account. The relationship between them reflects the relationship between the structure of "care" [*Sorge*] and that of temporality in Heidegger's *Sein und Zeit*.

In view of his constructive program, Sartre has to demonstrate the derivation of temporality from the notion of the original for-itself. He does this by showing, both in a phenomenological and in an ontological analysis, that time is incomprehensible unless viewed in the light of a structure which has the form of the for-itself. Conversely, the for-itself, so far discussed in the formal terms of in-itself and negativity, is enriched by an interpretation in terms of temporality. We concentrate on the ontological analysis.

87. Viewed in this light, Sartre's theory of the for-itself is the attempt to do for Heidegger what Fichte did for Kant: to deduce the categories (or existentialia, respectively) from a ground.

Preliminary Ontological Considerations

SARTRE GIVES US an ontological analysis of time, drawing for his systematic purpose on historical views of time. The irreversible succession of before and after, which is a universally admitted characteristic of time, is incomprehensible if the before and the after are regarded as separate because this would involve a disintegration of time into an infinity of instants.[88]

The associationist theory posits impressions only "externally" related with each other, but without prior unification their connection remains incomprehensible. One might resort, however, to the idea of a "witness" who unites successive contents.[89] But if the problem is not to recur in the case of the witness, we have to assume that he is at two temporal points at once, which means that he is atemporal. This, in Sartre's mind, is the upshot of Descartes' and Kant's solutions. The unity of time stems from an atemporal entity: from God, who exercises his *creatio continua,* or from the "I think." (In Descartes, time is unified by the material content maintained in being; in Kant, the form of intuition itself is determined by concepts of the understanding.) The instants to be unified are themselves atemporal; therefore, according to Sartre, a reconstruction of time is bound to fail. If time is to be real, God himself would be affected by it and would have to wait for a future event; God would be subject to a temporality comprehensible only in terms of self-externality. Or, to take the other alternative, time becomes an illusion of finite man. If we argue that, in Kant, the temporal form of intuition is already a unity, Sartre replies that what matters is not a total intuited unity but the intratemporal references between the before and the after. Quite generally, the idea of unifying isolated atemporal beings-in-themselves is as incomprehensible to Sartre as is that of a virtual temporality. Atemporal entities either remain unaffected by the introduction into them of cross-references, or must change into entities with a new type of unity, ecstatic unity. For Sartre, the before and after are conceivable only by virtue of the incompleteness of a before which refers to an after. An atemporal "I think," however, cannot bring about such a change of being.[90] How the "I

88. EN, p. 176; BN, p. 131.
89. EN, pp. 178f.; BN, pp. 132f. For the following analysis of Sartre, cf. Bergson, *L'Évolution créatrice, Œuvres* (Paris, 1959), pp. 787, 781, 795–801.
90. Sartre sees here the Kantian "I think" as a necessary condition rather than as a factual function of consciousness (cf. "La Transcendance de l'égo," pp. 85–87). Therefore, the "I think" becomes atemporal. Cf. Heidegger, who interprets the "I think" in terms of pure self-affection on the part of the subject (*Kant und*

think" could transform atemporal entities into a succession is incomprehensible. Time cannot be projected by an atemporal entity, nor can it be imprinted on something atemporal.

We note the following difficulty: succession need not be admitted universally. The pure unchanging persistence of a thing, or of being *in toto*, is not atemporal, at least not in the sense in which an instant is atemporal. We find, in fact, a twofold use of the notion of the in-itself: First, it means that which suffers no relations and, *a fortiori,* since before and after are relations, no time; the in-itself would in this way be a continuum, ever-existent being, or a perpetual now.[91] Second, the notion refers to discrete and isolated entities, including instants, which are regarded as successive although it cannot be seen how their succession is possible. If time is succession both notions of the in-itself drop out, and for contrary reasons.

Sartre also discusses the continuum theory of time.[92] His criticism is that, due to a lack of caesuras, there could be no before and after. For Leibniz the temporal sequence in fact turns into a logical immanence. By contrast, we have to maintain that time is also separation. Bergson's solution, a penetration of the present by the past, Sartre regards as rhetoric. How could an inactive past make itself felt in the present? [93]

In terms of the critical reflections discussed above, Sartre's objection to the continuum view of time means that time would require an in-itself along the lines of a non-relational, ever-existent being, such that the problem of determinateness of temporal content would have to be left open. But is not Sartre's *being* such an in-itself? He himself has to admit, though, that in being there are "abolitions and apparitions." Such successions, Sartre says, cannot be conceived from the standpoint either of the structures of the for-itself or of those of the in-itself; they do not belong to ontology but constitute a subject for metaphysics.[94] But does not ontology have to disclose the conditions of all succession in being? Sartre is here led to a distinction between ontology and metaphysics according to which the latter studies those successions in being which are not amenable to his "ecstatic" theory of time (to be discussed presently).

---

das Problem der Metaphysik, 2nd ed. [Frankfurt, 1951], § 34), and who in fact says (p. 174): "Zeit und 'ich denke' sind dasselbe." Sartre has failed to see the possibility of an "existential" interpretation of Kant.

91. Cf. chap. 4, sec. 3, below, "Excursus on Hegel."
92. EN, pp. 179–81; BN, pp. 134f.
93. Cf. Bergson, *Matière et mémoire, Œuvres* (Paris, 1959), pp. 283, 290, 370.
94. EN, p. 257; BN, p. 206. Cf. chap. 6, sec. 5, below.

In line with Sartre's intention of giving a comprehensible theory of time—that this is his aim is clear from the fact that a metaphysical element of time is set apart—it is not so much of time that we have to speak but of temporality as a feature attributable to an ecstatic being. Temporality stands for a unity which diversifies itself; it has to be interpreted as a reference in terms of being within a being.[95] "Temporality must have the structure of selfness." [96] Only a being of such a structure can be temporal. Such a being is being-for-itself with its ecstatic unity. Now if we require discreteness of time, but regard man as the only alternative to being-in-itself, temporality can only be a feature of human reality.[97] Worldly time originates with the for-itself.[98] With this thesis, Sartre follows Heidegger.[99]

The For-Itself as Temporal

IN AN ANALYSIS parallel to his general ontological discussion of time, Sartre points out that a separation of the temporal dimensions is equally unsatisfactory in the case of the subject. The subject has to be understood as the unity of the three dimensions, or ecstases. To use Sartre's expression, it is "dispersive" [diasporique].[100]

According to the popular view the past either "is no longer" or has some kind of shadow existence.[101] In both cases time has been interpreted from the standpoint of the in-itself. It cannot be shown, although it is phenomenologically evident, that the past is mine. The isolation of the past has to be abandoned in favor of its interpretation in terms of a type of being which has a past as its ecstasis. Human reality is clearly such a being having a past. Sartre analyzes this "having" in some detail.[102] My having a past

95. EN, p. 181: ". . . la temporalité est une force dissolvante mais au sein d'un acte unificateur, c'est moins une multiplicité réelle—qui ne saurait recevoir ensuite aucune unité et, par suite, qui n'existerait même pas comme multiplicité —qu'une quasi-multiplicité, qu'une ébauche de dissociation au sein de l'unité." BN, p. 136.

96. EN, p. 182; BN, p. 136.

97. In view of his notion of the in-itself, Sartre does not consider the possibility of raising the notion of the for-itself to a universal concept of being. Whitehead, in his cosmology (cf. Process and Reality [New York, 1929]), has attempted to introduce succession or process as a universal feature of the universe, leaving no opposition of a temporal subject and an atemporal object, by using the notion of "actual entity" which connotes the structure of the for-itself.

98. See pp. 90, 92n. 122, 106f., below.

99. Cf. Sein und Zeit, § 80.

100. EN, p. 182; BN, p. 136. "Dispersive" is my term.

101. EN, p. 152; BN, p. 109.

102. EN, pp. 156ff.; BN, pp. 112ff.

does not mean that I have a representation of past events; I "am" my past and yet "am not" my past because I "was" it. I "have to be" my past. The for-itself is negation of the in-itself which it is. As we see, it is the past which now plays the role of the in-itself.[103] It exemplifies the relation of the for-itself to its being. Accordingly, the past shares the feature of contingency. It is facticity,[104] substance,[105] or my essence.[106]

Sartre wonders how the structural requirement of a past can be reconciled with the fact of man's beginning in birth.[107] Birth is, for Sartre, the "absolute event" in the sense of a "nihilation of the in-itself." We should not say, then, that the for-itself must have a past in the sense of a "prior consciousness fixed in the in-itself." Rather, the past, as a necessary structural moment of the for-itself, hides a "reference of the for-itself to the pure in-itself," an original reference to the in-itself as such. Because the negation occurs, the in-itself figures as the "before"; it is what is "outside," "behind" the for-itself.[108] In view of this basic identity, Sartre can equate the in-itself of the world and the in-itself of one's own past. So we find him saying that one's past becomes a being in the world.[109]

The present is not just in opposition to the past, which is no longer, and to the future, which is not yet, and as such a mere limit or nothingness. Its primary feature is its presenting of something, its being presence to . . . [*présence à . . .*].[110] The "for-itself makes itself presence to being by making itself be for-itself. . . ." [111] Being remains unaffected by this presence. And yet, what we have is not just two beings which coexist for a third, a witness, or which stand in "external" relation to each other. Rather, ". . . in an original manner, the for-itself is presence to being, insofar as the for-itself is to itself its own witness of coexistence." [112]

103. EN, p. 162: "Le passé c'est l'en-soi que je suis en tant que dépassé." BN, p. 118.
104. EN, p. 162; BN, p. 118.
105. EN, p. 163; BN, p. 119.
106. EN, p. 164; BN, p. 120.
107. EN, pp. 184–86; BN, pp. 138–40.
108. EN, p. 184; BN, p. 139.
109. EN, p. 193: "Autrement dit, le Pour-soi tombant au Passé comme ex-présence à l'être devenue en-soi, devient un être 'au milieu du monde,' et le monde est retenu dans la dimension passée comme ce au milieu de quoi le Pour-soi passé est en soi." BN, p. 146.
110. EN, p. 165; BN, p. 121.
111. EN, p. 166; BN, p. 121.
112. EN, *ibid.*; BN, p. 122.

What has been said about the past applies *mutatis mutandis* to the future. Again, a relation in terms of being, rather than of representation, has to be assumed. "The future is *what I have to be* in so far as I can not be it." [113] If the for-itself is negation of its past and of the being it is present to—Sartre calls this negation a "flight"—the future is the goal of such flight. The future thus coincides with the possible and the ideal of the for-itself. It is a moment necessary to the for-itself; without reference to the future it would not be presence to the world either. The for-itself is beyond being in a twofold sense: it flees the being it is present to and the being which is its past. Its goal is equally twofold: the for-itself flees to itself as the possible for-itself and to the correlative of this possible for itself [*être cofutur*]. The future implies an in-itself in the future. It is the "meaning" of the in-itself in the present; through it the world receives the dimension of a future.[114]

The same impossibility that prevents the for-itself, interpreted as a lack, from coinciding with the ideal and the possible holds for the for-itself qua temporal: it cannot bring the future into the present. The future stands for the synthesis of selfness, but it is never reached. All the for-itself reaches is a for-itself "designated" by a project. The future, as such, "slides into the past as a bygone future, and the present for-itself . . . is revealed once again as the lack of a new future." [115]

The future is distinguished from the past in that the latter is the being I am without the possibility of not being it. The future, by contrast, is a being such that "I *can* only be it," i.e., it is open, it only "pre-outlines the frame" within which the for-itself can embrace certain possibilities. My possibilities have a hierarchical order distinct from the homogeneous sequence of moments in time.[116]

Sartre poses the question of an ontological condition of the *dynamic* of time.[117] Has not the account of temporality so far given been static in terms of a "structure" of the for-itself? In what sense has temporality reality-value, and why does the for-itself endure and constitute an ever renewed present?

113. EN, p. 170; BN, p. 125.
114. EN, pp. 171f.; BN, pp. 126f. Cf. the same objectification of references in the case of the pragmatic interpretation of the for-itself as a lack, pp. 83f., above. The future is distinguished from fantasy in that the for-itself I have in the case of fantasy does not emerge on the ground of the world as it is but from the ground of a nihilation of the world, apart from the world of being (EN, p. 172; BN, p. 127).
115. EN, p. 173; BN, p. 128.
116. EN, pp. 173f.; BN, pp. 128f.
117. EN, pp. 188–96; BN, pp. 142–49.

Sartre rejects the notion [118] that change implies permanence. In that view there would be an insoluble problem concerning the unity of that which changes and that which remains. His own solution is to say that change is "absolute," or "what changes *is* its former state in the past mode." For the for-itself to be such an absolute change, no change in the world is required. In such a changeless world, the for-itself would have to be "without change what it is in the form of having been it." The present has to pass away and become a before, and a new present has to emerge and constitute itself as an after. Both passing away and emerging are interdependent; the one coimplies the other. The present transforms the former present into past, thereby effecting a global modification: past becomes anterior past, or pluperfect—i.e., the relation between present and past becomes a relation in the mode of the in-itself. The future, in turn, is not realized by this modification; it becomes an ideal in-itself, the former future of a past. The remote future might lose the character of being my possibility; it would then become the former possibility of a past.[119]

This process could be interpreted, conversely, as the "reapprehension of the for-itself by being," such that the for-itself no longer has "the strength to sustain its own nothingness" and thus becomes a quality of the in-itself. The past of the for-itself and the being of the world merge. But this merger calls for the emergence of a new for-itself. Failing that, the result is "death" which is the "victory" of the in-itself over the for-itself.[120]

But have we now laid hold of the dynamic of time? Are we not merely offered formulas for "static structures"? It would be misleading to ask the question of how the ever new present can be explained if this present is taken as an isolated in-itself. We have to start from the for-itself. The constant renewal of the for-itself could be explained by spontaneity,[121] but this notion, too, is misleading, unless we regard spontaneity as something which sublates itself again and again, since, otherwise, it would become a being. "A for-itself which did not endure would remain of course a negation of the transcendent in-itself and a nihilation of its own being. . . . But this nihilation would become a *given;* that is, it would acquire the contingency of the in-itself, and the for-itself would cease to be the foundation of its own nothingness; . . .

118. EN, p. 189; BN, p. 143.
119. As we see, Sartre reproduces the distinctions Husserl makes in his *Vorlesungen zur Phänomenologie des inneren Zeitbewusstseins,* such as "protentions" in recollection.
120. EN, p. 193; BN, p. 147.
121. EN, p. 194; BN, p. 148.

it would be." In its flight, the for-itself is the "refusal of contingency by the very act which constitutes [it] as being the foundation of its nothingness." And yet it becomes contingent qua left behind and past. Thus totality is never achieved; the for-itself never "is."

The argument for a dynamic of time, or process, amounts to saying that temporality is *yet another dimension* in which a "being" of the for-itself has to be negated. The for-itself "flees" itself, inasmuch as it is in the present. The present is therefore transition to a new present, always on the way to being negated and transcended.[122] The dynamic positing of an ever renewed present has its ground in its self-diremption. The present is negativity, and to remain that—to be the "existent principle" it is—it must not remain but dirempt itself. In Sartre's terms, the for-itself has to negate itself so as not to become an in-itself. The for-itself "flees" its completion; it takes a negative attitude toward itself, qua positive. As a present it dirempts itself, opposes itself to itself, and constitutes what is left behind it as an in-itself which it is not.

In both cases, that of the for-itself's reference to the future and that of its reference to the past, the in-itself stands for a mode of being of the for-itself which is negated. In the case of the future, the in-itself involves a coincidence of the for-itself with itself in such a way that it would be the free foundation of itself. In the case of the past, it involves a coincidence which is pure contingency.[123] As such, the past logically collapses with the transcendent in-itself which is the environment of the for-itself. This is why Sartre can, as we saw when discussing the problem of man's beginning, identify the in-itself of the world and that of a past for-itself. The in-itself of the world is always on the way to being transcended, and so the for-itself as past and the world as past coincide. And yet, presence to the in-itself and reference to the past have to be distinguished. Phenomenologically, this distinction is expressed by the "non-positional" character of the for-itself's reference to itself, in contrast to the "positional" reference of its presence to the surrounding in-itself.[124] (In discussing the problem of the temporal beginning of the for-itself, Sartre collapses the two in a speculative fashion.)

122. This applies *mutatis mutandis* to the for-itself's presence to the world. Inasmuch as an in-itself is a *correlative* of the present and the present is always on the way to being transcended, that which is presented is equally transcended. The for-itself is always beyond its location, and the former location supplies the perspective for a new presence to the world. Cf. EN, p. 166; BN, pp. 121f.
123. Cf. EN, p. 164; BN, p. 120.
124. Cf. the parallel in the case of possibility and worldly goal. A for-itself objectified in "positional" negation will the other person. See chap. 5.

For a better understanding of the relationship between the analysis of temporality and that of the "immediate structures" of the for-itself, we will take up an earlier suggestion,[125] using Hegel to determine the difference between them. In his analysis of temporality, Sartre interprets the negativity of the for-itself as externality. If this determination of the for-itself is maintained without passing "logically" to a synthesis (totality, ideal) as a third stage, negativity assumes a temporal meaning. The for-itself is always ahead of itself and opposed to a past in-itself. The in-itself is the past, i.e., the for-itself as negated from the vantage point of the present, and the world as past. (The past exhibits "logically" the same state of affairs as the totality of the for-itself, which is one of the "immediate" structures.)[126] The for-itself takes position vis-à-vis itself in the present; qua "for" it, it is an in-itself, something contingent of which it is not the foundation.

The analysis of temporality may be regarded as a more complete account of the self-diremption of the for-itself (compared to that of its "immediate" structures), in that the present, or presence-to-itself, is now flanked on either side by a totality. The former analysis of the for-itself as determinate being [*Dasein*] had not featured this analogy with the factual temporality of the subject.

We have now come to know "functional" temporality as a structure of the for-itself. More explicit phenomena, such as recollection, expectation, and, more generally, the immanent intuition of time, will now have to be construed.[127] Such phenomena are, for Sartre, performances of *reflection*, which objectifies its givens and makes them an in-itself. It is in reflection that psychic time and a psychic, existent ego appear.[128] Sartre distinguishes two kinds of reflection, a *réflexion pure* and a *réflexion complice*, and it is the latter which is responsible for the actual objectification of temporal processes in terms of psychical givens.[129] The former may be attained from the latter by a sort of "catharsis" and constitutes a consciousness of the three temporal ecstases in terms of non-substantive temporality.[130]

For our purposes we can ignore Sartre's theory of reflection.

125. See pp. 76 and 82, above.
126. To distinguish the in-itself-for-itself qua past and qua ideal, material or existential content is required (possibility, facticity). For Hegel, too, abstract time would have a dimension but no definite direction.
127. For "innerworldly" time, see p. 106, below.
128. EN, pp. 209f.; BN, pp. 162f. Cf. "La Transcendance de l'égo," pp. 91ff.
129. EN, pp. 206ff.; BN, pp. 159ff.
130. EN, pp. 204ff.; BN, pp. 157ff.

Essentially, it amounts to an adaptation of his ontological analysis to the phenomenological account of reflection, with the addition of a second type of reflection. The dialectic has to explain how a diremption of the for-itself is possible to a point that, within the unity of consciousness, there can occur an opposition of subject and object. In contrast to the self-reference of the for-itself as a negation of itself, this opposition is, as it were, a more extended reference to itself, a unity "pushed further." The extreme extension of this reference to itself will be the reference of the for-itself to another for-itself. The ontological account of the possibility of the for-itself's reference to itself in reflection looks more like a "formulation" in ontological terms than like a new insight into its possibility. It reproduces the phenomenological findings in its own idiom.

Excursus on Hegel's View of Time

SARTRE'S INTERPRETATION OF TIME has a twofold basis: Husserl's and Heidegger's phenomenological analyses, and Hegel's dialectic of the for-itself. In our discussion we have noted Sartre's indebtedness to Husserl's notion of consciousness. But we saw him follow Heidegger in framing an ontological notion of consciousness; consciousness is a "being-there" [Dasein] which is unified with its past and its future not by intentionality references but by "being" them ecstatically. In Heidegger, these ecstases are adumbrated by a hermeneutics of the human subject; they are so-called existentialia, stated in terms of material content without formal reduction. It is through the question of a formal basis for these existentialia that Sartre comes to lean on Hegel.

In his view of time, Hegel is not the immediate paradigm for Sartre. Hegel's definition of time, according to which it is "the being which, in that it is, is not, and which, in that it is not, is," [131] looks similar to Sartre's definition of human reality or consciousness, according to which it is a being which "is what it is not and which is not what it is." [132] But this parallel is, as yet, a superficial one.

Hegel may be regarded as the philosopher of the movement of the notion. This movement is atemporal, categorial movement. Hegel shows how being—if viewed from the encompassing triadic perspectives of indifferent determination (qualitative being), unity

131. Hegel, Enzyklopädie, § 258: "Sie ist das Sein, das, indem es ist, nicht ist, und indem es nicht ist, ist."
132. EN, pp. 103, 116; BN, pp. 63, 74.

in reflection (essence), and self-comprehension (notion)—generates from itself all categorial determinations. Thus, Hegel can treat categorial modalities like contingency, possibility, and necessity as determinations of actuality. He realizes that a being (at the stage of actuality where these determinations occur) transcends its contingency while at the same time remaining bound to it. We find the relationship of facticity and coincidence with itself (necessity) treated as a categorial determination which moves on to a higher one, that of substance. A finite entity moves on the level of its applicable categorial determinations, but this temporal movement—a vacillation between opposites, a loitering about on its level—possesses no ontological rationale. It cuts across the line of the dialectical determinative process. Occasionally, Hegel himself draws attention to such repetitive processes, which fail to collapse in a higher categorial stage, as, e.g., when he discusses desire or external purpose. Time provides, as it were, the margin of free play for such repetitions and meanderings between opposite determinations which, in the movement of the dialectic, yield to a higher categorial synthesis. For something actual to move on its level it has to be a real, which as such is subject to the sphere of externality, including temporal externality. It will be external to itself since it cannot collapse with itself in a higher determination. This general determination of externality is indifferent to the categorial determination of actuality. Externality and actuality are only *externally* coincident.

Time is treated by Hegel as a topic in his philosophy of nature.[133] It is "negativity which, with reference to space, is a point." As such it is "for itself" while at the same time it posits its determination in the "sphere of externality." [134] As N. Hartmann says, it "opens another manifold of externality." [135] "It is the being which, in that it *is*, is *not*, and which, in that it is *not, is;* it is *intuited* becoming." [136] That is to say, it is, as a form of intuition, the unity of externality. As such it is not merely for a subject; "it is indifferent to the distinction of objectivity and a subjective consciousness over against it." [137]

Qua negativity, which is for itself, time is "self-referent negativity"—failure to remain a point, self-diremption. But time is this

133. Hegel, *Enzyklopädie*, §§ 257–59. The following translations are my own.
134. *Ibid.*, § 257.
135. N. Hartmann, *Hegel* (Berlin, 1929), p. 289.
136. Hegel, *Enzyklopädie*, § 258.
137. *Ibid.*

negativity in a "continuous" mode since, at this level of abstraction, there is not yet any difference to take account of. The real comes to be and passes away not "in" time, but "rather, time is itself this *becoming*, coming-to-be and passing-away, *existent abstraction*. . . . The real differs from time but is also essentially identical with it. It is restricted, and the Other involved in this negation is *outside* it; the determinateness qualifying it is therefore *external* to itself, and thus the contradiction of its being; time is the abstraction of this externality of the contradictory determinateness and of the unrest of the real. The finite is transient and *temporal* because it is not, like the notion, by itself total negativity; it has this for its general essence, ingredient in itself, but it is not in harmony with it, remains *one-sided* and so is subject to negativity as its governing *power*." [138]

In short, time is the "abstraction . . . of the unrest of the real." [139] What in the abstract account of time figures as a for-itself which is negation of space and self-diremption in a point, becomes, once reality is substituted, an account of a restricted entity as such. The Other—in a formal sense, "the Other of this negation," i.e., restriction—is "outside it"; the determinateness qualifying it is therefore "external to itself." [140] The concrete time of enduring and becoming is therefore the relatedness of the real to its Other, such that the real is barred from ever reaching a coincidence with it and thus a higher categorial determination. The Other is the real qua external to itself. In a modern expression, the real is "ecstatic"; a real being involves an external Other which is identical with it. [141]

"In nature," Hegel says, "time is the *now*." "The past and the future of time, taken as *existent* in *nature*, are space. . . ." [142] On the one hand, time is "indifferent to the distinction of objectivity and a subjective consciousness over against it"; on the other hand, "if these determinations are applied to space and time, space would figure as abstract objectivity" while time would be "abstract subjectivity." [143] It is in the subject only that the distinct temporal dimensions of present, future, and past "subsist"; "they are necessary

138. *Ibid.*
139. *Ibid.*
140. *Ibid.*
141. The real can be defined as "external to itself" since, in the Hegelian system, it comes under nature (which is the otherness of the idea). It therefore has a potential teleology, it "ought" to coincide with itself (in spirit). The diremption of the real cannot be detached from the system.
142. Hegel, *Enzyklopädie*, § 259. Hegel's point here corresponds to the atemporality of Sartre's in-itself.
143. *Ibid.*, § 258.

only in subjective representation, in *recollection*, and in *fear* or *hope*." [144]

"Time is the same principle as the I (= I of pure self-consciousness), but it is this principle or the simple notion in the form of utter externality and abstraction." [145]

Thus, time is differentiated into the dimensional time of a subject and a *nunc stans* of nature. The subject is temporal in an eminent sense since in it time becomes apparent.

Hegel regards the dimensions of time as "the *becoming* as such of externality and its dissolution into the differences of being, which is transition into nothing, and of nothing, which is transition into being." [146] "The immediate disappearance of these differences into *individuality* is the present as a *Now* that, qua individual, *excludes* others and yet, qua *continuously* passing into the other moments, is nothing but this disappearance of its being into nothing and of nothing into its being." [147] The *finite* present is "the *Now* as fixed in its *being* . . . as concrete unity. . . ." [148]

It is Hegel's idea that time is the *temporality* of the real. The emphasis is on coming-to-be and passing away; the finite is subjected to negativity as a power. Connected with this, however, is the structural insight that in becoming the finite always tends to be united with its Other, as that which would give it being. This becoming is, for Hegel, a general characteristic of finitude rather than that of a certain finite being with an ecstatic unity, the human subject, although Hegel did see the affinity of time with subjectivity and the notion.

Time is "the *notion* as *existent*," [149] and spirit "appears in time so long as it does not *grasp* its pure notion, i.e., so long as it does not annul time." [150] Hegel's interpretation of time can thus be seen to be inspired by the basic scheme of the dialectic of spirit; time is the incomplete notion. As such it is unspecific, not the temporality of man, for the basic scheme of the dialectic is universal. This explains Heidegger's criticism: [151]

Hegel demonstrates the possibility of a historical realization of spirit "in time" by going back to the *identity, in terms of formal structure, of spirit*

144. *Ibid.*, § 259.
145. *Ibid.*, § 258.
146. *Ibid.*, § 259.
147. *Ibid.*
148. *Ibid.*
149. Hegel, *The Phenomenology of Mind*, p. 800.
150. *Ibid.*
151. *Sein und Zeit*, p. 435. The translation is my own. Cf. *Being and Time*, trans. J. Macquarrie & E. Robinson (London, 1962), p. 485.

and time both of which are negation of the negation. Only by reducing spirit and time to the emptiest formal-ontological and formal-apophantic abstraction is it possible to establish the affinity of both. But as time is nevertheless conceived of as homogeneous world time, its origin is left totally obscure; it confronts spirit as something inert which simply is [*Vorhandenes*]. This is why spirit, to establish a rapport, *has to drop* "into time."

While the affinity of spirit and time on account of their formal identity is a point of criticism for Heidegger, Sartre seems to have been inspired by it. Human reality is temporal because it is negativity. Sartre tries to fuse Heidegger's concrete temporality with Hegel's abstract temporality. Possibility and facticity, future and past, are self-diremptions of the for-itself; self-diremption is the ground of existential time. In this thesis Sartre has taken over Hegel's idea that time is the deficient form of infinity or of the self-comprehensive notion. The for-itself is continually haunted by its coincidence with itself. For Hegel, as for Sartre, the finite is to be viewed from the perspective of the infinite, with the difference that Sartre knows of no categorial dialectic of spirit in terms of which spirit can eventually "comprehend" itself.

Clearly, Sartre's account of time shares the defects of Hegel's and even exacerbates them. We said that for Hegel time cuts across the line of the dialectical determinative progression. Like the latter, it is accounted for by the logical tool of negation, and so this progression in terms of the bad infinite "overlays" without mediation the categorial progression in which a real is placed by its very notion.

In Sartre there is no progression of categorial content, only existential "horizons" and temporal progression. Even so, he fails to distinguish time, by the logical tool of negation, from other relations or to establish negation as the sufficient condition of temporality. The unspecific character of Sartre's theory is clearly apparent. Hegel can place time within the categorial progression; it follows after space and so is propped up by its place in the system. In Sartre, the negative references are merely subject to different "interpretations." Also, in view of the degree of abstraction, temporality as a structure cannot be distinguished from temporal process. The dialectic of in-itself and for-itself has no room for an alternative approach to factual reality.

[4] THE FOR-ITSELF AS TRANSCENDENCE

WE SAID ABOVE [152] that Sartre proceeds on two paths: that of unfolding the structures of the for-itself in a "subjective

152. Pp. 69.

logic," and that of unfolding the opposition of the for-itself to being as transcending consciousness. This duality, and the inevitable relegation of one of these projects to second place, creates the impression that intentionality is posterior to the for-itself. Although this is not Sartre's intention,[153] the construction of intentionality points in this direction.

In discussing the immediate structures of the for-itself, we have already dealt with its reference to the world. Facticity involved presence to the world, and later, in the analysis of temporality, this reference took the more precise form of an ecstatic present. This shows that reference to the world, or transcendence, is already involved in instantaneous consciousness. Instantaneity figures once more as the point of departure for the development of a concrete self.

The Basic Reference to Being

ACCORDING TO SARTRE'S SPECULATIVE INTERPRETATION, the for-itself is the emergence of nothingness in being, turning the in-itself into a for-itself. But nothingness is not, by itself, an adequate notion of the subject. This is apparent from the ambivalence of this impoverished model: the subject is a nothingness over against being but it is also being because nothingness, as such, is not and so could not be negation of, and reference to, being. The subject therefore takes the form of a nothingness sustained by being; the subject has its own being, is its own type of being, is being and nothingness in unity, presence-to-itself. Drawing on the phenomenological notion of consciousness, Sartre was able to say that every consciousness is consciousness of something, or that presence-to-itself is presence-to-itself of a reference to being. Ontologically, this reference was termed a negation. How now can this reference be established on the basis of, or as deriving from, such a presence-to-itself? It will not suffice to say with cryptic briefness that consciousness is negativity; what is needed is a clarification of the reference to being issuing from an existent consciousness. Sartre's aim must be to show that the for-itself, in being negation of itself, is also consciousness of something.[154]

Sartre proceeds by the following argument: Presence-to-itself is a "phantom dyad" of "shine and countershine," the ideal sphere

153. Cf. EN, pp. 165f.: ". . . on ne saurait concevoir un type d'existant qui serait *d'abord* Pour-soi pour être *ensuite* présent à l'être." BN, p. 121.
154. EN, p. 269: ". . . tout se passe en effet comme si le Pour-soi, par sa néantisation même, se constituait en 'conscience de. . . .' . . . Le Pour-soi par sa négation de soi devient affirmation *de* l'En-soi." BN, pp. 216f.

of the for-itself. Now if either moment of this unity were only for the sake of the other, they would dissolve into nothing. On the other hand, if the shine is "something" there would be an in-itself within this sphere of pure self-appearance causing the destruction of the for-itself. If the shine is to be shine of something,[155] without taking on the character of an in-itself, it has to determine itself by "something other than itself." The shine "reflects" or "recoups" itself in being a reference to an outside which it is not. This argument would also do justice to the fact that percepts, and also subjective experiences (such as joy), are given "outside" as a character of things.[156]

The ideal sphere of the for-itself cannot be conceived as empty; its shine must be shine of something. But is it not just the shine of psychic being? It is true that Sartre has rejected the notion of a consciousness restricted to the sphere of immanence by pointing to phenomenological evidence and by devising an ontological interpretation of this evidence. If consciousness is to be construed, it must be shown that it can reach out beyond itself. And yet, we notice a difficulty besetting this important issue of the relationship between immanence and transcendence, for the subject is both nihilated psychic being and presence to the world.

Sartre wants to escape the problem that the subject might contain within itself a "representation" of the object. Presence-to-itself takes, therefore, the form of pure negativity, or of a phantom. On the other hand, the for-itself is a "being" of a type all its own, nihilated psychic being. The solution would seem to be that the shine is the negation of the being it reflects, such that it is determined by what it is not.[157] Being surrounds me, while I am simply the negation by which my presence-to-myself excludes all being from itself, thus separated from it and therefore connected with it.[158]

Of what type is this negation? It has a twofold task. In the first place, it causes being to be "there" for the for-itself; the for-itself is ecstatically submerged in being.[159] As the other end of this relation, the subject is intuitive and cognitive negation of being; it has taken on a general determination. In the second place, the for-itself

155. EN, p. 221: "quelque chose à refléter." BN, p. 173.
156. Cf. EN, pp. 222f.; BN, p. 174.
157. EN, p. 223: ". . . . le pour soi ne peut être que sur le mode d'un reflet se faisant refléter comme n'étant pas un certain être." BN, p. 174.
158. Cf. EN, p. 269: "Mais cet être qui 'm'investit' de toute part et dont *rien* me sépare, c'est précisément *rien* que m'en sépare. . . ." BN, p. 217.
159. Sartre reminds the reader of the phenomenon of fascination. EN, p. 226; BN, p. 177.

is equally negation of determinate being: if being is disclosed as "extended," the for-itself is given to itself as "unextended." [160] The disclosure of a determinateness of being is grounded in the very negation constituting the for-itself.[161] It is due to the negation which causes it to be "there" that a thing is determinate; or, more correctly, in that being is "there" for the for-itself, it is a determinate thing. Both a recoil from being and an access to it are ingredient in this negation of the for-itself. Thus, the negative reference of the for-itself to being is at the same time a positive reference, a "having," an affirmation,[162] and a negative reference, the relation of not being the Other.

This negation is not determinate negation, as in Hegel's categorial dialectic, but formal negation. The for-itself is transcending consciousness in that it excludes its objects from itself. Therefore, consciousness possesses only formal identity and abstract generality. And yet this negation is constitutive of consciousness; it is "internal" negation.[163] On the provisional level of the present analysis, the negation is abstract reference to being; to reach concreteness we will have to consider the reference to being entertained by the full self with its existential structures.

But will not the shine [*reflet*] be materially determined in such a way that it might constitute a "something" for consciousness? Consciousness negates its shine, but will this suffice to show that it transcends it? Has transcendence been established on the basis, and from the standpoint, of the subject? Is it not conceivable that what is given is an immanent shine, as in the case of Hegel's account of immanence instanced by the "feeling soul"? [164] And would this not destroy the possibility of ecstatic transcendence?

One might say the shine is a mediation. On the one hand, it is a materially determined moment of immanence or presence-to-itself; on the other, it reflects on an "outside" which the for-itself is not. It is through this shine that the for-itself mediates itself with being as its Other. But in this case the shine is ontologically prior, and one cannot see how the for-itself is able to take the shine "as" the negation of an Other. It is therefore misleading to say that the

160. EN, p. 228; BN, p. 179.

161. *Ibid.*: "en ce sens tout dévoilement d'un caractère positif de l'être est la contre-partie d'une détermination ontologique du pour-soi dans son être comme négativité pure." BN, p. 179.

162. EN, p. 269; BN, p. 217.

163. EN, p. 223: "Par négation interne, nous entendons une relation telle entre deux êtres que celui qui est nié de l'autre qualifie l'autre, par son absence même, au coeur de son essence. La négation devient alors un lien d'être essentiel. . . ." BN, p. 175.

164. See p. 68, above.

shine is the negation of being,[165] for taken in this isolation it is, rather, a positive immanent entity which, for the philosopher, may stand in a relation to something else. It is the for-itself which must constitute its unity as the negation of being. The shine must not acquire independent being; the unity of the for-itself, as qualified by the shine, must be negativity related to being. Viewed from the subject the shine must be prior because it belongs to the sphere of immanence and mediates the ecstasis. And yet the whole sphere of immanence is the negation of being, so that being is, for the for-itself, unmediated and immediate. The conflict between ontological and epistemological analysis is tied in a knot in this thesis. By negating itself the for-itself is presence to being.

Sartre's solution rests on the dialectical status of the shine qua moment of the unity of the for-itself and qua carrier of an ontic determinateness. In spite of its paradox, it is the consistent ontological formulation of Husserl's account of intentionality. Viewed in the light of Hegel, it appears more complicated than the corresponding Hegelian passages, if only because, for Hegel, self-consciousness and consciousness of objects are severed into stages of the dialectic. The sphere of immanence is first considered by itself; transcendence toward objects, in turn, constitutes a second stage, in which the former is "preserved." This is Hegel's way of saying that the two are one and that their unity need not be construed. However, Sartre, with his phenomenological orientation, has to show how consciousness and self-consciousness can coexist.[166]

The Articulation of Being

ONLY A BASIC REFERENCE of the for-itself to being has thus far been established. But we do not transcend to being qua undifferentiated plenitude, but to individuals within the framework of a world. The preceding discussion has, in fact, implied a

165. EN, p. 221: "[le reflet] . . . se reflète en tant que relation à un dehors qu'il n'est pas." BN, p. 173.

166. The above comparison is, of course, superficial in its limitation to the unity of two structures of consciousness (cf. p. 68, above). We might say, with a view to a more general comparison, that transcendence for Hegel does not pose the problem of how a subject can reach out toward something *existentially* "Other." It is a relation of otherness within an *essentialist* framework where any Other proves, in the course of the dialectic, to be amenable to integration with the subject. Transcendence is established as a logical mediation—a restricted subject is contradictory and, to avoid contradiction, transcends itself to its Other (cf. pp. 76f., above)—while Sartre's problem is to establish an existential bond to being which is also to be a bond of knowledge.

concreteness which in theory constitutes a further stage where "secondary" or "concrete" negations operate.[167]

In the ensuing analyses, Sartre will be found to lean more heavily than before on phenomenological findings, which he tries to formulate in the idiom of negation. Our factual object is a "this" [*ceci*], and, just as an object from a phenomenological perspective appears set off against a horizon which is ultimately the background of the world, Sartre regards the "this" conditioned by the disclosure of a world. The for-itself's presence to a "this" is bound up with the transformation of being to a *totality* or *world*. Conversely, its presence to the world is conditioned by its presence to "one or several particular things." [168]

For Sartre, the thesis that the world of the for-itself amounts to a totality follows from the fact that the for-itself "has to be . . . its own totality as a detotalized totality." It excludes itself from being as "*all* which is not being" and "being stands before it as *all* which the for-itself is not." [169] It is through the totality of being that the for-itself makes itself known to itself as a detotalized totality. This "meaning of being" as totality of the world appears only through the for-itself, although the latter "adds nothing to being." Sartre opposes the suggestion of a "subjective modification" in virtue of which being is available as a world. The nothingness whereby "there is" being, on the contrary, causes all subjectivity to be possible.[170]

The for-itself determines itself by the concrete negation of a "this." The emergence of such a "this" has to be presupposed; a partial negative structure is simply bound to appear. The "this" is "the being which I at present *am not*" and makes "known to me the concrete negation which I have to be. . . ." [171] The negation of a "this" is "determinate" negation in the restricted formal sense mentioned earlier. But the for-itself would not be a totality, even a detotalized one, if it did not transcend the "this." Its rationale of having to be a totality is matched by the necessity of referring to other "thises." [172]

167. EN, p. 229; BN, p. 180.

168. *Ibid.*

169. EN, p. 230; BN, p. 181.

170. *Ibid.* In Sartre's subsequent analyses we see him interpret transcendence as negation in a literal spirit. Of course, he does not mean to exclude "meaning"; indeed, the negative construction is intended as a ground for all material discourse on transcendence. And yet, his dialectic is only formally related to content.

171. EN, p. 231: ". . . pour m'annoncer la négation concrète que j'ai à être. . . ." BN, p. 182.

172. *Ibid.* By comparison with Hegel's transition from one "this" to another

The "this" "always appears on a ground; that is, on the un-differentiated totality of being inasmuch as the for-itself is the radical and syncretic negation of it"—a thesis which Sartre con-nects with the *Gestalt* theory. We have now two negations: the basic reference to being which is negation, and the negation of the "this" which is, therefore, "negation of the negation." [173] But the secondary negation, although negation of the negation, is not position. Sartre says it "has to be the radical negation which it denies." It does not "cease reattaching itself to it by an ontological thread" and "remains ready to dissolve in the radical negation at the upsurge of another this." [174]

Once several "thises" are disclosed, another relation, which in turn can be nothing but negation, comes up—that of "thises" between one another. Such relations are, as we have seen earlier when discussing the question of discreteness in the in-itself, "ex-ternal" negations, i.e., they leave the referents unaffected. [175]

With these negations Sartre has found a principle of *space*. The world has the "ambiguous character" of a "synthetic totality" and a "purely additive collection of all the thises," [176] in short, spatiality. Potentially, the world is many "thises"—they emerge from it and retreat into it—and yet an undifferentiated con-tinuum. Space is the "perpetual evanescence of the totality into collection, of the continuous into the discontinuous." [177] Space cannot be apprehended "by concrete intuition," "for it is not"; all that can be said is that it is continually "spatialized." [178] Space is only in the transcending of "thises" toward an order of "thises." It is no "form imposed in phenomena," for the for-itself adds noth-ing to the in-itself when space is realized. It is simply based on negation, and so its status with reference to the in-itself is the same as that of all other determinations.

The case of *quantity* is similar: it is the "indifference of being." Space and quantity are only "one and the same type of negation." [179]

(*The Phenomenology of Mind*, pp. 151ff.), which hinges on the abstract ostensive character of a "this," as exemplified by a turn of one's eyes or the passage of time, Sartre links this transition with the pragmatic character of human temporality.

173. EN, p. 232; BN, p. 183.
174. *Ibid*. The negation clearly has to do justice to all meaningful acts of the subject. A similar problem of differentiating a basic type of reference occurs in the case of Whitehead's prehensions.
175. EN, p. 234: ". . . sans les toucher. . . ." BN, p. 185.
176. EN, p. 232; BN, p. 183.
177. EN, p. 233; BN, pp. 183f.
178. EN, *ibid.*; BN, p. 184.
179. EN, p. 241; BN, p. 191.

Sartre's account of the relationship of "thises" is inspired by Hegel, for whom space is "the wholly ideal side-by-sideness" as the "first or immediate determination of nature." [180] For Sartre, contrary to Hegel, place, the place of a "this," precedes space. Sartre's external relations are grounded in an "internal" relation between the for-itself and the in-itself. The for-itself entertains internal relations to "thises" between which, cutting across these "radial" relations, as it were, there are external relations.[181] The order of "thises" is "ideal."

What has been constituted thus far is an ideal relational framework. The "this" is itself *qualitative*, however, and so Sartre, starting from quality, construes the "thing" as a perceptual and eventually pragmatic object.

From this perspective the "this" reveals the characteristic feature of the Sartrean in-itself, which is plenitude. The "this" is a "total interpenetration" of qualities. They are revelations of being on the condition that "there is" a "this." Quality is "the whole of being revealing itself within the limits of the 'there is.' " [182] From a "this" we can single out a quality, or rather a quality is already there singled out for us, while the other qualities remain an undifferentiated ground. The singling out, or apprehension, is an "abstraction." In it the subject transcends its instantaneity so that abstraction comes under the perspective of the subject's possibility. Abstraction is, however, only one case of transcending a "this," namely, by means of an increase of "precision." Generally, the for-itself's reference to a "this" has to be viewed from the perspective of its self-transcendence. A number of further characteristics of the "this" can be developed from this passage of the for-itself from one "this" to another in terms of its own possibility: the for-itself may interpret a "this" in terms of permanence,[183] potentiality,[184] probability,[185] or instrumentality.[186]

Let us once again return to Sartre's construction of such meanings. The "this" appears to me as something I transcend toward myself. Since I am negation in my reference to the "this," I

180. Hegel, *Enzyklopädie*, § 254. Cf. J. Findlay, *Hegel, A Re-examination* (London, 1958), p. 274. Cf., also, *Enzyklopädie*, § 261.
181. This state of affairs once again reminds us of Whitehead who, in his account of *presentational immediacy*, has to constitute relations of spatial neutrality out of internal relations (prehensions).
182. EN, p. 236; BN, p. 187. As a *Gestalt* the "this" is essentially variable; it ranges from point to thing. Cf. pp. 49f., above, n. 24.
183. EN, p. 243; BN, p. 193.
184. EN, pp. 245f.; BN, pp. 195f.
185. EN, p. 247; BN, p. 197.
186. EN, pp. 248ff.; BN, pp. 197ff.

"flee this negation in the direction of a complementary negation" which is to bring me closer to my ideal, the in-itself-for-itself. This "possible" negation is in turn related to a being "beyond" the "this" as the object of the previous negation. In this way a reference between the "thises" is established which stands "in exact correlation with the relation of the for-itself to its future," or possibility. The negation of a "this" is always engaged in the next negation. Or, in object language, the "this" of the first negation refers to that of the second.[187] In this way the pragmatic rationale of things [Bewandtnis] and innerworldly time, as well as other conferments of meaning, can be built up. Even for the ideal of the for-itself, the in-itself-for-itself, Sartre conceives of a meaning-correlate: it is beauty.[188]

Sartre's construction of transcendence, or mundane disclosure, follows the same pattern as his theory of the for-itself as such: he starts from instantaneity and develops from there a concrete totality which relegates the starting-point to an abstraction. In the analysis of the for-itself proper, presence-to-itself is the original for-itself from which the immediate structures and temporality were derived. In our present case, it is the transcendent object or "this" which serves as a starting-point, but it is rendered abstract in view of the network of references to other "thises" and, ultimately, to a world; a negation pure and simple would lose its meaning qua negation. The sequence of construction, culminating in a construed unity, corresponds to layers in the object which are united in a "this." The full structure on both the subject and object sides must "match" the full phenomenological description of being-in-the-world. The articulation of being, construed by way of negations, runs parallel with disclosures of qualities and pragmatic meanings which man, in correlation with his projected possibilities, confers on the world and on things.

It is not our aim to judge whether Sartre's theory of transcendence can do justice to the distinctions phenomenology has made in connection with our intending of objects. No doubt we would notice deficiencies, especially concerning the treatment of meaning as something which has ideal status, categorial relevance, and logical self-sufficiency. Sartre wants to make transcendence comprehensible by grounding it in the for-itself; as for meaning and material content, he merely offers a "scheme" for its constitution or construction. Leaving aside the basic question of whether such "empty" constructionism can be illuminating, we

187. EN, p. 242; BN, p. 192.
188. EN, p. 244; BN, pp. 194f.

must turn to a criticism of the constructive scheme itself. In an earlier section,[189] we raised doubts as to whether a subjective constitution, with the world as a correlative, is satisfactory, or whether the Other, toward which the subject transcends, would not have to be dialectically implicated. In other words, the question was raised as to whether a genesis of meaning and, at one with this, a projecting of the for-itself toward selfhood, are conceivable in this way. Sartre calls the subject's reference to the world an "internal" relation, which would imply that both subject and object are affected. In the game of Sartre's constructive scheme this requirement can be met in the abstract. But, discounting transcendental phenomenology, which we cannot discuss here, only a "categorial" dialectic can claim to *show* how meaning can be regarded as derived from an interplay of the subject with being as its Other. If we reduce the role the Other plays in such a categorial dialectic to that of an Other which is only "existentially" or by its mode of being an Other, the specific function of this being as a "mean" or "mediating middle" for possibility and object meaning can only be pointed to in terms of the abstract scheme: being runs parallel to, is a correlative of, the subject and is also constitutive for it. Consequently, we are once again faced with the question of whether it is illuminating to establish in ontology "existential" conditions of concrete subjectivity or, more specifically, of the subject's reference to the world.

189. Chap. 4, sec. 2, above, "Complement."

5 / Being-For-Others

THE OTHER PERSON presents a special problem: he occurs in the world, but is not exhausted by being the object of a subject. A theory which gives an account of one's relationship to the world—the stage to which the analysis has taken us—does not *ipso facto* encompass the other person. And, once he comes into view, we are faced as well with the necessity of regarding the subject as a concrete individual. Just as another person will not face us as a "structure" but as a concrete individual, so we, as a subject encountering another person, cannot be taken as a "structure" either. Although the transcendental objective of Sartre's analysis of the subject so far may have made us forgetful of this point, what has to be discussed now are concrete, contingent, individual subjects. And yet, in view of its transcendental objective, the subsequent analysis cannot help replacing the idiom of concreteness by one of abstraction.

Man exhibits patterns of behavior, such as shame, fear, and pride,[1] which *imply* others by referring to them. These phenomena indicate that we "count" on others and that a description of man ignoring these references to others would be incomplete. On the other hand, there is the problem of the *givenness* of others: the other person appears as a body. As for this mode of givenness, the Other does not differ from other objects: his appearance is incomplete. A theory like realism, taking thinglike realities as its basis, cannot but regard the other person as hypothetical.[2] In fact, such a theory treats him on idealist lines and makes him my construct. Idealism, in turn, cannot account for the Other as self-legislative; idealism has to presuppose him as real, and so turns

1. EN, pp. 275, 319, 348–52; BN, pp. 221, 261, 288–91.
2. EN, pp. 277–79; BN, pp. 223–25.

into dogmatic realism.[3] In either case, my reference to the Other is taken as an "external" cognitive relation. The being or not-being of the other person does not affect my being. Only a theory claiming an "internal" relation, i.e., a relation in terms of being, between me and the Other can show a way out of the difficulties. This is how Sartre locates the problem.[4]

Theories claiming an implicative relation between me and the Other are not, as such, satisfactory to Sartre. In Husserl, for example, the other person is on a par with my worldly ego; I qua being in the world dispose of object meanings implying others.[5] For Sartre, this is not sufficient to demonstrate a connection between my transcendental subjectivity and other such subjectivities.[6] In Hegel, too, Sartre finds an implicative relation between me and the Other. Hegel makes me "depend on the Other in my being," [7] granted that I am to be self-consciousness. We will discuss Sartre's criticism of Hegel at a later stage, but we may note here that Hegel's notion of a "general self-consciousness," which emerges from the mutual recognition of two immediate self-consciousnesses, does not satisfy Sartre. He is not concerned with the "truth" of self-consciousness as such but with the relation between subjects in the plural.[8] Heidegger, to take Sartre's last example, takes account of the Other by including the "existentiale" of "being-with" [*Mitsein*] in the notion of the human subject [*Dasein*]. This is tantamount to claiming an a priori openness toward others on the part of the human subject. The difficulty here, for Sartre, is that this implication of others will not be a basis for a concrete encounter with others. Solipsism has not been overcome.[9]

For Sartre, a theory about the relation between me and the Other need not give a proof of his existence or a refutation of solipsism. It can take my comprehension of the Other for granted. We do not, in fact, conjecture the existence of the Other, but simply experience him. The explication of this fact, however, must not take the form of a deduction of the Other from a higher totality; it has to point out a relationship in terms of being between him and myself on the basis of my cogito, such that the encounter with the concrete Other is accounted for. By way of anticipation it could be said that, for Sartre, no theory will

3. EN, pp. 279–85; BN pp. 225–30.
4. EN, pp. 275–88; BN, pp. 221–32.
5. Cf. Husserl, *Cartesianische Meditationen* (The Hague, 1950), §§ 50ff.
6. Cf. EN, pp. 288–91; BN, pp. 233–35.
7. EN, p. 293; BN, p. 237.
8. Cf. EN, pp. 291–301; BN, pp. 235–44.
9. Cf. EN, pp. 301–7; BN, pp. 244–50.

be successful which makes the Other merely a cognitive object.

Accordingly, what Sartre tries to give is a theory of the *encounter with the Other* and a theory of the *ontological reference to the Other*. Both will have to mesh: starting from the cogito, we will have to establish the encounter with the Other, and the encounter with the Other must be shown to "interest" our being.[10]

[1] THE ENCOUNTER WITH THE OTHER

IN ONE WAY, the Other is available to me as an object, granted his being is disclosed to me. As such his existence is, epistemologically speaking, merely probable; he might, in fact, be a dummy. Still, qua object, the Other presents himself to me not merely as a body but as a modification of my world. The objects of my world in the vicinity of the Other will appear oriented toward him.[11]

Sartre describes this modification of my world in a subtle analysis of my encounter with the *object-Other*. The projects the Other entertains as his possibilities have assumed object status and form "enclaves" within my world. If the Other is seen reading, for example, he may be comparatively closed in upon himself; if he comes my way, however, my world will be affected to a greater degree. The Other is not, qua an object appearing in my world, hidden from me; in my objectification he is given to me as a totality.[12] An uncomprehended individual trait is, in principle, amenable to explication with the help of additional objective data which I attribute to a subjectivity escaping me. (The situation resembles the relationship between being-in-itself and phenomenon: phenomena refer to other phenomena, not to being.) This is not a plea for behaviorism. The Other is for me a "total organization of the world" of which he is the "key." He is a "center of autonomous and intramundane reference in *my* world." [13]

I encounter the Other in another way when he looks at me: he faces me in his look [*regard*] as a subject.[14] This encounter is characterized by the disappearance of the Other-as-object; I cease to observe him and could not, for example, describe his eyes any more.[15] I experience an essential modification of my being and my

10. EN, p. 309; BN, p. 252.
11. EN, pp. 311f., 314; BN, pp. 254, 256.
12. EN, pp. 353f.; BN, p. 292f.
13. EN, p. 356; BN, p. 295.
14. EN, p. 314; BN, p. 256.
15. EN, p. 316; BN, p. 258.

world; I react with feelings like embarrassment, shame, etc.[16]

My world, which had been immediate to me and distanceless, becomes integrated, in the light of my experience, into the Other's world and his possibility projects. What was, in the case of my looking at the Other, his world as a world "given" to me is now my "experienced" [*erlebte, vécu*] world as transcended by the Other. I experience myself as situated in an objective world: I *am* someone, I am situated at certain distances from things and places, and my possibilities have vanished.[17] The Other, qua subject, is not encountered in my world;[18] he is merely "the *fact* of the presence of a strange freedom."[19] I am alienated from myself.

My reacting to the Other in fear, shame, or pride may prompt a reversal of the relation between me and the Other, such that I come to make him an object, i.e., a "transcended transcendence."[20] Conversely, I comprehend the object-Other as someone I might experience as a subject.[21] This possibility, however, is not *my* possibility, but rather an "absolute possibility . . . that . . . there may occur the upsurge of an Other-as-subject. . . ."[22] The relation between me and the Other is reciprocal and alternating, a constant conflict. "Conflict is the original meaning of being-for-others."[23]

But when the Other appears to me as a subject, can I not be mistaken? Thus I might, for example, "experience" my being looked at even though no one is there. However, "to be looked at" cannot be taken in the literal sense of two eyes seen as looking at me. According to Sartre, this is precisely not the case when the Other looks at me.[24] Any conventional sign of an Other—a rustle, an open window, etc.—can produce in me an experience of being looked at. I may peer through a keyhole out of jealousy and feel suddenly caught redhanded at the occasion of a noise in the

16. EN, pp. 319, 328; BN, pp. 261, 269.
17. EN, pp. 312–31; BN, pp. 263–72.
18. EN, p. 328; BN, p. 270.
19. EN, p. 334; BN, p. 275.
20. EN, p. 352; BN, p. 291.
21. EN, p. 357; BN, p. 296.
22. EN, p. 358; BN, pp. 296f. The upsurge of the Other is a metaphysical event. Cf. p. 41, above and chap. 6, sec. 5, below.
23. EN, p. 431; BN, p. 364. In subsequent sections, Sartre gives a rich analysis of various forms and accentuations of this conflict: love, language, and masochism (EN, pp. 431–47; BN, pp. 364–79) correspond to my being an object vis-à-vis the Other; indifference, desire, hate, and sadism (EN, pp. 447–84; BN, pp. 379–412) testify to my being a subject over against him. We cannot here discuss these analyses; they exemplify the elucidating character of a "structural" analysis of man in conjunction with phenomenological description.
24. EN, p. 316; BN, pp. 258f.

corridor, although there is in fact no one there.[25] Would it not be a fallacy to experience a subject-Other who does not exist?

Sartre works on the assumption that the Other-as-object is only a *probable* Other, while my relationship to him as subject is *apodictic*. When there occurs in me an experience of being looked at, e.g., in the form of an experience of shame, the validity of this experience must not be made dependent on the merely probable givenness of the Other; otherwise, the apodictic character of my experience could not be maintained. The given object-Other is no more than an "occasion" for my experience of being looked at.[26]

Sartre's solution of the problem is most peculiar. The objectification of me by the Other is no error for I remain affected by the Other in any case. What is doubtful and, in a given case, erroneous is merely the facticity of the Other. The Other may in fact be absent.[27] Absence is a "particular way of . . . being present":[28] it makes no difference to the relevance the Other has for me, and an absent Other may, as in the case of a present subject-Other, effect a rearrangement of my world in such a way that I consider myself at a distance from the Other as object while the subject-Other is present to me without distance. Although we will normally think here of a contracted relationship, as in the case of the friendship between two persons, Sartre holds that the function of the absent Other can be generalized. It is in relation to every other living man that I am "present or absent on the ground of an original presence."[29] Whatever I do, my actions are only "empirical variations on the fundamental theme of my being-for-others."[30] I may be mistaken in individual cases, but the presence to me of all humanity is not thereby affected. My certitude of the existence of the Other is independent of individual experiences and is, on the contrary, "that which makes them possible."[31] I may be mistaken in a given case as to whether I exist for the Other as "this" person or "as a European, as a Frenchman, or a Parisian."[32] The subject-Other is a reality not specified as to singleness or plurality; plurality belongs only to objects. The subject-Other is a *prenumerical* reality;[33] he is not a collective, like a class or an

25. EN, pp. 335–45, esp. 336; BN, pp. 276–85, esp. 277.
26. EN, p. 336; BN, p. 277.
27. EN, p. 337; BN, p. 277.
28. EN, p. 338; BN, p. 278.
29. EN, p. 339; BN, p. 279.
30. EN, *ibid.;* BN, p. 280.
31. EN, p. 340; BN, p. 280.
32. *Ibid.*
33. EN, pp. 341f.; BN, pp. 281f.

audience, but a prenumerical "one." (For Sartre, Heidegger's "one" [*Man*] is only applicable to a subject-Other.) It is when I objectify the Other that "he" can be counted and found to be a plurality or an individual.[34]

With this train of thought the theory of the *encounter* with the Other has turned into a theory claiming an *implicative relation* between me and the Other. I am always for an Other in general simply because there are many human beings in the world. The theory fuses the idea of my reaction to the Other in concrete experiences such as embarrassment, etc., with that of an inescapable relationship to some Other. So when I experience shame there will exist a subject-Other, if not necessarily the particular one assumed. The assumed subject-Other affecting me is an individual Other; but this is only a concrete version of my relation to an indefinite Other on the occasion of the upsurge of an object which indicates by the way it looks that I am looked at. The subject-Other thus turns into a hypostasis of what is basically an a priori reference to the Other. This hypostasis is apparently supported by the plurality of Others in the world who, as subjects, are not numerically a plurality for me.[35]

A thoroughgoing phenomenological interpretation of Sartre's theory of the Other would have to distinguish more carefully between the *direct* encounter in the look and implicative phenomena like embarrassment, etc., which can be regarded as *indirect* encounters with the Other. Bowing to the universality of our relationship to the Other, who is so frequently absent, Sartre places greater emphasis on the indirect encounter.[36] This may lead to the objection that in such an indirect encounter we are not really encountering the subject-Other. As for the rearrangement of my world in reaction to the Other, which is one form the indirect encounter takes, a phenomenological interpretation

34. *Ibid.*

35. The subject-Other has now become an Other who is not usually encountered as an object, but is simply supposed. In view of this extension of the notion, a refutation of Sartre's thesis would involve the fictitious assumption that there is no one else in the world but me, for we might then ask whether I would still feel ashamed in an a priori manner, as it were. However, this fictitious assumption is not available to us precisely because Sartre is not here giving a description of man's essence, but is pointing out an apodictic reference which is, by itself, factual. But is it then necessary for Sartre to have recourse to the factual existence of others where these do not confront me as objects? In view of the idea of prenumerical existence, there is no one-to-one relationship between my experience and concrete others. Sartre's thesis strikes us as an unsuccessful attempt to avoid the a priori character of our reference to the Other. The theory remains confined to subjectivity.

36. Cf. the ontological analysis in the following section.

would have to clarify whether Sartre's idea of a "hemorrhage" and a "flow" of my world toward the pole of the Other who "absorbs" it constitutes a persuasive phenomenological description. By and large, Sartre's descriptions may be regarded as refinements of Husserl's theory of "appresentation," [37] with the difference that Sartre is not dealing with successive stages of interpersonal meaning-constructs but with the factual upsurge of the Other, if only of a presumed one. However, the fact that the event of such an upsurge is understood in its meaning seems to presuppose the constitution of interpersonal meaning, ranging from objective space and nature to the comprehension of the possibilities of other persons.[38]

[2] THE ONTOLOGICAL REFERENCE TO THE OTHER

SARTRE DEMANDS that my reference to the Other should be a relation in terms of being. He is guided by Hegel's idea that I am myself only in distinguishing myself from the Other. My *opposition to the Other* is, for Hegel, bound up with a *recognition of myself in the Other*. This latter point is of particular importance to Sartre's theory.

The for-itself is not, as such, by its very structure, dependent on the Other. In ontological rather than anthropological terms, being-for-others is not a structure of the for-itself.[39] It only so happens that we are for others. And yet, Sartre regards my reference to the Other, by analogy with my basic reference to being in negation, as an "internal" or constitutive relation. I am everywhere surrounded by the Other.

If, in general there is an Other, it is necessary above all that I be the one who is not the Other, and it is in this very negation effected by me upon myself, that I make myself be and that the Other arises as the Other. . . . [T]he for-itself as itself includes the being of the Other in its being in so far as its being is in question as not being the Other. . . . This very detachment, which is the being of the for-itself, causes there to be an Other.[40]

Compared to the case of the for-itself as a negation of being, however, there is this essential difference: the relationship between the for-itself and the Other is reciprocal. "The Other exists for consciousness only as a *refused self*"; "I make myself not-be a being who is making himself not-be me." For I can, according to

37. Cf. *Cartesianische Meditationen*, §§ 5off.
38. Cf. Husserl, *Cartesianische Meditationen*, § 58; and A. Schuetz, "Sartre's Theory of the Alter Ego," *Philosophy and Phenomenological Research*, IX, 197f.
39. EN, p. 342; BN, p. 282.
40. EN, p. 343; BN, p. 283.

Sartre, "neither apprehend nor conceive of a consciousness which does not apprehend me. . . . Thus the Other whom I recognize in order to refuse to be him is before all else the one for whom my for-itself is," i.e., the one who negates my for-itself.[41]

Can this relationship be called a recognition of myself in the Other? Sartre sees a dilemma: Either, the Other is an object for me and in that case he has become something entirely different, if not for himself [42] then for me. If the Other appears to me as an object, I cannot seize myself as objectified in him since for that to be possible the Other would have to be a subject having me for his object. Qua object, he is not the alter ego turning me into an object; qua object, he cannot be the mirror in which I can appear to myself. It is true, I do experience that the Other has reference to me; his intentions aiming at me appear, according to Sartre, objectified in my world. But I apprehend myself only internally, not in the Other.[43] Or, to take the alternative case, I am the object: then I cannot negate the Other and so he cannot appear to me.[44] The dilemma remains that the Other is the "not-me-not-object." [45] "He cannot be revealed in the same upsurge by which I deny being him." [46] In keeping with the phenomenological analysis, the Other cannot qua Other be an object; there is "nothing on which [my negation] can be brought to bear." Thus, a recognition of myself in the Other is not possible for Sartre. I am myself in negating the Other. As in the case of my negating being-in-itself, my reference to the Other is a negation of exclusion.

For Sartre, negation and negatedness, answering to subject and object, constitute a contradictory opposition. Accordingly, recognizing oneself in the Other involves the contradiction that a subject is available to itself as object, or that in the object a subject has access to itself qua subject. We can appreciate this view as a transformation of the epistemological insight, that a cogito only refers to phenomena, to the more radical ontological thesis that what is given to a cogito can only be being-in-itself and not being-for-itself. The for-itself is non-identity; as objectified, however, it assumes the status of identity. This idea, which for Sartre is self-evident in terms of structure, runs parallel to the more explicit classical theory according to which the Other is given as a body credited with an inferred subjectivity. The Other

41. EN, p. 435; BN, p. 284.
42. See pp. 116, above and 124, below.
43. EN, pp. 299f., 345; BN, pp. 243f., 285.
44. EN, p. 345; BN, p. 285.
45. *Ibid.*
46. *Ibid.*

turns into a construct, a conceptual object, so that the cogito is barred from ever reaching the Other's subjectivity. This antagonism between subject and object, which makes it impossible to have cognitive access to the Other as a subjectivity, or to recognize oneself in the Other, forms one of Sartre's basic convictions. It contrasts with Hegel's basic conviction that the progress of the dialectic mediates the subjective and the objective, a conviction which makes Sartre regard Hegel as guilty of "epistemological optimism." [47]

Sartre's argument is based on the idea of a reciprocal exclusion of subject and object. What is surprising is that, through my reference to him, an Other should be prevented from making me an object, although it is only "for me" that he is an object. Sartre agrees, in his ontological treatment of the problem, to the idea of reciprocity involved in Hegel's thesis of a constitutive relation between me and the Other, although, as a phenomenologist, he places my own self in the center. Thus the reciprocity means, from my perspective, that when the Other objectifies me I cannot objectify him. As we have seen in an account of his phenomenological theory of the alter ego, Sartre expressly subscribes to this thesis. As the object of an Other I am paralyzed.

Now, since self-recognition in the Other fails, we are left with negation of the Other in the sense of an "infliction" or a "disqualification." Such a negation is not characterized by reciprocity proper but by alternating reciprocity. A disqualified for-itself has to retrieve itself before it can disqualify in turn. Although presented as the result of epistemological argument, Sartre's account of a person's reference to the Other and vice versa contains an element of interpretation, such that conflict comes to be the general characteristic of this double reference. Sartre can use as a paradigm for this interpretation certain features of Hegel's chapter on "Lordship and Bondage" in the *Phenomenology of Spirit;* [48] it is here that he can find a struggle between two unequal self-consciousnesses which proves exemplary for his own position. Sartre's theory of the Other is, in a way, a subtle transformation of Hegel's richer and more complex configuration into a simpler and more general one which nevertheless retains Hegel's concrete meaning. The line of argument in each case is completely different, however.

47. EN, p. 296; BN, p. 240.
48. Pp. 141ff. (J. Baillie, pp. 229–40.) Our account follows the shorter version of the *Encyclopedia*, (§§ 430–35).

Hegel begins with the confrontation of two self-consciousnesses:

[T]here is, to begin with, a self-consciousness for a self-consciousness, an Other for an *Other in immediacy*. In the Other qua ego I intuit myself in immediacy, but I also intuit in the Other an immediate existent object absolutely independent and different from me.[49] . . . This contradiction impels each to *show* himself as a free self and, as such, to be *there* for the Other in a process of mutual recognition.[50]

For Hegel, this mutual recognition of self-consciousnesses is a struggle, "for insofar as the Other is to me an immediate existent Other I cannot know myself in the Other as myself; I am therefore working toward a sublation of his immediacy." [51] In Sartre, this idea of the Other's immediacy is replaced by my objectification of him; I only have access to the Other as an object, while what I want is to encounter him as a subject.

Hegel's next step is to say that one self-consciousness is ready to renounce its immediacy—which is now interpreted as its "life" —while the other holds on to it: the one the master, the other the slave. The inequality is not deduced but assumed as a factual distinction which makes the Hegelian figure possible. With this assumption Hegel can also do justice to a process in reality, the supposed conditions at the dawn of human statehood. Submission and rule stand for two opposite decisions: self-effacing commitment and option for survival, respectively. In Sartre, submission turns into an inevitable objectification at the hands of the Other. It is in view of his immediacy that, for Hegel, the slave fails to be the Other in which the master can recognize himself. His immediacy is not inevitable but, on the contrary, to be overcome. In view of his instrumental role vis-à-vis the master, he shares something with him: there exists a *"common need* and a common concern for its satisfaction." Furthermore, the slave loses his immediacy—now interpreted as "stubbornness"—in fear of his master and rises through his work to the level of self-consciousness.

49. *Enzyklopädie,* § 430: "Es ist ein Selbstbewusstsein für ein Selbstbewusstsein, zunächst *unmittelbar* als ein anderes für ein *anderes.* Ich schaue in ihm als Ich unmittelbar mich selbst an, aber auch darin ein unmittelbar daseiendes, als Ich absolut gegen mich selbständiges anderes Objekt." The translations are my own.

50. *Ibid.:* "Dieser Widerspruch gibt den Trieb, sich als freies Selbst zu *zeigen* und für den anderen als solches *da* zu sein—den Prozess des Anerkennens."

51. *Ibid.,* § 431: ". . . denn ich kann mich im Andern nicht als mich selbst wissen, insofern der Andere ein unmittelbares anderes Dasein für mich ist; ich bin daher auf die Aufhebung dieser seiner Unmittelbarkeit gerichtet."

He now stands on his own feet, on a par with his master. In the process of mutual recognition the individuality and immediacy of the slave vanishes in favor of the identity of master and slave. The process is not limited to interpersonal relations between the two, but presupposes a relationship of the slave to the world in his work. Sartre's transformation discounts this latter point and makes the relationship an immediate interpersonal one. He imputes to Hegel the contention that self-recognition can take place in the Other as immediate. Hegel's view, however, is that for such a self-recognition to be possible a transformation has to take place. It is not possible unless a for-itself and a for-itself, both, cease to confront each other as immediate existents. It is not Hegel's aim to show how self-recognition in intuition is epistemologically possible—that is, if intuition is taken as ultimate. Rather, what he says is that the immediate "having" of the Other in intuition would not constitute the "determinate negation" required on the level of self-consciousness. Self-recognition of self-consciousness in the Other presupposes a sublation of immediacy; e.g., the master has to risk his life, and the slave has to work away his stubbornness. Once immediacy is sublated in this way on either side, self-recognition, in view of the identity achieved on either side, is already granted. Self-recognition is the illustration, in terms of concrete content, of double negation. (This can also be gathered from the first occurrence of self-consciousness in what the *Phenomenology of Spirit* calls "explanation" [*Erklären*]: consciousness grasps an infinite [viz., the interdependence of the factors of a scientific law] and, since consciousness is itself an infinite, it collapses with its object. Hegel has in mind the conceptual identity, in this case qua infinity.)

For Sartre, Hegel's epistemological optimism, in that it fails to show how my own consciousness reaches the Other,[52] is rooted in an ontological optimism. Hegel "places himself at the vantage point of truth, i.e., of the Whole," considering the two consciousnesses "from the point of view of the Absolute."[53] Once again, we can urge our divergent notion of what Hegel is doing. The self-consciousnesses Hegel deals with in the *Phenomenology of Spirit* are not "moments" of a metaphysical whole. He wants to say, rather, that the subject entails transformations which are explications of its principle, so that, at the end of these transformations, spirit fulfills its principle and is present to itself. To this end, the line of progression passes through renewed confrontations with

52. EN, pp. 296ff.; BN, p. 240.
53. EN, p. 299; BN, p. 243.

immediate opposites. These oppositions are not existent pluralities but dialectical oppositions. What Hegel intends to show is that spirit as such, or the subject as such, have to be regarded as mediated with opposites on the level of the determinateness concerned. How this is possible in real terms is not Hegel's problem. All he needs to say is that for a fulfillment of the subject principle immediacy (existence, life, etc.) has to be sublated. The *Phenomenology of Spirit,* although designed to unfold the principle of the subject in a conceptual dialetic, permits, in its oppositional stages, the substitution of real pluralities as illustrations. It is therefore tempting to interpret it in terms of a real dialectic or a metaphysical hypostasis.

Let us return to the formal analysis of the ontological reference of the subject to the Other. Now that the cogito has proved unable to establish cognitive access to the Other, or recognition in the Other, Sartre calls for a relation to the subject-Other *in terms of being* to make the encounter with the Other possible. The difficulty is that I, as an object vis-à-vis the subject-Other, have to gain access to him as subject-Other. To get out of this difficulty my negation of, or reference to, the Other has to be construed as an *indirect negation.* Instead of negating the Other in an immediate way, I negate my ego as objectified and negated by him. In refusing the Other I assume "my being-as-object for the Other. . . . I assume and recognize as mine this alienated Me." [54] The Other is given only in virtue of my assumed objectivity. [55] My Me-as-object is my "bond" with the Other and the "symbol of our absolute separation." But it is not mine only; ". . . insofar as the Other is co-responsible for our original separation, this Me escapes me." I claim as mine a "Me which escapes me." It is "not an image . . . growing in a strange consciousness" but "*my* being as the condition of my selfness confronting the Other and of the Other's selfness confronting me." It is "*my* outside" [mon *dehors*]. [56]

Sartre regards such an object-Me as the only possibility of construing the separation of one consciousness from another. Through this object-Me the Other can limit me. The object-Me is my limit, and as such not ideal but real: this being-for-others is my body. [57]

54. EN, p. 345; BN, p. 285.
55. *Ibid.*
56. EN, pp. 345f.; BN, pp. 285f.
57. EN, pp. 346f., 364; BN, pp. 286f., 302. Note the apparent conflict between the thesis that I "negate" my object-Me, and thus have reference to the Other, and the thesis that I "am" my object-Me. My relationship to my being-for-others corresponds to that type of negation which Sartre terms a "having-to-be" and

The change-over from my being objectified by the subject-Other to my objectifying him means, in formal terms, that I must control the negation issuing from the Other: i.e., I must negate his negation. In other words, I can attain an "explicit self-consciousness" because this is tantamount to being the negation of the Other; this negation of the Other is simply my possibility. The "consciousness (of) wrenching myself away from the Other" is "consciousness (of) my free spontaneity," whereby I put the Other "out of play." The occasion for this change-over is empirically contingent and subject to emotional experience.[58]

Given this ontological analysis of being-for-others, we now have two contrasting ontological constructions: a *direct* one, answering to Hegel's immediate opposition, in which my relationship to the Other is that of a formal, limiting negation causing me to be myself and to have the Other as an Other; and an *indirect* one, which construes, as it were, the transcendental condition for such a relationship, at variance with an epistemological explanation in that being-for-others constitutes an ontological reference to the Other rather than a cognitive one. Or, to put it with greater precision: since, for Sartre, cognition already is a relation in terms of being, but a relation simply to ontologically nondescript being, my reference to the Other, who is not ontologically nondescript, has to be a reference transcending mere cognitive reference. For Sartre, only the account in terms of a transcendental ontology can serve as a foundation of the objectively ontological plurality of subjects interconnected by a bond of being. This procedure reflects Sartre's commitment to a subjective orientation. Where—as in Hegel's case in Sartre's interpretation—this construction starting from the subject is dispensed with, we are left with an unjustified position, such as a philosopher might propose who is removed from reality.

In possession of this ontological construction starting from the cogito, Sartre himself assumes the role of the exalted philosopher and considers the relationship between the for-itself and the Other from the perspective of an encompassing unity.[59] By comparison with the references of the for-itself to itself in terms of possibility and future, and with another type of reference to itself in reflection or introspection, the relationship between the for-itself and the Other constitutes the most extended detour of the for-itself on

---

distinguishes from the negation of exclusion. The exclusive negation of the Other, which is "positional," is mediated by a negation which is "non-positional."
58. EN, p. 348; BN, pp. 287f.
59. EN, pp. 360–62; BN, pp. 299–301.

the way to itself. In self-consciousness, the unity is most tightly knit; shine and countershine prove inseparable. In reflection, the reflecting and the reflected tend toward separate existence, although their unity is maintained. In the relationship between me and the Other, however, there occur two reciprocal negations. Since they are "internal" negations, I and the Other meet within me as non-external to each other. There seems to be a need for a unified being "ego-alter ego" which divides itself into me and the Other in a manner not dissimilar to reflection. I and the Other would seem to constitute the attempt at a self-division of a totality in order to apprehend itself as an object.

However, by "its effort to be consciousness of itself the totality-for-itself would be constituted in the face *of* the self as a self-as-consciousness which has to not-be the self of which it is consciousness. Conversely the self-as-object in order to *be* would have to experience itself as *made-to-be* by and for a consciousness which it has to not-be if it wishes to be." [60] In other words, Sartre urges here the impossibility of a totality of the for-itself, which occurred earlier in EN, on yet another level. The for-itself entertains a bond of being only in view of its incompleteness. The moments of the totality cannot recoup themselves or, if they do, will not share a unity of being qua totality. The totality, if assumed as a metaphysical hypostasis, dirempts itself.

A transition from me to an encompassing totality, such as Hegel proposes in the *Phenomenology of Spirit,* is mistaken in view of its unipolarity: ". . . *simultaneously* with my negation of myself, the Other denies concerning himself that he is me." [61] The two negations are "indispensable" and cannot be reunited by any synthesis for, in that case, each negation would not-be the other (in the manner of an it-itself, not in the manner of "having to not-be" that which is negated; I and the Other would be without a constitutive relation to each other's opposite). The relationship possesses an element of facticity, an irreducible contingency: the separation is not due to just *one* for-itself but requires a duality or plurality.[62]

In one way then, being-for-others seems to presuppose a *totality of spirit*—the totality would be *metaphysically* prior—: in another, the *facticity of plurality* is irreducible. "The multiplicity of consciousnesses appears to us as a *synthesis* and not as a

60. EN, p. 361; BN, p. 300. Cf., by contrast, Hegel's being-for-one, p. 65, above.
61. *Ibid.*
62. EN, p. 362; BN, pp. 300f.

collection, but it is a synthesis whose totality is inconceivable." [63]
Sartre denies the possibility of regarding spirit, from a higher
vantage point, as a dialectical unity: there is no such vantage
point on totality.[64]

As in the case of the immanent structures of the for-itself,
totality stands for a *horizon of meaning* supplying the for-itself
with its ideal. Any relationship between me and the Other is
surrounded by a halo of totality. Totality is thus a structure, a
principle or idea, and no encompassing metaphysical absolute. It
is man's predicament to be incapable of ever attaining the totality
hovering above him. And, since the horizon of totality transcends
the immanence of any one for-itself and cannot be derived in a
dialectic of the for-itself as such, it is a contingent ideal.[65]

Sartre's comments on an encompassing notion of spirit and
his criticism of Hegel on that score testify to his divergent aim.
What he has in mind is the immediate ontic relationship of concrete subjects, and he is looking for the general ontological
condition making it possible. My negation of the Other—the formulation is reminiscent of Hegel's level of abstraction—is insufficient
since it would give me the Other as an object only, and, conversely, the Other's negation of myself would simply make me his
object. A concrete and contingent bond of being such as Sartre
means to propose cannot be established in this way. A priori
theories like those of Hegel, Husserl, and Heidegger fail to satisfy
Sartre because they do not provide a foundation for a concrete
encounter with the Other and because, in Hegel's case as Sartre

63. EN, p. 363; BN, p. 301.
64. *Ibid.* Accordingly, Sartre rejects in EN any concrete community of subjects [*nous-sujet*]. Such a plural unity fails in view of the objectification of all the
others issuing from each subjective center. For detailed analyses, see J. Kopper's
articles cited in the bibliography and his book, *Die Dialektik der Gemeinschaft*
(Frankfurt, 1960). As indicated above, Kopper's interpretation is indebted to
Hegel's notion of spirit. Accordingly, the irreducible plurality so dear to Sartre
appears as something yet to be overcome in a mysticism of spirit. Still, for Kopper,
Sartre is superior to Hegel, in that he takes account of the body and the various
forms of self-knowledge of spirit occasioned by the body. In our context, restricted
as it is to the outlines of Sartre's ontology, we cannot enlarge on Kopper's
analyses.
65. In his new work, *Critique de la raison dialectique*, I, Sartre has given a
further development of the problem of the Other. The conflict between the subject
and the Other, which in EN appears as their basic relationship, is expanded into a
theory of determinate "totalizations" corresponding to various types of community. We now have solidarity, couples, "serial" alignment of subjects as others of
others, the group as a subject-We, etc. Insofar as the individual subject remains
the center, conflict is not thereby overcome. But Sartre now acknowledges the
mediation of individuals, effective in complex types of community.

sees it, a hypostatized totality is introduced. To provide for an ontological foundation, the requisite theory has to be an a priori theory and yet, to provide for concrete encounter and contingency, a phenomenological theory as well.

Let us attempt a concise restatement of Sartre's theory about the Other. His solution of the problem is somewhat confusing in view of the conflict of an *objectively ontological perspective*, on the one hand, and a *subject-oriented perspective* in terms of phenomenology and *transcendental ontology*, on the other. In the earlier analyses, it was possible to maintain a subjective orientation and to "re-shape" the phenomenological analysis of human existence in dialectical terms. The conflict between the two orientations, the subjective one and the objectively ontological one, was reflected in a division of being into two types of which one, being-in-itself, had to be left undetermined. Being-in-itself was regarded as ontologically prior, but at the same time relegated to formal emptiness. In the analysis of the relationship between ego and alter ego, the case is changed. The Other is given to me in subjective orientation and yet, as far as an objectively ontological account of him is concerned, cannot be left empty and undetermined since he is an opposite ego. In the ego-alter ego relationship we have to take account of an opposite orientation, apprehended from my center of orientation. The conflict is manifested in a reciprocity in which the orientation of the relationship alternates.

This conflict cuts across the conflict of a priori implication of, and empirical encounter with, the Other. The a priori implication of the Other can be justified by implicative phenomena (such as embarrassment, etc.) and the experience of the Other. Ontologically, it involves the positing of a prenumerical Other as a contingent structure of the for-itself or, if we like, as a transcendent existentiale—in short, a hypostasis. The for-itself (or any for-itself) is determined by a limitative relationship to the Other (or any Other). The limitative relationship of any one couple of ego and alter ego is reciprocal. The structural account of such a state of affairs is an objectively ontological thesis about something like a plurality of monads.

The relationship is not one of simultaneous reciprocity, however; rather, it is one of alternation, inasmuch as the "structural" ego-alter ego relationship "occurs" factually in the form of a concrete encounter in such a way that the opposite orientation of the Other is given in subjective orientation. Phenomenologically, this is shown in the analysis of the "look." There is an apodictic

awareness of being looked at and thus of the presence of a subject-Other. I am an object of the Other, whereas he is not my
object.

Sartre's aim now is to provide an ontological foundation for
such an encounter, over and above a mere a priori reciprocity. The
requisite foundation is once again rooted in a structure of the for-
itself and yet a going beyond the idea of an a priori implication of
the Other. The for-itself "has" (or "is") a being-for-others. This
being-for-others is not just something posited by the aloof philoso-
pher-ontologist, nor is it a mere "horizon" or "pre-comprehension"
of a concrete encounter; it is, rather, a "being" of the for-itself
which makes an indirect reference to the Other possible. This
being is my body as an object for the Other. Qua being, this being-
for-others permits a dialectic on the lines of the previous analyses
of the for-itself: the for-itself is always beyond its being and
therefore, in the present case, negates its being-for-others. This
dialectic accordingly *construes* the alternating reciprocity of the
encounter. The Other, in negating me, makes me an in-itself, and
I in turn negate this negation inasmuch as I am a for-itself. The
relation is not just a reciprocal a priori limitation, but a relation
experienced in subjective orientation which has its transcendental
ground in the subject. As a result of Sartre's abstract dialectic,
being-for-others stands for a concrete foundation of the encounter,
as well as for a basic structure of the for-itself as such.

One might ask whether this subjective foundation of a bond of
being between me and the Other is sufficient. In abstract terms,
the difficulty is why I should be "affected" by the negation issuing
from the Other. Is it only "for the Other" that I turn into an in-
itself, or is this true also in the light of objective ontology? How
can someone else's negation affect me? If we say it must affect
me, we have fallen back on the idea of a limitative and implicative
relationship between me and the Other within the horizon of
totality, although it is clear that such an implication or pre-comprehension differs from a concrete, contingent encounter. We
cannot, so it seems, expect an existential ontology to "prove" the
occurrence of an encounter with the Other. We have reached the
limits of an ontology which sets itself the task, however impossible in the case of the ego-alter ego relationship, of encompassing
subjective orientation and ontology properly so called—and this
without being restricted to an a priori account such as Hegel's, but
with due regard for contingency. Hegel's procedure of securing
the relationship to the Other by way of categorial implication,
such that higher stages of spirit and, lastly, the Absolute presup-

pose it, or Husserl's way of regarding interpersonal meaning as a construct implying communing monads, need not be discounted: as "essentialist" doctrines they remain side by side with Sartre's "existentialist" doctrine which, in view of its abstract dialectic, has to disregard the categorial and meaning elements of the relationship between the subject and its Other.

6 / Sartre's Ontology as a Whole and Its Relationship to Hegel

IN THE PRECEDING ANALYSES we have examined Sartre's main work in the spirit of critical interpretation. We joined him at his phenomenological starting point in order to see his dialectical ontology develop from there. In the course of our analyses we pointed out what is already apparent from his use of notions like "being-in-itself," "being-for-itself," and "negation," namely, his many-sided indebtedness to Hegel's *Logic*. What is missing thus far, owing to the "dissociated" state of our analyses, is a summary interpretation of Sartre's total ontological framework, as related to Hegel's philosophy.

If we can attach weight to the Introduction to EN, Sartre can be said to be prompted by a dissatisfaction with phenomenology, particularly as concerns the problem of being: he wonders how that which is given to consciousness can be saved from mere subjectivity, or, in other words, how realism can be established. In answer to this problem, Sartre claims a being of phenomena. With this newly established basis the scientific method of phenomenology has already been left behind, although another essential element of phenomenology, the subjective orientation involved in the starting point of the cogito, has been retained. We spoke of a phenomenology with ontological foundation. Sartre's philosophy is characterized by such a confrontation of two realms of being; it is an ontology of intentionality.

We find in Sartre's philosophy the idea that the meaning of the being of phenomena and of the subject calls for elucidation.[1] But this idea may easily mislead us. Sartre is not concerned with the quest for the "meaning of being" in the way Heidegger seeks it,

1. EN, p. 34; BN, p. lxvii.

namely, by turning to a human subject [*Dasein*], whose ontological analysis is to furnish a horizon for the comprehension and interpretation of being.[2] We find ourselves in the midst of a different line of thought when Sartre asks what solution can be offered to explain the relations between the two realms of being if idealism and (traditional) realism fail.[3] This question is more formal than the inquiry into the meaning of being. One of the two types of being has to be interpreted in such a way as to make its reference to the other, which figures as being in the mode of the in-itself, intelligible. Sartre's guiding idea is that ontology has to establish a bond of being [*lien d'être*] between the two realms of being. This means that ontology, if it is to lead to an understanding of this bond, has to offer an interpretation of the being of the subject, for it is the subject which entertains this relation. Thus, Sartre is clearly looking for interpretative comprehension, but from a formalist perspective since the two realms, subject and being, are primarily seen in their relational aspect as confronting each other. Notions like being-in-itself and being-for-itself, which are brought in to account for this relation, seem to meet the demand made on them.

We repeat the question we asked earlier: Are we not dealing with a mere "scheme" of thought, designed to account for intentionality? In asking for the "ultimate meaning of the two types of being," or for the reasons why they "both belong to being in general," [4] Sartre has already admitted that these ontological questions will be answered in formal abstraction only. Is it legitimate to make the resulting abstract notions the basic notions of a "regional" ontology dealing with man and the world? Why is ontology restricted to such abstract notions? Clearly, we must raise the problem of formal abstraction in EN. In fact, it may be well to make this problem the central issue of our final considerations.

To solve our problem we will try to appraise Sartre's use of Hegelian notions not merely in the schematic recasting of the intentionality theory of phenomenology, but also as a transformation of Hegel's *Logic*. An appreciation of the coincidence of these two trains of thought may contribute to an understanding of Sartre's position and, more specifically, of the formal abstraction of his ontology.

Thus far, Hegel has served us in making certain notions of

2. Heidegger, *Sein und Zeit*, pp. 14, 29.
3. EN, p. 34; BN, p. lxvii.
4. *Ibid.*

Sartre's appear plausible. For example, the notion of the for-itself only proved intelligible as a dialectical Hegelian notion and not as an "ontological act" or as "nothingness of being." Similarly, the unfolding of the existential structures of the for-itself into "lack," "totality," and "being-for-others" owes its intelligibility to Hegel's dialectic. But in Hegel we found not one but a number of analogies: from the *Logic* and from the philosophies of nature and of spirit in the *Encyclopedia*. We spoke of higher "levels" or "stages" in Hegel's philosophy. His philosophy is not restricted to the abstract notions used by Sartre, and yet they are hardly picked at random from the first part of the *Logic*. What, then, is their function in Hegel's philosophy?

[I] HEGEL'S FORMAL INTERPRETATION OF BEING

BEFORE DISCUSSING THE FUNCTION in Hegel of the key notions of being-in-itself and being-for-itself, we must glance at the methodological framework which determines all other features of his doctrine of being.

For Hegel, philosophy can be defined as the "*thinking study* of objects,"[5] whereas "the human contents of consciousness, though founded in thought, do not initially appear *in the form of thought*, but as a feeling, an intuition, or representation."[6] Philosophy "puts *thoughts, categories*, or, in more precise language, *notions* in the place of representations."[7] The "real *import* of our consciousness is *retained* . . . when translated into the form of thought and the notion."[8] The content of philosophy "is no other than the content which, originally produced and producing itself in the domain of living spirit, has become the *world*, the inward and outward world, of consciousness"; its "content" is "*actuality*."[9] Inasmuch as "*thinking* things *over* stands for the principle . . . of philosophy,"[10] "subjective reason desires *in point of form* a further satisfaction; and this form is, in the widest sense of the term, *necessity*."[11] "Hence reflection, inasmuch as it sets itself to satisfy this desire, becomes *speculative thinking*, the thinking proper to philosophy."[12] "This thought, which is proposed as the

5. Hegel, *Enzyklopädie*, § 2. The translations are adapted from W. Wallace, *The Logic of Hegel*.
6. *Ibid.*
7. *Ibid.*, § 3.
8. *Ibid.*, § 5.
9. *Ibid.*, § 6.
10. *Ibid.*, § 7.
11. *Ibid.*, § 9.
12. *Ibid.*

instrument of philosophic knowledge, calls for the justification of its necessity and of its claims to be capable of apprehending the absolute objects. Such an insight into its justification is itself an instance of philosophic knowledge, and properly falls *within the scope* of philosophy itself." [13] Philosophy "owes its development to the empirical sciences," it is true, but "it gives their contents what is so vital to them, the form of *free* thought (or the a priori). These contents no longer depend on authentication through finding and experiencing facts, but are *accounted for* by *necessity*. The fact as experienced thus becomes an illustration and a copy of the original and completely autonomous activity of thought." [14] "It may seem as if philosophy, in order to start its course, had, like the rest of the sciences, to begin with a subjective presupposition" and that it had to "postulate *thought* as the pre-existent object of thought. But, by contrast, it is by the free act of thought that thought occupies a point of view, in which it is for itself, and thus *gives itself an object of its own production.* . . . The very point of view, which originally is taken on its *immediate* evidence only, must in the course of the science be converted to a *result,* its ultimate result. . . ." [15]

For Hegel, thought establishes itself as self-warranting and self-evident knowledge; it remains within its own immanence. In contrast to Kant's foundation of knowledge, in which an uncomprehended opposite, the thing in itself, is retained, Hegel's account makes knowledge absolute in virtue of its very principle; it reaches totality, or the Absolute, and this first in the domain of the *Logic.* The *Logic* constitutes the transcendental sphere of origin from where the subsequent unfolding of philosophy starts. For Hegel, a priori knowledge reaches beyond the *Logic.* Still in a systematic context, he makes the transition to nature and spirit, and, at a further remove, he introduces time and arrives at the philosophy of history. The transition to nature and spirit is effected by transcendental thought itself: it releases itself into externality or nature, regarded as that in which thought is external to itself, if only to devise its return to itself. In its final stage, Hegel's philosophy amounts to a knowledge which comprehends itself as the activity not only of logical but of absolute spirit. Philosophical knowlege is, in the final analysis, the re-enacted process of the Absolute grounding itself.

We do not intend to enlarge here on the transcendental project

13. *Ibid.,* § 10.
14. *Ibid.,* § 12.
15. *Ibid.,* § 17.

of Hegel just outlined, i.e., on the process of self-foundation of thought and the dialectical movement governing its traversal. Nor is there a need to comment on its inception from being and on its mediation with negation; these features of Hegel's philosophy are presupposed.[16] Instead, we focus on a characteristic of this movement which may help us to understand Sartre's position. Hegel's philosophical system is laid out in an architectonic order, which might be called a "projective" order: notions occuring at the beginning of the *Logic*—being, determinate being, being-for-itself— have analogies in subsequent notions or recur in them in an amplified manner. Thus, notions like "notion" or "spirit" are amplifications of being-for-itself, and notions from the philosophy of nature are amplifications of determinate being. The *qualitative* notions of determinate being and being-for-itself are "ingrediences of negation in being" and can be understood as first principles which recur in the more determinate notions constituting their *principiata*.

We can distinguish a *macroscopic differentiation* in terms of being, essence, and notion (repeated as idea, nature, and spirit), constituting an amplification of the first principles, and a *microscopic differentiation* which governs the notions of each sphere, in that it arranges them in dialectical oppositions corresponding to those mediating the first principles. The *macroscopic order* of being, essence, and notion (or idea, nature, and spirit, respectively) exhibits an amplification and interlacing of first principles in a twice reiterated movement: in one of the resulting triads, being internalizes itself in essence, becomes a negative opposed to being, and sublates this opposition in the notion; in the other, the idea externalizes itself to become nature and returns to itself in spirit. The *miscroscopic order* articulates each notion in terms of the first principles, which thus prove to be the principles of the dialectical method, in that it is regarded first as an in-itself, next as affected by an opposition, and finally as a for-itself. According to the two orders, Hegel's dialectical movement of thought can be considered a process of self-foundation in a linear sequence of negation and double negation, and, equally, as a structured architectonic, arrived at by way of amplification and interlacing of first principles.

Within this architectonic, which coincides with a deductive sequence, notions of principle are prototypes of more determinate or more material notions regarded as having been generated from

16. Cf. p. 37f., above.

them. Thus, being-for-itself is the prototype of the notion and of the subject or spirit. By itself it is a form or structure, insofar as being, on the level of qualitative being, which is also the level of first principles, is characterized only by opposition and identity, i.e., in terms of relation or negation. Hegel's doctrine of first principles amounts to an *interpretation* or *hermeneutic* of being. Being is differentiated by *modes* or *types:* pure being is the zero instance of determinateness, determinate being [*Dasein*] exemplifies determinateness, and being-for-itself is being with absolute determinateness. These types of being do not stand for beings but for modes of being governing beings under them (determinate beings [*Daseiendes*] or beings-for-self [*Fürsichseiendes*]). We thus find in Hegel a formal interpretation of being which undertakes to evolve the determinateness of being from the principles of determinateness and absolute determinateness. Qua determinate being, being is qualified by opposition; qua being-for-itself, it is qualified by identity with itself.

The division of being just outlined is not one of a "regional" ontology, according to which the various modes of being would each apply to certain beings only. In a way this is nevertheless true, inasmuch as the dialectic culminates in the absolute subject. Subject and Absolute have their distinction as *principiata* of being-for-itself. Being-for-itself constitutes, in fact, the final interpretation of being. But in the dialectical sequence, any determinate being comes, qua immediate, under the mode of being (being-in-itself); qua opposed to an Other, under that of determinate being; and qua synthesized with it, under that of being-for-itself. All beings are regarded as on the way toward subjectivity, each stage being a relative subject by itself and with reference to other stages. By its place in the macroscopic order, each is also found to be regionally fixed as a *principiatum* either of determinate being (essence or nature, respectively) or of being-for-itself (notion or spirit, respectively).[17]

In stressing the formal aspect of Hegel's philosophy, our interpretation has also brought out its existential aspect. We did not place weight on the categorial and "essentialist" cause of Hegel's system—the movement of the notion as a determinative process

17. This account of Hegel's *Logic* as an interpretation of being—an account which, for this general thesis, is indebted to H. Marcuse's book, *Hegels Ontologie* (Frankfurt, 1932)—is not at variance with statements made earlier in which we held the determinations of Hegel's *Logic* to be determinations in terms of thought. The principles we spoke of are evolved by transcendental thought: this means that being, interpreted as capable of a mediation with negation and as progressively self-determining, can be apprehended in its truth.

leading to higher and higher determinateness of content—but insisted instead on the converse thesis, namely, that all categorial content derives from an existential interpretation of being in terms of pure being, determinate being, and being-for-itself. The architectonic of Hegel's *Logic* makes it clear that existential determinations—Hegel calls them qualitative ones—are principles for the whole of being such that the categorial sequence hinges on them. The negative, which on our interpretation seems unduly suppressed, may be regarded as an element of being mediated by thought: by disclosing nothingness as identical with pure being, thought can derive the principles of determinate being and being-for-itself from pure being. In this way all explications of being, including being itself, belong to the immanence of thought. Eventually, this immanence is tantamount to being returned unto itself.

[2] SARTRE'S FORMAL INTERPRETATION OF BEING

THE PERSPECTIVE on Hegel's *Logic* and *Encyclopedia* given above, one-sided as it is compared to other possible perspectives, throws Sartre's relationship to Hegel into relief. Sartre's philosophy in EN is found to be the consistent transformation of Hegel's *Logic,* resulting from a rejection of the immanence of thought.

A steppingstone toward this transformation can be seen in Sartre's remodeling of phenomenology which, as previously noted, led to a confrontation of being, regarded as existential moment, being-in-itself, or being of the phenomenon, and the subject, regarded as being-for-itself. Hegel's *Logic* can now serve as a paradigm for an interpretation of being in terms of which the phenomenological confrontation of beings may be reassessed as an opposition of *modes or principles of being,* for on the authority of Hegel the basic distinction of subject and being can be reduced to a distinction of first principles.

Let us consider the resulting union of phenomenology and Hegelian dialectic in a systematic summary. Sartre's ontological scheme covering being and subject is restricted to the notions of being-in-itself and being-for-itself. He rejects a dialectical determinative process; accordingly, there can be no mediation between being and nothingness. Being simply "is." It is the same *existent* being as that borne out by Sartre's analysis of the ontological implications of phenomenology. Being-for-itself, by itself a dialectical mediation of being and negation, is retained as a fixed opposite to being. This is perfectly consistent: if the immanence of thought is rejected and, with it, the logical mediation presupposing such an immanence, the ontological principles become irreducible. Being and its modes posses no logical connection. Negation is ontologically unique: an event rather than a logical relation that would constitute ontological principles and, further afield, categories and essences within the immanence of thought. Accordingly, Hegel's tripartite division of being into pure being, determinate being, and being-for-itself is replaced by a duality of *being* and *being-with-negation,* or of being-in-itself and being-for-itself in Sartre's acceptation of these terms. Hegel's articulation of ontological principles now takes on regional relevance: only the human subject is a for-itself, just as in Heidegger only man is a being in the mode of *Dasein.* All other being is being-in-itself, in accordance with Heidegger's disjunction of *Dasein* and being of a non-*Dasein* (inert) character.

Consistently, the for-itself is given a non-logical and undialectical foundation. As we saw, Sartre conceives of a regressive analysis, designed to establish the necessity of a negative ground by inferring such a ground from negative phenomena. The for-itself must be a negative, but one requiring being for its support, so that it is in fact a dialectical unity, a type of being of its own. Similarly, being-in-itself, which in view of its fixed opposition to the for-itself is deprived of categorial explication and determination, receives a non-logical foundation by being assigned the function of the existential moment of the phenomenon. Being must be a transdeterminate existential ground; its internal oppositions are merely phenomenal oppositions calling for a for-itself to constitute or disclose them.

Once the negative character of the for-itself has come to light, Sartre avows his interest in dialectical mediation as a transcendental device: if the for-itself is a dialectical unity it can serve, in its original core of presence-to-itself, as a ground for the derivation of the concrete subject with its existential, temporal, and intentional structures. In this dialectic the Hegelian notions of determinate being, as distinct from being-in-itself and being-for-itself, and of finitude and infinity, reappear.

The resulting situation is this: In view of the architectonic in terms of ontological principles, what are, for Hegel, general notions (determinate being, being-for-itself) functioning as generalities or abbreviations of more determinate or concrete ones (essence, notion, nature, spirit), are in EN notions "meant" as concrete material notions, deputizing for world and subject, and yet found to be irreducible to more general principles. They are already ultimate notions; a further reduction of the for-itself to nothingness in isolation would be mere abstraction. The specific structures to be covered in EN by the dialectical notion of the for-itself, which Hegel develops in his dialectical process, are in fact accounted for by the ambiguity as to specific content of that notion. Sartre's basic notions generally stand in a formal relationship to material content. Or, conversely, in these notions distinct categorial stages of Hegel's dialectic are collapsed into one. The unity of being and nothingness defining the for-itself, for example, is made to stand for presence-to-itself, existential ecstases, temporality, transcendence, and being-for-others. Being-in-itself, in turn, is made to stand for the object, for transdeterminate transcendent being, facticity, the for-itself-as-ideal, and being-for-others. To permit of an unambiguous specific interpretation, the first principles would have to be developed as in Hegel, provided the dialectic is to be constitutive for specific content and that such content is to be generated or accounted for by the dialectic. But Sartre's first principles are from the start identified with concrete beings and, accordingly, the specific contents and structures are simultaneous. These are not only ambiguous categorially or as existential structures, but they are, in the acceptation of dialectical existential modes, applicable to any concrete content: I am courageous and not courageous, I am any concrete determination and not it, my ideal is the totality of any concrete determination, etc.[18] It is existence, not essence, which is dialectical.

The collapsing of different subjective structures in the notions of the for-itself and the in-itself entails, furthermore, that these notions become ambiguous not only as to specific content but as to their dialectical import, in such a way that their meaning reverses itself abruptly. The subject qua for-itself is *existence*, determinate being or being-there [*Dasein*], externality, finite being, whereas qua transcendence and freedom it is *negativity*. Sartre cannot, like Hegel, mediate these shifts of emphasis between the positive and the negative (in keeping with the distinctions of being, essence, and notion, or idea, nature, and spirit, respectively). Positive and negative constitute an antithesis for Sartre, and yet they collapse into each other. Similarly, being-in-itself displays an abrupt dialectic: as we saw, it is not merely the positive, nor the moment of being of the for-itself qua determinate being or being-there, but also the totality of the for-itself. This may remind us

18. Cf. pp. 79 and 84, above.

that in Hegel, too, being is immediate as well as mediated: essence is also being, and yet being is its opposite because essence is negative. And the same applies *mutatis mutandis* to the notion where this opposition is overcome. But in Sartre such shifts from the positive to the negative are not made plausible dialectically; his notion of being is abruptly ambiguous in view of the missing mediation.[19]

In Sartre, Hegel's categorial ontology is reduced and repristinated to a doctrine of formal principles. These are not regarded as transcendental conditions, such that ontological truth can be unfolded from them as their logical conclusion, but rather as contingent features of being. Hegel succeeds in generating or construing the determinations of reality by deductive differentiation of first principles, culminating in the Absolute. Sartre, in his ontology, limits himself to an interpretation, or rather "division," of reality in terms of two principles, being-in-itself and being-for-itself. There are no ontological principles or categories of higher determinateness.

Sartre's ontology, accordingly, is unable to account for what there is per se from an objectively ontological perspective, namely, individual things and individual persons. His theory of the phenomenon makes allowance for a delimitation of phenomenal individuals (in virtue of external relations), but for beings taken by themselves (things and subjects) there exists no principle of individuation. This is due to his reducing ontology to existential principles in order to fit the correlativistic position of phenomenology. All there is, is being and being-for-itself; the subject is an existent principle. No ontological principles concur so as to constitute beings per se, i.e., individuals, whether things or subjects. (One might wish to say that the for-itself, by analogy with the negation which makes individual phenomena appear, is the constitutive principle for the individuation of the subject as well, so that the subject is individuated in virtue of its negation of being. We remember that Sartre has claimed negation as an event. However, the distinction of the for-itself qua individual will, on that interpretation, rests with being, with qualitative and situative factors, which *are* only *for* negation. The subject will be a self-phenomenon, i.e., something which causes itself to be a determinate being. But a negation capable of such a feat is not a general but already an existent principle, an individual in the metaphys-

19. Cf. W. Biemel's criticism that the introduction of contradiction into consciousness in Sartre is not properly justified ("Das Wesen der Dialektik bei Hegel und Sartre," *Tijdschrift voor Philosophie*, XX [1958], 300).

ical sense.) Sartre shares the difficulties concerning the problem of discreteness and individuality with all correlativistic epistemologies which—like Kant, Husserl, and even Heidegger—posit a transcendental subjectivity. An *ontology* of intentionality shares equally the implications of the subject-oriented starting point: it cannot show the mediation of principle and individual. In this connection, Sartre's analyses of the alter ego are revealing. In the case of the Other a distinction between principle or mode of being and individual has to be made. Sartre's solution is, as we saw, to incorporate the plurality of individual subjects in the structure of each subject in the manner of a priori implication, and, in a manner accessible to phenomenological description, to identify such a for-itself with the concrete subject encountering an Other. Being-for-others, as an aspect of the for-itself's being, is both structural and concrete.

We might speak of a *dialectic of orientations* in this connection, namely, of the subjective and the objective ontological perspectives. In subjective orientation, as in transcendental philosophy generally, there exists no determinateness of the subject as such with reference to other subjects; individuality and principle coincide. Inasmuch as the subject is an absolute, it cannot be assigned a place in objective ontology. Determinateness of the subject over against other subjects is the result of the objectification of Others and of the reappropriation of such objectification by the subject itself (appresentation). The objective ontological perspective is called for, but cannot be assumed as long as the subjective one is imperative.[20]

It seems that Hegel does not share the implications of the correlativistic starting point. The inclusion of all determinations of being in a world of thought surpassing them all is not equivalent to a denial of the determinateness and discreteness of the real. Hegel need not explain individuation; all he has to do, in view of his concern for transcendental foundation, is to establish the determinateness of being in thought. His notions of principle, rather than being isolated from things determinate, are mediated with them in the immanence of thought, for it is in that immanence that the determinateness of being and subject is thought. In view of the fact that the perspective of transcendental thought is claimed to hold good for all of being, including the subject, the problem of an objective ontological perspective militating against

20. Cf. N. Hartmann's aporetic with regard to this problem in his *Grundzüge einer Metaphysik der Erkenntnis*, chap. VI, and his attempt at a solution, chap. XLIV.

the subjective one does not arise. Sartre's abstract principles, on the other hand, must cause things to be real abruptly, must make them appear determinate and individuated without mediation. Thus, his ontology is a *formal, real dialectic: formal*, in that it is existential, restricted to qualities of being; *real*, in that it is concerned with the immediate confrontation of a being with being. The being "for" which there is being cannot justifiably attain the ontological truth of determinate being, whether this be objective ontological truth or absolute transcendental truth.

[3] EXISTENTIAL EPISTEMOLOGY

IN THE PRECEDING SECTION Sartre's ontology was interpreted as a concurrence of the correlativistic position of phenomenology and Hegel's interpretation of being. We noted the ontological difficulties besetting this union, which, though designed to pass for an ontology and to arrive at objectively ontological statements, is pledged to a subjective orientation. Are we not left with an opposition of thing-in-itself and transcendental subjectivity in the Kantian manner? We would do well, therefore, to summarize Sartre's ontology from an epistemological perspective. The question is, in a nutshell, what is the transcendental constitution or a priori factor enabling the subject to be related to being in such a way that a world presents itself?

The subject lacks all self-constituted meaning, all categorial or essential determination, and yet is not altogether undetermined. It is accounted for by an existential structure derived from a ground, and the phenomenon, inasmuch as it is conditioned by a differentiated negation of being, can be regarded as constituted by it. But this a priori factor visible in the constituting of the phenomenon is not categorial, it is *pre-categorial* or *unspecifically transcendental*. We might call Sartre's ontology an *existential transcendental philosophy*, granting the ambiguity inherent in such a notion. His ontology is a transcendental philosophy inasmuch as an ontological principle, the for-itself, is invoked as a ground enabling the subject to encounter a world, the ground being the mode of being of the subject stated in formal generality. The constitution, or construction, of world and subject remains on the level of a formal scheme. What we find is a formal theory of constitution rather than an epistemology or a theory of cognitive validity. This harmonizes with Sartre's thesis that the subject adds nothing to being, which is a virtual denial of any material constituting of phenomena. Sartre's for-itself comes under the transcendental type of subject notion which is designed to establish experience by means of a subjective operation, or negation, rather than by means of presupposed categorial elements. But, in contrast to a transcendental theory such as Fichte's, which provides for stages of categorial constitution, Sartre's theory calls for unmediated constitution by means of formal negation, all material content being a matter of being.

The scheme of formal constitution is differentiated according to structural moments of the subject, which result from a complex dialectic of being and nothingness as moments of the for-itself. The for-itself and its dialectic have been found to presuppose a logical principle, the principle of synthesis by way of double negation (the totality haunting the for-itself), which is interlaced with the reality principle of a finite being. In fact, this principle of finitude, the determinate being of the for-itself, is by itself a conflict of thought and being: logically, it involves the dialectic of the limit (the relation of the for-itself to itself as Other), but qua real it also involves the *being* or *fixation* of this dialectic—i.e., the for-itself is transition and non-transition, failure to reach the destination of transition, and thus mere "reference" to its destination (expressed in the structures of existentiality and temporality). The transcendent given, which is a correlative of the for-itself, must be regarded as differentiated accordingly. Again, Sartre gives us a formal scheme of constitution which, in correspondence to the existential structures of the subject, is to account for pragmatic meaning.

With respect to the subject as a transcendental ground, Sartre's dialectic of the for-itself expresses the heterogeneity of thought and being on the level of formal principles. The for-itself is the thought of being impersonated by finite being. The for-itself involves a logical dialectic of finite being, or the finite existence of the logical dialectic. Such a subject notion cannot, in spite of its logical import, be derived logically. We have to put up with the real dialectic of the for-itself and the antithesis of thought and being as an ontico-ontological fact. Accordingly, we might call Sartre's dialectic of the for-itself a descriptive dialectic. In it, Sartre construes, under the inspiration of Heidegger's analytic of the human subject, a contingent and concrete subject in dialectical abstraction.

With respect to the reference of the subject to being, or its encounter with the world, all that Sartre offers is, as we have seen, the idea of a correlation between the structural moments of the for-itself and the world; no essences enter the existential dialectic. Accordingly, the constitutive function of these structures for phenomena remains empty. A philosophy maintaining this position can be regarded as transcendental in character inasmuch as the subject, in its structural differentiation, is held responsible for a disclosure of the world. But such a philosophy yields no returns, inasmuch as it cannot justify any material content and has to regard such content as a matter of empirical experience. Thus, despite its transcendental character, Sartre's philosophy has no cognitive value; i.e., there are no consequential insights, such as synthetic judgments a priori in Kantian epistemology, which flow from it. But this absence of consequential insights also applies to less formal transcendental theories dealing with the mere "disclosure" of a world, such as Heidegger's.

[4]   Excursus on Sartre's Relationship to Phenomenology

INASMUCH as our analysis is not limited to a study of Sartre's ontology in the light of Hegel's *Logic,* but deals, from a wider perspective, with his philosophy as a union of phenomenology and Hegelian dialectic, we will follow up the summary of Sartre's epistemological position by a comment on his relationship to Husserl's phenomenology.

We have repeatedly discussed phenomenology as an antecedent of Sartre's philosophy which serves him as a starting point. To what extent, however, is the basic conception of his developed philosophy compatible with phenomenology? And to what extent can his philosophy in EN, which is subtitled "Essai d'ontologie phénoménologique," be called phenomenological? Can he integrate phenomenological descriptions and interpretations into the body of his philosophy?

We noted before that Sartre is an empiricist. He does not intend to "generate" content, either of consciousness or of phenomena. Discounting further ontological ramifications, we can say that all he intends to do is to establish a relationship in terms of being, or a bond of being, between subject and object. Accordingly, he gives what, for him, is the imperative ontological interpretation of the subject, the interpretation in terms of the for-itself. The subject is being-for-itself, i.e., a unity of contingent being and negation. For something to be consciousness it has to be capable of interpretation in terms of such a unity. This thesis does not conflict with descriptive phenomenology. Sartre can, in fact, accept the bulk of phenomenological descriptions. And in common with phenomenologists, he makes use of reflection, with the difference that he distinguishes two kinds of reflection, *réflexion pure* and *réflexion complice*.[21] He even makes contributions of his own toward phenomenological description, e.g., in his analysis of the pre-reflective cogito, which is surpassed by a dialectical interpretation but is not called into question qua descriptive analysis.

The same applies *mutatis mutandis* to the phenomenology of time-consciousness. Sartre reinterprets the subjective time references in terms of his dialectical principle, but the resulting ontological references are congruent with the intentional references claimed in Husserl's study of time-consciousness. Sartre links these time references with existential meaning—the haunting totality of the for-itself—in a manner not to be found in Husserl. It can be said, then, that Sartre preserves the formal aspect of Husserl's descriptions while, for existential meaning, he leans on Heidegger's interpretations.

Sartre's ontological position calls for a reappraisal of phenomenology, however, in point not of description but of philosophical theory. Discounting reflection, consciousness is in immediacy present to its content. This relation is not one between ego and content but is being-for-itself, unity of consciousness and a contingent element. The body, for example, is a structure of man's non-positional self-consciousness; [22] i.e., the body is a moment of the for-itself involving internality and being-in-itself. There is no problem of how the body can be given "from within": it simply belongs to the for-itself, or, as Sartre says, "I exist my body." [23] There is no problem concerning the interaction of body and soul or of their unity; the notion of the for-itself, the prototype of any unity of consciousness and being-in-itself and of any referential structure of the subject, is regarded as an adequate philosophical analysis. Thus far, Sartre's theoretical reappraisal involves no conflict with phenomenology; he merely adds a philosophical theory.

There seems to be a difficulty, though, concerning the problem of conscious awareness, so important to phenomenology. In principle, all subjective references follow the same pattern of analysis. But are they equally instances of self-consciousness? Sartre sticks throughout to his contention that all references of the for-itself are conscious references, but, to allow for phenomenological differences, he distinguishes between "collateral awareness" [*conscience lateral*] and an awareness (of) myself as attending to

21. EN, pp. 201–9; BN, pp. 155–62.
22. EN, p. 394; BN, p. 330.
23. EN, p. 418; BN, p. 351.

something,[24] both types of awareness being cases of non-positional consciousness. The formal identity of the dialectical account does not mean that all subjective references are equally conscious. All that Sartre does is to fit the various references into an ontological framework whose identical pattern induces him to claim an awareness, however attenuated. It is significant that the specific character of the various types of consciousness, e.g., of positional and non-positional consciousness, can be accounted for by phenomenological distinctions only. Such distinctions, helping to differentiate what is otherwise mere negation, are indispensable if the dialectical account of subjective immanence is to have any definiteness.

There is open conflict between Sartre's ontological position and phenomenology in cases where the latter makes theoretical assumptions of its own. The notion of the for-itself does not, for example, permit of any real [*reell*] elements within consciousness, such as Husserl's "hyle," since these would not be "for" consciousness. For sense data, Sartre has to take refuge in evasive phraseology: e.g., pain is termed a "translucent matter of consciousness." [25]

Another item of phenomenological theory, the *noema*, which for Husserl constitutes the correlative of the noesis, is at least subjected to a reinterpretation. Husserl's noema is a result of phenomenological reduction and, as such, is ontologically problematic. (It will be remembered that Sartre, in his ontological proof, takes the opposite line and, starting from the alleged noema entity, discloses the transcendent phenomenon.) So we cannot really say that the noema is abolished, except as a subjective entity. Sartre's theory of the subject cannot distinguish between the noema and the object. (Perhaps, though, his notion of a "shine" [*reflet*] mediating consciousness with the world betrays a subtle reversion to a subjective entity—a subjective entity which, incidentally, Husserl's noema is not intended to be since it merely serves the purpose of a transcendental theory of meaning.) As for Husserl's *noesis* correlating with the noema, Sartre's reinterpretation is similarly unspecific: whereas the noesis, symbolized by a ray or arrow, is a positive act [*reeller Akt*] with ingredient meaning, content, Sartre's analogue is negation or a nothingness sepa-

---

24. Cf. EN, p. 395: "conscience (de) soi en tant que project libre vers une possibilité qui est sienne. . . ." *Ibid.*: "La conscience (du) corps est conscience latérale et rétrospective; le corps est *négligé*. . . ." BN, p. 330.

25. EN, p. 398; BN, p. 333.

rating subject and object. His account is too inexplicit to do justice to Husserl's distinctions; on the contrary, Sartre has to introduce phenomenological distinctions to make it definite. Discounting these, the whole problem of meaning is, as we saw, covered only by the thesis that the subject, in virtue of its negating, articulates being so as to be present to meaningful phenomena. In Sartre's idiom a theoretical explication of thought or of empty intentions unaccompanied by percepts is hardly conceivable.

As concerns the problem of intersubjectivity, Sartre omits an account of interpersonal meaning, limiting himself to facts like the encounter and the mutual implication of existent subjects. In this field he far surpasses Husserl as to phenomenological acumen (e.g., in his account of the "look"). However, in restricting intersubjectivity to the references between existences, he is led to the radical conception of alternating reciprocity between them. The phenomenologist would want to deny the radicalism of this consequence in view of the fact that there is mutually coordinated encounter and interpersonal communication. Sartre's existential theory presents, in a sense, the converse of Husserl's essentialist theory of intersubjectivity.

Discounting the divergencies mentioned, we note a peculiar congruence between Husserl's phenomenology and Sartre's ontology. Phenomenology remains the school of description and the stronghold to retreat to in the face of pressing problems of theory —there can be no doubt, for example, that Sartre accepts empty intentions, though he cannot account for them—but it is subjected to a far-reaching reinterpretation insofar as its theoretical assumptions are concerned. In the field of the alter ego, on the other hand, phenomenology is enriched in its own domain of description. Ultimately, the basis for the convergence of phenomenology and Sartre's ontology is found in his notion of negation, which can serve as an analogue of any intentional reference. But since his dialectic condemns him to utter abstraction, he helps himself to the requisite material content by drawing on phenomenological description, whether Husserl's, Heidegger's, or his own.

[5] ONTOLOGY AND METAPHYSICS

THE EPISTEMOLOGICAL OPPOSITION of a transcendental subject and a nondescript in-itself or transdeterminate thing-in-itself is not Sartre's last word. In his ontology the in-itself is, in fact, implicated in the dialectic of the for-itself. Sartre's dialectic transcends appearance, if only on the level of abstract principles.

Therefore, we must, in conclusion, discuss Sartre's philosophy as an ontology in the sense of a doctrine of being in general. This will take us once more into the vicinity of Hegel.

How Sartre intends to deal with the unity of being has thus far escaped us. One type of being, the in-itself, was found to be non-referential being, whereas the other, the for-itself, is negation of being and thus connection with being or a unity encompassing being. But with this notion of the for-itself we are thrown back on the opposition of the intentionality relation, and so look for a being above the two types of being. In our interpretation we regarded the two types of being as a realization or fixation of Hegelian principles of qualitative being. The question remained unanswered as to how Hegel's account of the unity of being, which is grounded in the determinative process stretching from pure being to the Absolute, has to be reinterpreted to be applicable to Sartre.

Sartre cannot accept an encompassing unity of being. For purposes of ontology, he limits himself to the idea that the types of being are related just as the for-itself is related to the in-itself: "The for-itself and the in-itself are reunited by a synthetic connection which is nothing other than the for-itself itself." [26] This leaves us with a hiatus in being. To overcome it, being would have to be regarded as a whole [ὅλον] in which being-in-itself is no longer non-referential but in need of the for-itself. This, for Sartre, is an ideal totality and thus impossible. [27] Such an ideal is the project of a for-itself and, on that analogy, real being is "an abortive effort to attain to the dignity of the causa sui. . . . Everything happens therefore as if the in-itself and the for-itself were presented in a state of *disintegration* in relation to an ideal synthesis." [28] We can raise the question as to the totality of being, but we cannot "adopt a point of view on this totality; . . . I am both one of the terms of the relation and the relation itself." [29] The for-itself "makes itself other in relation to the in-itself," but the in-itself "is in no way other than the for-itself in its being; the in-itself purely and simply is." [30] It is up to metaphysics to assume *one* being behind this duality. Metaphysics constitutes the philosophical discipline which forms hypotheses offering the possibility of "unifying the *givens* of ontology," and which must attempt to determine the nature and the

26. EN, p. 711; cf. pp. 716f. BN, p. 617; cf. p. 622.
27. EN, p. 717; BN, pp. 622f.
28. EN, *ibid.;* BN, p. 623.
29. EN, p. 719; BN, p. 624.
30. EN, p. 718; BN, p. 624.

meaning of the pre-historic process which is the articulation of the in-itself by the for-itself.[31]

Clearly, it is Sartre's notion of being-in-itself which makes a successful dialectical unity of being impossible. There is an immanence of being, but only in dissociation, only as a duality. The determinateness of being appearing within this immanence is not objectively ontological, but phenomenal. Ontology, therefore, cannot grasp the determinateness of being. It is the attempt to transcend the subjective orientation toward a point from where it can comprehend the subject as a dialectical unity with the in-itself which by itself remains non-referential. Being appears unto itself, but ontology is unable to say what and how being is by itself. The remaining problem is thus twofold: first, *to re-establish the unity of the two types of being;* and, second, *to attain a knowledge of being as determinate by itself* that would allow the for-itself and its articulation of the in-itself to be grasped as a *function* of being itself.

Hegel, too, views being in terms of dissociation and re-established unity. His philosophy is intended as a reproduction of this process and as its final stage of complete reflection. Qua transcendental thought, philosophy traverses the sphere of determinateness, which is that of dissociation of being, and transcends it since, followed up by thought to its logical conclusion, being proves to be the Absolute, or unity, or immanence. The determinateness of the real is not denied but regarded as untrue, as the provisional truth of dissociative understanding (as opposed to that of reason). Hegel thus refrains from making a statement on the objectively ontological determinateness of being. Philosophy, in possession of the truth of being, sublates all determinateness in the Absolute.

Sartre's interpretation of being in terms of reflection or immanence is stated in the abstract, as a relation of qualitative principles. For him, there is no transcendence of the dissociation by means of a dialectical movement because such a movement seems impossible for existent being. The unity remains an ideal; all there is, is the unsuccessful unity of the for-itself. Each for-itself is an instance of this attempt at unity on the part of being, wherever and in whichever form it occurs. Ontology limits itself to regarding being as if being were striving toward an overcoming of the dissociation of ontological principles, with each attempt at unity an instance of the self-foundation of being.[32]

31. EN, p. 715; BN, p. 621.
32. Cf. *ibid.*

Metaphysics, on the other hand, is seeking the per se determinateness of the one being, or what we called the objectively ontological account of being. For Sartre, its task is, as we have seen, first, to form hypotheses on the unity of being and, second, to inquire into the origin of all occurrences. (In ontology, these occurrences are interpreted as to their ontological type but not pursued to their ultimate ontological origin.) In the latter capacity, metaphysics must therefore seek to determine the grounds for individuality and discrete things whose grounds are, for ontology, covered by the blanket term of transdeterminate being. So we might say that only qua ontology, dealing with types of being along the lines of intentionality, is Sartre's philosophy restricted to an abstract formalism, whereas over and above that metaphysics can range freely. In a way, the Kantian position is thus reestablished. The novelty of Sartre's philosophy can be seen in the fact, that, prior to any metaphysics, it offers an ontology in subjective orientation while, at the same time, denying Hegel's absolute thought. Sartre makes Kant's abstention from metaphysical assertions concerning the thing-in-itself appear as a positive virtue: in applying Hegelian tools to an interpretation of man's relation to being-in-itself, he discloses, on that pre-metaphysical level, a self-contained field of study.

Retrospect

HITHERTO, the discussion of Sartre's philosophy has been largely made up of contributions probing into its ultimate metaphysical implications. For some time, especially in the early postwar period, its existentialist traces exerted a certain fascination; many were attracted by the refinement of its phenomenological and psychological analyses, and yet the polemical spirit prevailed, taking exception to the absurdity of this ontology, to the denial of God and the suppression of a harmonious and meaningful order of being. In this situation, I felt that the discussion of Sartre's philosophy ought to take a more conciliatory course. Such an improvement of attitude seems feasible if attention focuses on the sources of inspiration of this philosophy. When we follow this recipe it appears that Sartre has a bent for *strict philosophy* and is interested in specific problems of traditional philosophy rather than in ideological solutions. In this spirit we can understand his work as the latest metamorphosis of the Western philosophical heritage, designed to take up some of its unsolved problems. It may well be that his theory is built on too narrow a basis and that, accordingly, the "ultimate implications" for an overall view of being and for the ethical problem of freedom prove unsatisfactory. For our purposes, however, an analysis of his solutions seems justified if we can be certain of Sartre's serious commitment to philosophical questioning in the field of specific philosophical problems. Perhaps our analysis has helped to show that Sartre is not simply offering us an idiosyncratic doctrine of nothingness.[1] Rather, what he seems to be doing is, as we said, tackling certain

1. Some early comments on EN testify to the appreciation of Sartre's treatment of nothingness. Cf. C. E. Magny's article, "Système de Sartre," *Esprit*, XIII (1945), 564–80, 709–24.

basic, unsolved problems of traditional philosophy from the presuppositions of his philosophical orientation.

The problems whose solution Sartre seeks to advance converge
ultimately on one, namely, the problem of the subject's relation to
being. This problem is twofold, inasmuch as it covers the subject's
reference to the given as well as the ontological relation between
the subject and being. Sartre's attempt at a solution by way of an
ontological theory about this relation involves two basic steps.
First, to transcend mere givens, he discloses a being of the given,
or of phenomena. This being, distinguished from determinate
beings, is opposed to the subject as its ontological referent. In this
way the givenness of the phenomenon, as well as the per se character of being, are accounted for. Sartre goes on to link this analysis
with the complementary idea, stemming through Heidegger
from Hegel and Kierkegaard, that a similar severance of being
and essence is to be assumed in the case of the subject. On the
ontological level thus reached, being-in-itself and subjective being
confront each other. Sartre's second step is to view these two types
of being as dialectically related. For this he makes use of Hegel's
Logic in a transformed version suitable to his purpose. The introduction of the dialectic enables him also to do justice to the
transcendental motif, i.e., to rationalize the constitution of
the concrete subject and its part in the disclosure of a world.

We have discussed at length the inherent difficulties of this
doctrine: its questionable title to the dialectic, the conflict between contingent being and logical dialectic, the lack of material
determinations, the ambiguity of the subjective structures, and its
abstract formalism in general. Sartre's ontology falls short of true
constitutivity, i.e., it fails to provide reasons sufficient for the
comprehension of being, as divided into subject and object, and of
the relation between these. What it provides is an abstract formalism, a rational model, attaching itself only to the existential
moment of being. And yet it is genuine theory in that it supplies a
coherent interpretation of the relation between subject and object
and of the dilemma of subjective and objectively ontological orientations—problems otherwise likely to remain incomprehensible.
However, it supplies only an *interpretation* of being and not a
foundation establishing its own cogency.

Sartre's ontology appears, from what we have said, as a special
type of philosophical theory meriting closer study. From one angle, it is an attempt to solve the problems mentioned at the price
of sacrificing the classical ontological doctrine, which regards beings as concrescences of essence and existence. It is a price which

may have to be paid if we want to understand the subject-object relation. From another angle, this ontology constitutes a transformation of Hegel's *Logic,* deriving from it a dialectic and, along with it, a rationality for concrete reality. Sartre's ontology ought to be appreciated, therefore, as a proposal worth discussing, especially since it is clear that Sartre's delimitation of the problem does not preclude metaphysics. In fact, the polemic against Sartre can be reduced to a difference of opinion with regard to the question of whether or not his ontology prejudices metaphysics. One might say that the solution offered for the aporetic dualities of idealism versus realism and of subjective orientation versus objective ontology is traded for an uncompromising antagonism between ontology in Sartre's new sense and metaphysics, the aporetic dualities retreating into the doctrine of being itself. Ontology would appear to be a modest discipline, committed to a subjective orientation, which, in renouncing an apprehension of the per se determinateness of being, is able to interpret being in terms of existential structures. The dialectic introduced to permit this interpretation rests for its justification on a basis which, as we have seen, cannot ground it. Understandably, therefore, criticism from a Hegelian angle, such as we had to raise in our analysis, tends to be more stringent than the appraisal of Sartre's project as a whole. Clearly, what is needed is greater familiarity with the existential dialectic. Meanwhile, we cannot deny being impressed by the *rationality* inherent in the attempted reduction of the subject to a principle accounting for existentiality and temporality as well as for reference to totality and the alter ego. At the same time, we may have to admit that this principle is by itself complex, and so testifies to the fact that the problem of thought versus being has merely retreated to its innermost core. Accordingly, the assumptions involved in Sartre's comparative rationality, namely, the interpretation of existence as dialectical being on Hegelian lines and the rejection of classical ontology in favor of a priority of existence, pose problems which call for renewed efforts in ontology.

Appendix: Excursus on Solger

ALTHOUGH OUR ANALYSIS of Sartre's ontology is concerned with systematic questions rather than with questions of historical influence, it may be permissible to draw attention to the curious fact that his ontology has been anticipated in a number of points by Solger, an early nineteenth-century philosopher under the influence of Hegel. The work we have in mind is Solger's posthumous essay, *Über Sein, Nichtsein und Erkennen* (*On Being, Non-Being and Knowledge*).[1] The intriguing point is that Hegel commented on this essay and other writings by Solger in a commemorative article. We thus possess evidence, as it were, of Hegel's criticism of Sartre, however little his charges can be said to go beyond the findings of a systematic comparison of Sartre's and Hegel's philosophies.

We begin by giving a short account of Solger's ideas. In his essay, which takes the form of a dialogue, he first analyzes things: any thing is something for itself.[2] Things possess characteristics which, in one way, are positive and general features, but which, in another way, stand for the differences of things in relation to each other and thus are negative. Now a thing is something for itself not simply in virtue of its difference from others; all differences deducted, there remains an indefinite inner core without characteristics and qualities, that which its characteristics and qualities are not.[3] The true being of a thing is a dark and quality-less

1. *Solgers Nachgelassene Schriften und Briefwechsel*, II, eds. L. Tieck and F. von Raumer (Leipzig, 1826). In the following account quotation marks have not been used to set off what could—but for the elimination of dialogue forms—pass for translated quotes.
2. *Ibid.*, p. 210.
3. *Ibid.*, pp. 211f.

essence.[4] Each of the infinitely many things must have its pure being individually for itself.[5]

Things owe their non-being—their determinateness [6]—to their being known: non-being is not an object of knowledge, but is rather identical with an object's being known; [7] therefore, the non-being of all other things is bound up with our own being.[8]

Limitative non-being, like being, is shared by all things. Non-being, as a common element of things, is none other than our knowledge of them.[9] Thus, non-being can never deny any particular determinate being or that which makes a being determinate, but only being in general. All determinations must therefore be contained in non-being in a non-existent way. The determinations must, however, contain a general and unique being which is negated by general non-being.[10] Whatever we might regard as individual real things are, in fact, no more than the diversified forms of the common being, and the latter is at one with knowledge pure and simple. This general being is at the bottom of each thing, identical in each, and only as so supported are things facing us truly animated. For each is, qua individual, a mere appearance; in itself, however, it is identical with being in general.[11]

We have arrived at a general being which is entirely sublated by non-being. Either contains the totality of particulars.[12] There is a being and a non-being, both of them general. But if they are to coexist they must be related to each other in the manner of a mixture, such that the one becomes determinate with reference to the other.[13] In order that being and non-being should not sublate and annihilate each other completely, being must be being only in part, and in part become non-being.[14] By itself being is, of course, completely self-identical and, therefore, impervious to knowledge.[15] Knowledge, on the other hand, is not self-identical; it possesses an admixture of being.[16] Being, in turn, has an admixture

4. *Ibid.*, p. 214.
5. *Ibid.*
6. *Ibid.*, p. 215.
7. *Ibid.*
8. *Ibid.*, p. 217.
9. *Ibid.*, p. 223.
10. *Ibid.*, p. 225.
11. *Ibid.*, p. 228.
12. *Ibid.*, p. 230.
13. *Ibid.*
14. *Ibid.*, p. 231.
15. *Ibid.*
16. *Ibid.*

of knowledge, but not in the same way, not as something qualifying being in itself; what is added is merely non-being through which the original unity of being with itself is being sublated. Knowledge, by contrast, is, as consciousness teaches us, nothing but such a division and mixture. Being is, in itself, completely at one with itself and so cannot be known; it leaves, as it were, no gaps for knowledge to intrude. Therefore, we call it dark being.[17] Knowledge is, by itself, a mixture of being and non-being. It does not constitute a picture of being, but simply a unity of both being and non-being: being does not require an image of itself in knowledge, for it is completely at one with knowledge, in the sense that the one is what the other is not.[18]

Solger links these ideas with a doctrine of a synthetic dialectic issuing from being: being creates by itself non-being, and this in turn constitutes an impediment which being tends to transcend toward infinity. In this way the determinateness of being is deduced from being itself via non-being. And being wants, through the mediation of knowledge, to become once again identical with itself.[19]

We need not pursue here Solger's movement to such a synthesis of being and knowledge. Solger's systematic coincidence with Sartre in a number of points should be sufficiently clear. Solger posits a being which is, in one way, general being, but which, in another way, is individually determinate being, just like Sartre's being-in-itself. Knowledge, to Solger, is general non-being, which being creates by itself; Sartre thinks of an "ontological act." If non-being can be only in relation to being, this relation, the negation of being, can be taken as tantamount to knowledge—which is also Sartre's position. Things known then are *ipso facto* determinate beings, Sartrean phenomena. What strikes us is not so much the import of Solger's doctrine but the coincidence of his level of abstraction with that of Sartre. Like Sartre, Solger conceives of a *dialectical model* according to which the subject is the nothingness of being, as such in immediacy related to being, an existent nothingness, for which being is turned into determinate beings or phenomena. Similarly, we find in Solger a doctrine approaching the idea of a real dialectic couched in the abstract terms of being and nothingness. This dialectic lacks, however, the motivation

17. *Ibid.*, p. 232.
18. *Ibid.*, p. 244.
19. *Ibid.*, pp. 233ff.

Sartre tries to establish by the ontological and meontological proofs.

Here now are Hegel's comments: [20]

This attempt . . . has the disadvantage that the abstractions of being and non-being are mixed with more concrete notions, such as knowledge; the main theses amount to incommensurate combinations, with the effect that *non-being* is *knowledge*, that knowledge is non-being of an infinitely diversified being and, accordingly, also universality, etc. In other respects, however, [Solger] adheres to the general evolutionary notion of the idea, according to which the idea is at each stage synthesis and return unto itself; [in his work] the speculative character of the notion predominates. Solger does not hesitate to assert the unity of being and non-being; . . . However, in the quoted utterances contradiction is arrested in all its harshness, so that it appears as something that has come to stay rather than as something essentially involving its immediate disappearance and dissolution, which alone makes it tolerable to the imagination and to thought.[21]

With reference to other works by Solger, Hegel remarks earlier in his article: "The mixture in the ideas quoted of such concrete notions as God, sacrifice, humanity, knowledge, evil, etc. [notions occurring in Solger in connection with his treatment of the relationship between philosophy and revelation], with abstractions like being, nothingness, semblance, etc., is as disadvantageous to philosophy as to communication on the part of the author and comprehension on the part of the reader. We are jostled from one of these heterogeneous levels to the other; the realization that these abstract forms of thought are unsuited to the richness of the notions involved is by itself disturbing. . . ." [22] "The inconsistency in [Solger's] contemplation of things from such lofty points of view [Hegel refers to Solger's treatment of the relationship between consciousness and its opposite] . . . is apparently due to the fact that the meaning of comprehension, thought, and knowledge is presupposed in a vague way rather than grasped through analysis." [23] ". . . Solger has not found his way to the higher task of grasping this *progress* [of thought] by itself, i.e., the inner necessity inherent in knowledge, the true nature of the dialectic." [24]

There is little need for comment on our part. Hegel notes the

20. "Über 'Solgers Nachgelassene Schriften und Briefwechsel'," *Vermischte Schriften aus der Berliner Zeit, Sämtliche Werke,* Jubiläumsausgabe, XX, pp. 132–202. (The translations are my own.)

21. *Ibid.,* p. 200.

22. *Ibid.,* p. 170.

23. *Ibid.,* p. 180.

24. *Ibid.,* p. 171.

emptiness of the abstract determinations applied to concrete content, the *static contradiction,* and the *absence of any necessary development* of thought to arrive at the requisite notions. Solger's idea of a real positivity of being, as distinct from Hegel's notion of being, is reflected in Hegel's reproach that Solger starts with a "presupposed dualism" [25] which he intends to wind up in a "higher reality" in which this dualism will be reconciled. The oppositions to be reconciled—in connection with revelation, Solger thinks of God and humanity; in systematic contexts, of being and knowledge—are real oppositions. Hegel wants to reduce reality to its notions; Solger wants to grasp a real process conceptually. These comments suffice for an inference of what Hegel's criticism of Sartre would be like.

Should we say then that, in view of this parallel, Sartre stands closer to Solger than to Hegel and that we should have followed this line of approach in the first place? We must not forget that Solger's essay is no more than a philosophical sketch, the draft of a system in the form of a dialogue, without the requisite detail and strictness of argument. Solger does not follow Hegel as closely as Sartre does, when we consider that notions like being-for-itself and being-for-other(s), taken over by Sartre from Hegel, are not part of Solger's terminology; his essay sticks to the vague notion of a "mixture of being and nothingness." Since Sartre makes use of Hegel's dialectical detail, we, in turn, felt entitled to use Hegelian tools to clarify Sartre's meaning. It seems, therefore, that a Hegelian perspective on Sartre's ontology is legitimate after all. Last, and not least, Sartre's relationship to Solger is only a coincidence of ideas, and a limited coincidence at that; it is unlikely that Sartre has taken any notice of Solger's work. In his appropriation of Hegel, Sartre has taken a course in some ways similar to Solger's, but with an objective that is quite different. It might be tempting, though, to compare Solger's and Sartre's philosophies on a wider scale, taking into account Solger's key notion of *irony.* One would then want to draw a line from romantic irony, which may be said to stand for the insistence on negative subjective freedom in reaction against rationalism, to Sartre's negative subjective freedom which, in a reaction not altogether dissimilar as far as ideological motifs are concerned, has become once again the centerpiece of a major philosophical edifice.

25. *Ibid.,* p. 169.

Bibliography

THE FOLLOWING BIBLIOGRAPHY is a personal selection of philosophical writings by Sartre, of books and articles on his philosophy, and of other works incidental to the subject of the present study.

PHILOSOPHICAL WRITINGS OF SARTRE

L'Imagination, Paris, 1936.

"La Transcendance de l'égo," *Recherches philosophiques*, 1936–37, pp. 85–123; *The Transcendence of the Ego*, trans. F. WILLIAMS and R. KIRKPATRICK, New York, 1957.

"Une Idée fondamentale de la phénoménologie de Husserl," *Nouvelle Revue Française*, 1939, pp. 129–32.

Esquisse d'une théorie des émotions, Paris, 1939; *The Emotions: Outline of a Theory*, trans. B. FRECHTMAN, New York, 1948.

L'Imaginaire, Paris, 1940; *The Psychology of Imagination*, trans. anonymous, New York, 1948.

L'Être et le néant, Paris, 1943; *Being and Nothingness*, trans. H. E. BARNES, New York, 1956.

L'Existentialisme est un humanisme, Paris, 1946; *Existentialism*, trans. B. FRECHTMAN, New York, 1947.

Situations, I–III, Paris, 1947–49; *Literary and Philosophical Essays*, trans. A. MICHELSON, New York, 1955.

Critique de la raison dialectique, I, Paris, 1960.

BIBLIOGRAPHIES

BIEMEL, W. *Jean–Paul Sartre in Bildzeugnissen und Bilddokumenten*, "Rowohlts Monographien," Hamburg, 1964. (Best recent bibliography.)

Douglas, K. *A Critical Bibliography of Existentialism* (*The Paris School*), "Yale French Studies," No. 1, 1950.

Jolivet, R. *Französische Existenzphilosophie*, Berne, 1948.

Natanson, M. *A Critique of Jean–Paul Sartre's Ontology*, "University of Nebraska Studies," 1951, pp. 127–36.

Spiegelberg, H. *The Phenomenological Movement*, II, The Hague, 1960, 513–15. (Includes studies and articles in English up to 1959.)

Secondary Literature on Sartre's Philosophy

Alquié, F. "L'Être et le néant," *Cahiers du sud*, Marseille, 1945, pp. 273–74, 648–62, 807–16.

Ayer, A. J. "Novelist-Philosophers: J.-P. Sartre," *Horizon*, XII (1945), 12–26, 101–10.

Ayraud, P. "Réflexions sur l'Être et le néant," *Témoignages*, X, (1946), pp. 213–29.

Bertrand, R. "Note sur l'essence et l'existence," *Revue de métaphysique et de morale*, LI (1946), 193–99.

Biemel, W. "Das Wesen der Dialektik bei Hegel und Sartre," *Tijdschrift voor Philosophie*, XX (1958), 269–300.

Blackham, H. J. *Six Existentialist Thinkers*, London, 1951.

Blondel, M. "The Inconsistency of J.-P. Sartre's Logic," *The Thomist*, X (1947), 393–97.

Butts, R. E. "Does Intentionality Imply 'Being'?," *Journal of Philosophy*, LV (1958), 911–12; enlarged version: *Kant-Studien*, LII (1960–61), 426–32.

Caillois, R. "Analyse réflexive et réflexion," *Deucalion*, I, Neuchâtel, 1946, pp. 127–39.

Champigny, R. J. "Le Mot 'être' dans L'Être et le néant," *Revue de métaphysique et de morale*, LXI (1956), 155–65.

Colin, P. "La Phénoménologie existentielle et l'absolu," *Recherches et débats*, X (1955) 91–107.

Collins, J. "The Existentialism of J.-P. Sartre," *Thought*, XXIII (1948), 59–100.

Corvez, M. "L'Être de la conscience dans la philosophie de J.-P. Sartre," *Revue Thomiste*, L (1950), 563–74.

———. "L'Être en-soi dans la philosophie de J.-P. Sartre," *ibid.*, 360–72.

de Beauvoir, S. *La Force de l'âge*, Paris, 1960; *The Prime of Life*, trans. P. Green, Cleveland and New York, 1962.

———. S., "L'Existentialisme et la sagesse des nations," *Les Temps modernes*, I, No. 3 (December 1945), pp. 385–404.

DESAN, W. *The Tragic Finale*, Cambridge, Mass., 1954.

DE WAELHENS, A. "De la phénoménologie à l'existentialisme," *Le Choix, le monde, l'existence*, Paris, 1947.

———. "Heidegger et Sartre," *Deucalion*, I, Neuchâtel, 1946, pp. 15–37.

DUBARLE, D. "L'Ontologie phénoménologique," *Revue de philosophie*, (1946), 90–123.

DUMÉRY, H. "La Méthode complexe de J.-P. Sartre," *La Vie intellectuelle*, XVI (1948), 102–20.

ÉCOLE, J. "Essence et existence chez Sartre," *Les Études philosophiques*, I (1951), 161–74.

———. "La Création du moi par lui-même et l'optimisme Sartrien," *Les Études philosophiques*, XII (1957), 479–83.

GROOTEN, J. "Le Soi chez Kierkegaard et Sartre," *Revue philosophique de Louvain*, LI (1952), 64–89.

HARTMANN, K. "Das Realitätsproblem," *Lebendiger Realismus, Festschrift für Johannes Thyssen*, ed. K. HARTMANN in collaboration with H. WAGNER, Bonn, 1962, pp. 115–30.

HOLZ, H. H. *Der französische Existenzialismus*, München, 1958.

———. *J.-P. Sartre*, Meisenheim, 1951.

HÜBNER, K. "Fichte, Sartre und der Nihilismus," *Zeitschrift für philosophische Forschung*, X (1956), 29–43.

JEANSON, F. *Le Problème moral et la pensée de Sartre*, Paris, 1946.

JOLIVET, R. "J.-P. Sartre et le matérialisme," *Giornale di metafisica*, IV (1949), 510–18.

KOPPER, J. *Die Dialektik der Gemeinschaft*, Frankfurt, 1960.

———. "Die Dialektik im französischen Denken der Gegenwart, *Zeitschrift für philosophische Forschung*, XI (1957), 142–64.

———. "Sartres Verständnis der Lehre Hegels von der Gemeinschaft," *Kant-Studien*, LII (1960–61), 159–72.

KUHN, H. *Encounter with Nothingness*, London, 1951.

LUKÁCS, G. *Existentialisme ou Marxisme?*, Paris, 1946.

MAGNY, C.-E. "Systême de Sartre," *Esprit*, XIII (1945), 564–80, 709–24.

MARCUSE, H. "Existentialism: Remarks on J.-P. Sartre's L'Etre et le néant," *Philosophy and Phenomenological Research*, VIII (1948), 309–36.

MÖLLER, J. *Absurdes Sein?*, Stuttgart, 1959.

MÜLLER, M. *Existenzphilosophie im geistigen Leben der Gegenwart*, Heidelberg, 1949.

MURDOCH, I. *Sartre, Romantic Rationalist*, London, 1953.

NATANSON, M. *A Critique of Jean-Paul Sartre's Ontology,* "University of Nebraska Studies," 1951.

———. *Literature, Philosophy and the Social Sciences,* The Hague, 1962.

PAISSAC, H. *Le Dieu de Sartre,* Paris, 1950.

PODLECH, A. *Der Leib als Weise des In-der-Welt-Seins,* Bonn, 1956.

RICHTER, L. *J.-P. Sartre oder die Philosophie des Zwiespalts,* Berlin, 1949.

SCHUETZ, A. "Sartre's Theory of the Alter Ego," *Philosophy and Phenomenological Research,* IX (1948), 181–99.

SMITH, V. E. "Existentialism and Existence," *The Thomist,* XI (1948), 141–96.

SPIEGELBERG, H. *The Phenomenological Movement,* Vols. I and II, The Hague, 1960.

STERN, A. *Sartre: His Philosophy and Psychoanalysis,* New York, 1953.

THEUNISSEN, M. *Der Andere,* Berlin, 1965.

THYSSEN, J. "Vom Gegebenen zum Realen," *Kant-Studien,* XLVI (1954–55), 68–87, 157–71 (reprinted in *Realismus und moderne Philosophie,* Bonn, 1959, pp. 92–138).

TROISFONTAINES, R. *Le Choix de J.-P. Sartre,* Paris, 1946.

VARET, G. *L'Ontologie de Sartre,* Paris, 1948.

VERNEAUX, R. "Esquisse d'une ontologie du créé," *Revue des sciences religieuses,* XXIV (1950), 301–14.

VUILLEMIN, J. "La Dialectique négative dans la connaissance et l'existence," *Dialectica,* IV (1950), 21–42.

WAHL, J. "Essai sur le néant d'un problème," *Deucalion,* I, Neuchâtel, 1946, pp. 41–72.

———. "Freedom and Existence in Recent Philosophies," *Philosophy and Phenomenological Research,* IX (1948), pp. 538–56.

———. "Sur l'introduction à l'Être et le néant," *Deucalion,* III, Neuchâtel, 1950, pp. 143–66.

WEISS, P. "Existenz and Hegel," *Philosophy and Phenomenological Research,* VIII (1948), 206–16.

OTHER WORKS

ANSELM, SAINT. *S. Anselmi Cantuariensis Archiepiscopi Opera omnia,* ed F. S. SCHMITT, Secovii (i.e., Seckau), 1938.

ARISTOTLE. *De anima,* ed. W. D. Ross, Oxford, 1956.

BECKER, O. "Zwei phänomenologische Betrachtungen zum Realismusproblem," *Lebendiger Realismus,* Bonn, 1962.

BERGSON, H. Œuvres, Paris, 1959.

BRENTANO, F. Psychologie vom empirischen Standpunkt, Vol. I, Leipzig, 1924.

COHN, J. Theorie der Dialektik, Leipzig, 1923.

DESCARTES, R. Œuvres, eds. C. ADAM and P. TANNERY, Vol. III, Paris (reprint, no date).

DIELS, H. Die Fragmente der Vorsokratiker, 10th ed., Vol. I, Berlin, 1961,

FICHTE, J. G. Grundlage der gesamten Wissenschaftslehre (1794), ed. F. MEDICUS, Hamburg, 1956.

HARTMANN, N. Grundzüge einer Metaphysik der Erkenntnis, 4th ed., Berlin, 1949.

———. Hegel, Berlin, 1929.

———. Zur Grundlegung der Ontologie, 2nd ed., Berlin, 1941.

HEGEL, G. W. F. Enzyklopädie, ed. J. HOFFMEISTER, 5th ed., Leipzig, 1949; The Logic of Hegel (Encyclopedia, §§ 1–244), trans. W. WALLACE, Oxford, 1892.

———. Phänomenologie des Geistes, ed. J. HOFFMEISTER, Hamburg, 1952; The Phenomenology of Mind, trans. J. B. BAILLIE, 2nd ed., London, 1949.

———. Vermischte Schriften aus der Berliner Zeit, Sämtliche Werke (Jubiläumsausgabe), ed. H. GLOCKNER, Vol. XX, Stuttgart, 1930.

———. Vorlesungen über die Ästhetik, ibid., Vols. XII–XIV, Stuttgart, 1937–39.

———. Vorlesungen über die Philosophie der Religion, ibid., Vols. XV and XVI, Stuttgart, reprinted 1959.

———. Wissenschaft der Logik, Werke, Vols. III–V, Berlin, 1833–35; Hegel's Science of Logic, trans. W. H. JOHNSTON, and L. G. STRUTHERS, Vols. I and II, 2nd. ed., London, 1951.

HEIDEGGER, M. Sein und Zeit, 7th ed., Tübingen, 1953; Being and Time, trans. J. MACQUARRIE, and E. ROBINSON, London, 1962.

HELLER, J. Solgers Philosophie der ironischen Dialektik, Berlin, 1928.

HUSSERL, E. Cartesianische Meditationen, The Hague, 1950.

———. Die Idee der Phänomenologie, The Hague, 1950; The Idea of Phenomenology, trans. W. P. ALSTON and G. NAKHNIKIAN, The Hague, 1964.

———. Ideen zu einer reinen Phänomenologie und phänomenologischen Philosophie, Erstes Buch, The Hague, 1950 (my page references follow the 1st ed., Halle, 1913, which are noted in 1950 ed.); Ideas, trans. W. R. BOYCE-GIBSON, London, 1931.

———. Vorlesungen zur Phänomenologie des inneren Zeitbe-

wusstseins, ed. M. HEIDEGGER, *Jahrbuch für Philosophie und phänomenologische Forschung*, Vol. IX, Halle, 1928; *The Phenomenology of Internal Time-Consciousness*, trans. J. S. CHURCHILL, The Hague, 1964.

JAMES, W. "Does Consciousness Exist?" *Journal of Philosophy*, I 1904, 477–91.

JASPERS, K. *Philosophie*, 3rd ed., Vol. III, Berlin, 1956.

KANT, I. *Kritik der reinen Vernunft*, ed. Preussische Akademie der Wissenschaften, Vol. III, Berlin, 1904: *The Critique of Pure Reason*, trans. N. K. SMITH, London, 1929.

LEIBNIZ, G. W. *Nouveaux Essais, Philosophische Schriften*, Vol. V, ed. C. I. GERHARDT, Berlin, 1882.

LOCKE, J. *An Essay Concerning Human Understanding*, ed. C. FRASER, Oxford, 1894.

KIERKEGAARD, S. A. *The Concept of Dread*, trans. W. LOWRIE, Princeton, 1944.

MARCK, S. *Die Dialektik in der Philosophie der Gegenwart*, Tübingen, 1929, 1931.

MARCUSE, H. *Hegels Ontologie*, Frankfurt, 1932.

SCHELER, M. *Philosophische Weltanschauung*, München, 1954.

SCHOPENHAUER, A. *Die Welt als Wille und Vorstellung, Sämtliche Werke*, ed. P. DEUSSEN, Vol. II, München, 1911.

SOLGER, K. W. F. *Solgers nachgelassene Schriften und Briefwechsel*, eds. L. TIECK, and F. VON RAUMER, Vol. II, Leipzig, 1826.

WHITEHEAD, A. N. *The Concept of Nature*, Cambridge, 1920.

———. *Process and Reality*, New York, 1929.

Index